WHY WARS WIDEN

WHY WARS WIDEN
A Theory of Predation and Balancing

STACY BERGSTROM HALDI
US Naval War College

Foreword by

ROBERT A. PAPE

FRANK CASS
LONDON • PORTLAND, OR

First published in 2003 in Great Britain by
FRANK CASS PUBLISHERS
Crown House, 47 Chase Side, Southgate
London N14 5BP

and in the United States of America by
FRANK CASS PUBLISHERS
c/o ISBS, 920 NE 58th Avenue, Suite 300
Portland, Oregon, 97213-3786

Website: www.frankcass.com

British Library Cataloguing in Publication Data

Haldi, Stacy Bergstrom
   Why wars widen: a theory of predation and balancing
   1. Prolonged war 2. Military policy 3. Military history
   I. Title
   355'.02

ISBN 0-7146-5307-1 (cloth)

Library of Congress Cataloging-in-Publication Data

Haldi, Stacy Bergstrom, 1964–
   Why wars widen: a theory of predation and balancing /
Stacy Bergstrom Haldi; with a foreword by Robert A. Pape.
     p. cm.
   Includes bibliographical references and index.
   ISBN 0-7146-5307-1 (cloth)
   1. War. 2. Military history, Modern – Case studies. I. Title.

U21.2 .H345 2003
355.02–dc21
                                                            2002031501

Typeset in Aldine 11/13pt by Frank Cass Publishers
Printed in Great Britain by
MPG Books Ltd, Victoria Square, Bodmin, Cornwall

Contents

Foreword

Stacy Bergstrom Haldi's *Why Wars Widen* is an ambitious book, one that asks an important question and gives a strong answer to it. Since nuclear strategists in the 1960s began to distinguish between major wars that escalate geographically, as more and more states join the conflict, from those that escalate in intensity, as the existing rivals inflict greater and greater costs on each other,[1] scholars of international politics have attempted to provide general explanations for the escalation of major wars over time. Although there are notable exceptions, few social scientists have been able to provide compelling answers that hold across a significant number of cases over a broad period of time. This is especially true for the mystery of major power wars have had a tendency to widen since the rise of the modern nation state in the 17th century.

A central obstacle to explaining this phenomenon has been coming to grips with the fundamental changes in the technology of military power over the past several centuries. Major power wars occur infrequently, compelling scholars seeking to develop general theories of why previously neutral states intervene in major wars to work in an empirical laboratory that extends over several centuries. Over such broad periods of time, military technology and the nature of major power war itself have undergone vast transformations. In the 17th and 18th centuries, major wars were limited affairs, involving relatively infrequent combat between small and hard to replace military forces. From the Napoleonic Wars through World War II, the rise of nationalism and industrialization created the era of protracted wars of attrition, consisting of virtually constant combat between vast military forces that could replace large numbers of troops and equipment almost as quickly as they were destroyed, not just once but for years at a time. With the nuclear revolution, military technology changed again as did the nature of disputes between major powers which have been resolved in relatively short crises with little actual fighting.

Haldi tackles this challenge head on. In *Why Wars Widen*, she develops an important new theory for why neutral states intervene in on-going major power war that credibly cuts across the tremendous changes in military technology over the past three centuries. Haldi argues that the central factor in a neutral state's decision to intervene in a major war is how threatening participation in the war is to the survival of the state – which she calls 'the political cost of warfare' – a factor that closely reflects changes in military technology over time. The political cost of warfare determines whether a neutral state should take advantage of opportunities or respond to shifts in the balance of power that occur during the course of a major power war, and so is the key underlying cause of why major wars widen.

Haldi's theory is parsimonious, pertains to the decisions of major and minor states who are neutral at the start of a major power war, and applies broadly across basic changes in the nature of military technology over time. In addition, this theory yields straightforward predictions. When the political cost of intervention is expected to be low, states should often take advantage of opportunities to seize territory or make other gains to improve their relative power positions. Alternatively, when the political cost of intervention is expected to be high, states should be much more reluctant to intervene for profit and do so mainly to prevent the balance of power from shifting against them. Haldi subjects these propositions to detailed empirical analysis of the decisions of numerous states to intervene in cases that are crucial for her theory. She finds broad and significant support for her theory, forthrightly presents evidence that does not, and shows that her theory outperforms the most likely alternative explanations across a range of cases.

Why Wars Widen is highly relevant to contemporary international politics. September 11, 2001 has caused a major change in US national security policy, and the Bush administration is committed to waging a vigorous 'war against terrorism'. The United States has already conquered two countries – Afghanistan and Iraq – and may conquer others as well. Haldi's theory suggest that we should be confident that future US wars are unlikely to widen due to predatory policies by other states but has a note of caution. Wars could still widen if a major power were to act, deliberately or inadvertently, in a manner that shifted the balance of power in its favor. Accordingly, statesmen, scholars, and graduate students have good reason to carefully consider the conditions under which wars widen. Haldi's study is the place to start.

Robert A. Pape
Chicago, May 2003

1. Morton H. Halperin, *Limited War in the Nuclear Age* (New York: Wiley, 1963); Herman Kahn, *On Escalation* (New York: Praeger, 1965); and Bernard Brodie, *Escalation and the Nuclear Option* (Princeton, NJ: Princeton University Press, 1966).

Acknowledgements

I owe many, many debts of gratitude to people and institutions that have helped me with the research and writing of this book over the years. So much time has elapsed that I no doubt will neglect to mention several individuals. To them I sincerely apologize.

I have incurred my most lasting debt to John Mearsheimer, who instructed me and guided my research for close to two decades. With remarkable patience, he has helped me see this project through from initial idea to bound book. I will always be grateful.

I likewise am indebted to Steve Walt and Daniel Verdier for the generous comments, critiques and guidance they gave me on this research project. Their assistance was invaluable at each stage of the process.

I would also like to thank the Program on International Politics, Economics and Security at the University of Chicago. My friends and colleagues at PIPES, especially Ivan Toft, provided me with valuable comments and criticism on this research in its early stages. Michael Desch, Dale Copeland and Andy Kydd also read over early drafts and generously gave me helpful comments and suggestions.

I would like to thank Cynthia Thompson and the staff at the Amelia S. Givin Free Library for providing me with research assistance after I moved to Mt Holly Springs, Pennsylvania. In a similar vein, the library staff at the US Army War College and the Military History Institute, both at Carlisle Barracks, have provided me with generous access to their collections.

I am very grateful to the US Naval War College. Through many and varied discussions with faculty and my Strategy and Policy students in the College of Distance Education, I was able to hone my arguments, particularly with reference to the French Revolutionary/

Napoleonic Wars and World War I case studies. Particular thanks go
out to Stan Carpenter, Michael Creswell, Steven T. Ross and Chuck
Thomas.

More recently, I would like to thank Ed Rhodes, Jack Levy and
the Center for Global Security and Democracy at Rutgers for providing me with an intellectual home on the east coast. They have been of
great assistance to me the past two years.

I owe a special debt to the anonymous reader for Frank Cass, who
provided very detailed and concrete suggestions for improving the
manuscript. I have tried very hard to meet these expectations, and
where I fall short, it is entirely my own fault. I would also like to
thank Robert Bohrer and Donald Borock, both of Gettysburg College,
for reading through Chapter 1. I am also thankful for the kind atten-
tions of my editor at Frank Cass, Andrew Humphrys, and the copy-
editor, Penny Rogers.

Robert Pape has generously written the Foreword to this book. I
am honored that he has given me such time and attention. I am
indeed privileged.

Lastly, I would like to thank my family – my children, for putting
up with my work, and my husband, for never losing faith.

— 1 —

Introduction

President Clinton justified US/NATO military action in Kosovo with the words: 'We act to prevent a wider war, to defuse a powder keg at the heart of Europe that has exploded twice before in this century with catastrophic results.'[1] Was this conflict likely to widen? Were there sufficient grounds to justify expanding the war in order to prevent it widening of its own accord?

Scholars likewise point to the dangers of war widening. For example, in 'Back to the Future', John Mearsheimer writes: 'However, local wars tend to widen and escalate. Hence there is always a chance that a small war will trigger a general conflict.'[2] But nowhere in the essay does he explain how or why this could happen. The international relations literature provides little direct guidance on this important policy issue. This study seeks to fill that void.

I examine the widening[3] of interstate conflicts. Why and under what conditions are wars likely to widen? By 'widen', I mean when neutral states enter an ongoing conflict, such as the decisions by France and Great Britain to enter what would have been the ninth Russo-Turkish War, thereby turning it into the Crimean War (1853–56). There are some periods of European history where virtually every war widened; likewise, there are periods where war widening was the exception. This study encompasses almost three centuries of European history from 1700 to about 1973, precisely to examine the *changes* in the incidence of war widening. By understanding what made conflicts more or less likely to spread in the past, we can more fully predict what will make wars more or less likely to widen in the future and adjust our policy accordingly.

The argument that I develop in the following chapter is that the level of political cost of warfare – how threatening war is to the survival of a state – creates incentives for states to engage in predatory or balancing war widening. I argue that, when the political cost of war is low, states are very likely to widen wars for predatory motives. When the political cost is high, the incentives for predation diminish, but the incentive for balancing increases in situations where other balancing options have been exhausted. The existence of balancing options other than intervention in a war makes predation a greater cause of widening than balancing. Therefore, predation causes more war widening than balancing; by extension, war widening is most likely when the political cost of warfare is low. The political cost of warfare, which was fairly low in the eighteenth century, increased dramatically after the French Revolution, when Napoleon ushered in an era of total war and redrew the map of Europe.

This study specifically omits the widening of civil wars. There is ample reason to believe that the variables identified as causing interstate conflicts to widen would also apply to internecine wars. The outbreak of a civil war can also provide opportunities for predation or incentives for balancing just as wars between states. Nevertheless, civil wars differ enough from interstate wars to confuse matters. Civil wars are complicated by issues of multiple sovereignty.[4] The fact that one side must demobilize its armed forces at the war's conclusion means that civil wars almost always entail high political cost for the initial combatants that may or may not also translate into high political cost for neutrals seeking to intervene.[5] This line of reasoning would eliminate the variation on what I have identified as the independent variable, the political cost of warfare. Testing the applicability of the theory developed in this study to civil wars is a project in and of itself.

The study focuses primarily on wars involving the European states system. The reason for this is empirical, not theoretical. Indeed, I would expect that the theory applies equally to non-European conflicts. But, in the years since 1700, most of the great powers have been European. The major exceptions, of course, are the United States and Japan.

This analysis has concrete policy implications. First, it helps identify which wars are likely to widen and, just as important, which wars are *not* likely to widen. Second, it helps identify historical trends that will influence the possibility of wars widening. Third, it helps explain the role that foreign-policy activities, such as alliances, have on the likelihood of future conflicts spreading. In short, with all the struggles occurring around the world at any point in time, it gives policy-makers another tool to help decide which conflicts are worthy of closer scrutiny.

Next, this study helps fill an important gap within the international relations theory literature. The idea of war widening as a distinct phenomenon, something separate from war origination, has received remarkably little attention from international relations theorists. Most of the attention it has received has been through the study of alliances: do alliances make war more or less likely for their members? Does the alliance formed for deterrence guarantee a wider war if deterrence fails? This is an old idea, tracing its way back among American policy-makers to George Washington's Farewell Address.[6] This study, while revealing some interesting aspects of alliance behavior, shows that alliances do *not* cause wars to widen.

This study also brings some generally neglected concepts back into the forefront of international relations scholarship. Principally, it draws a distinction between balancing and predatory behavior.[7] Predatory behavior, the notion that states will act to increase their power when they are able, is something which has been downplayed in favor of the idea that states exclusively seek to enhance their security, which sometimes drives them to behave aggressively. While there is some validity to that position, I believe that collapsing the distinction between balancing and predatory behavior forsakes too much explanatory richness. The conditions under which a state is compelled to balance to ensure its survival are the opposite of those which prompt predatory behavior. Moreover, the policy prescription for deterring balancing war widening is different from predatory war widening. In its simplest terms, if one wants to deter predation, one must raise the costs, but raising the costs might provoke balancing behavior in the right circumstances.

Finally, I employ a broad historical perspective to answer the question of war widening. While there is not much existing scholarship on the question, much of the research that has been done has been quantitative, utilizing a database beginning in 1815. By reaching back into the eighteenth century, I have found that there is a significant difference in the amount of war widening across time, which cannot be captured by studies that focus solely on the post-1815 time period. Moreover, the case-study method is better suited to demonstrate the circumstances leading to predatory and balancing behavior.

TABLE 1.1
DATA ON WAR WIDENING, 1700–1973

	Mean corrected length*	Total % widening	% predatory widening	% great power widening by predation	% balancing widening	% great power widening by balancing
1700–1802	3.95	83.0	78.9	64.0	21.1	36.0
1803–1973	1.36	42.9	41.0	38.1	59.0	61.9
Total 1700–1973	2.66	55.0	63.5	52.2	36.5	47.8

Note: *The length of wars before 1866 was reduced by half because the campaigning season was generally only five to six months out of every year.

METHOD AND ORGANIZATION

I began my inquiry with a survey of European wars from 1700 to 1973. It was this historical review that led me to question why war widening was prevalent in some periods and not in others. While my primary focus is not quantitative, an examination of the pattern of warfare is revealing.

Table 1.1 presents data gathered on the incidence of war widening from 1700 to 1973. Of the 13 wars occurring before 1803, ten widened, or roughly 83 per cent. Of the 28 wars from 1803 to 1975, 12 widened, or roughly 43 per cent. In the post-Napoleonic period, therefore, wars were half as likely to widen than in the previous period. What accounts for the dramatic difference in levels of war widening across time?

I discovered that the single most important factor accounting for this variation is the political cost of warfare, by which I mean the pain of war most directly felt by a state's regime. As political cost rose, the amount of war widening decreased. There is also a strong correlation between the length of a war and the number of states engaged. Even correcting for the shorter campaign season, on average wars before 1803 were roughly twice as long as wars occurring after 1803. This is consistent with the argument put forth in this book, that initial wars create opportunities that other states can exploit; longer wars would seem to present more opportunities. Nevertheless, one cannot meaningfully assert that the length of a war causes it to widen, for that naturally begs the question, why were eighteenth-century wars longer? The answer is low political cost. The indecisiveness of eighteenth-century warfare prevented combatants from eliminating each other, and thus wars tended to be protracted.

In the period before 1803, 78.9 per cent of the states that entered ongoing conflicts did so for predatory reasons. In the period after 1803, only 41 per cent of the widening is caused by predation. So the amount of predatory war widening in the earlier period was substantially greater than the later period.

Prior to the outbreak of the Napoleonic Wars, 64 per cent of great power widening was caused by predation. Beginning with the Napoleonic Wars, roughly 38 per cent of great power widening was caused by predation. The difference between the two periods is 26 per cent, which is not as dramatic as the total level, but nonetheless significant. These descriptive data show distinct trends in overall widening, predation and balancing before and after 1803. But the data do not offer an explanation as to why these differences exist. To explain these differences, I use four case studies.

Political cost, I argue, rose dramatically in the midst of the Napoleonic Wars, as warfare itself became more decisive. Therefore, the Seven Years' War, where predation by Austria and Russia caused the war to widen, is presented to investigate war widening when political cost is low. Likewise, the Crimean War, where the failure of Austria and Prussia to join prevented a general war, is presented to examine war widening when political cost is high.

Two additional cases are presented for consideration. The French Revolutionary and Napoleonic Wars show how the political cost of warfare rose, and the contrast between the first and final coalitions exemplifies the transition from predation to balancing as the primary cause of war widening. World War I is included for two reasons. First, as an explosive case of widening in an era of high political cost, it is a difficult case for this theory. Second, and more importantly, it is a strong case for the counter-arguments: it is one of the chief cases for the alliance argument, because prewar alliances played an important role in the outbreak of the war. Moreover, it is an important case for the offense dominance argument. These four cases are presented in chronological order.

The concluding chapter summarizes the findings of the case studies. It assesses how well predation and balancing fared against the competing arguments. The chapter also offers directions for future research suggested by this study. It suggests trends, such as nuclear proliferation, which may perversely lower levels of political cost and make future wars more likely to widen. Finally, knowing whether predation or balancing is driving the likelihood of wars to widen is the key to choosing the appropriate policy response.

NOTES

1. *New York Times*, 25 March 1999, p. A1.
2. John Mearsheimer, 'Back to the Future', in Sean M. Lynn-Jones, ed., *The Cold War and After: Prospects for Peace* (Cambridge, MA: MIT Press, 1991), p. 151.
3. Another term for war widening is 'horizontal escalation'. However, horizontal escalation can also refer to opening a new front against an existing belligerent, which would not be war widening. For example, see Joshua M. Epstein, 'Horizontal Escalation: Sour Notes of a Recurrent Theme', in Robert J. Art and Kenneth N. Waltz, eds, *The Use of Force: Military Power and International Politics* (Lanham, MD: University Press of America, 1988), pp. 541–52.
4. Roy Licklider, 'The Consequences of Negotiated Settlements in Civil Wars, 1945–1993', *American Political Science Review*, 89, 3 (September 1995), pp. 681–90, see 682.
5. Barbara Walter, 'The Critical Barrier to Civil War Settlement', *International Organization*, 51, 3 (Summer 1997), pp. 335–64, see 335–6.
6. 'Europe has a set of primary interests, which to us have none, or a very remote, relation. Hence she must be engaged in frequent controversies, the causes of which are essentially foreign to our concerns. Hence therefore it must be unwise in us to implicate ourselves, by artificial ties, in the ordinary vicissitudes of her politics, or the ordinary combinations and collisions of her friendships or enmities.' George Washington, 'Farewell Address', 17 September 1796, reprinted in Charles Dudley Warner, ed., Hamilton Wright Mabie, Lucia Gilbert Runkle, George Henry Warner, assoc. eds, *A Library of the World's Best Literature* (New York: J. A. Hill, 1896–1902), pp. 15,667–82, see 15,679.
7. The most notable exception to this assertion is the recent scholarship of Randall Schweller, *Deadly Imbalances: Tripolarity and Hitler's Strategy of World Conquest* (New York: Columbia University Press, 1998).

— 2 —

Predation, Balancing and Political Cost

Why do wars widen? More specifically, why do states enter ongoing conflicts? States enter ongoing wars for one of two reasons: predation or balancing. Predation is the attempt to acquire strategic assets. Balancing is the attempt to prevent an adverse shift in the balance of power. The likelihood of predation or balancing to cause a war to widen depends on the level of political cost, or decisiveness of warfare, associated with a given era or state system. Therefore, the likelihood of wars to widen varies over time and can be predicted.

This chapter lays out the basic war widening argument. The logic behind predation and balancing is presented first, followed by the political cost variable which is used to predict both predation and balancing. Last, this chapter presents some of the alternative explanations found in the international relations literature.

A THEORY OF WAR WIDENING

In order to understand war widening, a critical, albeit basic distinction must be made: there are initial combatants and there are neutrals. Every war is initiated by at least two, and usually only two, combatants. Regardless of preexisting alliances or underlying hostilities, any state not party to the initiation of armed conflict is just that: a nonbelligerent or neutral. While the distinction between initial combatants and neutrals may be clouded in a given instance, the distinction is necessary to explain the underlying logic of war widening.

This study rejects the notion that there are separate causes of general wars and limited wars. Instead, it assumes that general wars originate as two-party wars that other states join.[1] By focusing on why neutrals enter other states' conflicts – why wars widen – this thesis also ignores the cause of the initial war. In doing so, the argument emphasizes the possibility that neutrals may have interests and policies entirely distinct from those of the initial combatants. This assumption is clearly supported by experience. The historical record is replete with examples of the difficulties diplomats and generals face when trying to reconcile war aims within coalitions.

Given this distinction between initial combatants and neutrals, a war may widen in one of two ways. In the most common form of widening, a neutral may choose to enter a war by attacking an initial combatant or another neutral. On rare occasions, one of the initial combatants may attack a neutral. This latter type of war widening has a causal logic entirely unrelated to the first. Initial combatants widen wars due to logistic imperatives: they need the neutral territory or assets in that territory to support their primary conflict against the other initial combatant.[2] Since this type of war widening is infrequent and due to an entirely different causal logic, it will not be discussed in this study. The war widening theory explains the most common form: when neutrals choose to widen wars. Neutrals widen wars for only two reasons: predation or balancing.

The predation and balancing arguments are related, in that they share an independent variable: political cost. When political cost is low, predation causes war widening. When political cost is high, balancing causes war widening. These arguments, therefore, will be presented first, beginning with the predation and balancing logic and then showing how predation and balancing can be predicted through political cost.

The theory bases both the predation and balancing arguments on two key assumptions. The first is that the international system is anarchic. The second is that states are sovereign. Therefore, states have no outside force to guarantee their survival; states must depend on their own strength or, conversely, on other states' weakness.

States are, of course, differentiated by strength and weakness; great powers and small powers often behave quite differently due to that disparity. Great power behavior is laid out first, because it has the greatest effect on the international system in general and war widening in particular. Small power behavior is then discussed, with particular emphasis on how it relates to great power action.

Predation

Predation is a state's attempt to acquire strategic assets – generally, territory – as a means to enhance state power.[3] Becoming more powerful is the most important measure a state can take to increase its security. Alliances with other states are never wholly reliable; the only power a state can depend on is its own. Therefore this argument assumes that most, if not all, states would like to increase their power.[4]

Often an ongoing war provides an opportunity for a neutral state to attack another state with a greater likelihood of success than prior to the outbreak of war.[5] The opportunity may be against one of the initial combatants or against another neutral. Against an initial combatant, the neutral may be offered incentives to join the war as an auxiliary. An auxiliary joins one of the initial combatants as a junior partner, so to speak. The auxiliary's contribution and reward are usually stipulated before the neutral enters the war. Such a formal relationship, while common, is not necessary. In certain situations, such as when both the initial combatant and neutral covet some of the same territory, there is no agreement at all: rewards are then left to the fortunes of war.

Wars may also create opportunities to attack other neutral states, rather than joining in a war against one of the initial combatants. Such an opportunity may be created if the initial conflict has tied down the intended victim's allies, leaving the victim state vulnerable. A similar opportunity may be created if a neutral had been restrained from attacking another neutral for fear that it would in turn be attacked by one of the initial combatants, even if there was no sort of defensive alliance between those states. In this sense, predation may also be thought of as opportunism.

Alliances with initial combatants are not necessary for predatory war widening. In some cases, they are useful to establish the quid pro quo relationship of the auxiliary or to formalize various strategic or operational agreements for a campaign. In other instances, particularly when there is conflict over division of the anticipated spoils, states prefer to forgo any alliance.

For predation to be successful, the neutral must choose a side likely to win or commit enough of its own assets to ensure victory. The existence of the initial conflict usually ensures that those combatants will be committing a significant portion of their own resources. This is the core of the opportunity. A great power can, by virtue of its relative size, usually bring victory to either side with proportionately less cost than the initial combatants who are already committed against each other. Thus the critical choice facing a great power is: which side offers the greatest gain at the least cost?

In predatory war widening, states use the opportunity presented by the initial war to seek gains. The opportunity arises when the initial war increases the likelihood of successful predation for neutral states. This predation may be either unilateral or allied, against an initial combatant or another neutral. The key aspect of predation is the desire to gain assets to increase state power.

Balancing

Balancing is acting to prevent an adverse shift in the balance of power. In this case, the potential outcome of a conflict threatens the security of a neutral state, which then enters the war on the side of the least menacing party (generally the weaker) to preserve its own security. Here the initial war threatens to leave the victor substantially stronger, creating a security risk for a neutral state or states. Thus, to protect its own position, a neutral attacks the stronger of the two initial combatants, usually in some form of alliance with the weaker state.

It should be noted that there is nothing in balancing logic that requires the neutral to have a strong preference, be it ideological, cultural or even security driven, for one initial combatant over the other. Quite the contrary, the motive may be to prevent either combatant from winning – an attempt to preserve the status quo ante. British behavior in the War of the Spanish Succession (1701–14) illustrates this situation. The Austrian Habsburgs and the French Bourbons held competing claims to the Spanish throne. If Spain were controlled by either France or Austria, it would adversely affect British interests. As the French claim was initially the stronger of the two, Britain allied with Austria. But in 1711, the political situation changed, strengthening Austria's claim. Britain therefore deserted Austria and supported France. While Britain's allies changed, its policy remained the same: to prevent the rise of a European hegemon.

Balancing and predation are differentiated by motive and behavior. Balancing seeks to prevent damage, usually by preserving the status quo; predation seeks gains. These different motives prompt different behaviors. For example, balancers usually side with the weaker belligerent, while predators often join the stronger one. While the gains sought through predation may ultimately enhance security, the motives and behaviors that drive predation and balancing are separate and distinct.

Predation and Balancing: Small Powers

Although accounting for the majority of states in the world, small powers enjoy a rather precarious existence. They are subject to the vagaries of great power politics over which they have little influence and less control. As much, or even more so than the great powers, small powers want to increase their power.

Predation, of course, means the same thing for a small power as a great power: an attempt to acquire strategic assets as a means to enhance state power. But predation is more difficult for small powers. Unlike the great powers that can make the difference between a winning and a losing coalition, small powers must be more careful to choose the winning side. This accounts for the not uncommon situation where smaller states enter wars late, when the outcome seems clear, or even change sides during a conflict. While Italy's behavior in World War I is one of the more notorious examples, there are many others. In the same war, Romania was induced to join the Allies with promises of territory, while Greece actually switched from being pro-Allied to pro-German when the fortunes of war seemed in Germany's favor.

Wars involving great powers can provide many predatory opportunities for smaller powers. Great powers already engaged in a conflict are less concerned with the regional balances that constrain small power behavior. Even when they are concerned, their engagement in the primary war may prevent great powers from being able to aid smaller allies. In this instance, a great power war may provide small powers with an opportunity to attack a neighbor with better prospects than during peacetime.

Great powers may also offer small powers inducements to join them in a coalition. If a war becomes protracted, small powers may be offered compensations in exchange for assistance in the belief that the small powers' contribution, while small, may be enough to tip the balance. An example of this is the generous package Great Britain gave to Sweden in the Wars of Liberation.[6] Britain provided Sweden with subsidies out of all proportion to the size of the Swedish contribution, but London believed this small additional force was necessary to ensure Napoleon's defeat.

Even if a small power's contribution is not believed to be necessary to win the war, great powers are often willing to provide significant inducements to small powers in an effort to preserve their own postwar position. Even a victorious great power has to be concerned about relative power vis-à-vis not only the defeated state, but also coalition partners and neutrals.[7]

Ironically, small powers can find some of their greatest predatory opportunities from great power balancers. The great power predator, or revisionist state, is after spoils that may conflict with the designs of the smaller powers. A balancing great power is not fighting for spoils, and is more likely to grant them to small powers, not only because the great power does not want them, but also as a means of enhancing the great power's security by reducing its foe.

Small power predation is the bandwagoning behavior theorized by Randall Schweller,[8] but a simpler concept, in that it does not distinguish between what Schweller refers to as jackal 'bandwagoning' and 'piling on'. There are two significant differences between small power predation used to explain war widening and bandwagoning in Schweller's work. The first is that, unlike Schweller, this argument does not view small power predation as buck-passing, because the small powers usually make some sort of contribution to the war, albeit a small one. The second, and most significant departure from Schweller, however, is the relationship between status quo and revisionist states. Schweller contends: 'status quo coalitions promise a smaller payoff to dissatisfied states than do revisionist coalitions, since the former cannot, in principle and for domestic political reasons, offer territorial incentives to wean the revisionist state away from a revisionist coalition.'[10] The argument here is quite different. Balancing coalitions are willing to carve up their adversaries to provide spoils for small powers precisely because they do not covet the territory themselves.

Balancing behavior is usually limited to great powers. Small states rarely balance against threats to the global order because they are generally unable to affect the balance in any meaningful way. Although concerned about their regional balance of power, they are relatively ineffective if great powers intervene. Therefore, small powers tend to seek security through alliances with great powers. Most small powers at some level would like to become great powers and thus be able to more effectively ensure their own security instead of depending on great power alliances. This creates predatory pressures which in ordinary circumstances are curbed through the regional balance of power and threat of great power intervention. But once a great-power war occurs, these restraints are removed. These conflicts present opportunities for gains because great powers offer concessions they would not otherwise make. Small powers try to limit their exposure by entering the conflict only after it becomes clear that their proposed allies will win, but not so late that their allies will not pay for their participation.

Unlike the great powers, small powers are only predatory war wideners. They have no incentive to intervene in the wars of great powers to affect the balance of power. Ironically, when great powers are balancing they can create more predatory opportunities for small powers than when the great powers themselves are widening a war for predatory motives.

PREDICTING PREDATION AND BALANCING

The primary determinant of whether neutral great powers will enter ongoing wars, whether for predation or balancing reasons, is political cost. When the political cost associated with warfare is low, the incentives for predation are high, and almost all wars will widen. When the political cost of warfare is high, states have little incentive for predation. This is offset somewhat by an increased incentive for balancing, as wars are more likely to shift the balance of power. But, since states can balance in ways other than direct intervention in a conflict, wars occurring in a high political cost environment are less likely to widen. Therefore, an era of low political cost fosters war widening, while high political cost does not. More simply put, predation produces more war widening than balancing does.

Political *cost* is the independent variable driving the likelihood of predatory or balancing behavior. Political cost refers to the cost of losing a war. The size of the cost is more important than the relationship between cost and gain. The anarchic nature of international relations requires that states must seek to ensure their own survival. Cost *must* be more important than benefit in determining predatory behavior because there is a point at which, regardless of how great the potential gain, the potential cost – annihilation – is too great. Thus, the independent variable is political cost, and not a cost–benefit ratio. States will risk their survival only when their survival is being threatened – a balancing behavior rather than a predatory one.

Defining Political Cost

Political cost is the price associated with warfare felt most directly by a state's regime. Conceptually, the costs associated with war can be divided into three distinct yet obviously related categories: economic, military and political. Economic costs include not only the financing of the campaign, but also lost trade and other opportunity costs. Military cost refers to casualties and expended materiel. Political cost is manifested in such areas as loss of influence, loss of territory and, in the extreme, loss of regime. Obviously, military and economic costs contribute to political cost, but political cost is distinctive in several ways.

First, and most important, political cost captures the decisiveness of warfare. A war may entail very high military and economic costs without threatening the survival of the states engaged in the conflict, and vice versa. Examples of the disparity between military and political cost are the Gulf War and the Tet Offensive in Vietnam. Saddam Hussein paid a high price militarily in the Gulf War, but has paid a lower price politically. The United States suffered a significant political cost as a result of Tet, despite winning the engagement and suffering a relatively low price militarily.

Second, by focusing on the political cost of warfare, this explanation of war widening allows for disparities in regimes or regime types. This study does not account for differences in regime types, for example, democratic or authoritarian; to the contrary, it asserts that the political cost of warfare is a system-wide variable, affecting all states in a similar fashion. However, should convincing evidence be produced that there is a significant difference in the political cost of warfare between regime types, then the war widening theory could be modified to take this into account.[10]

Third, there is a fundamental difference between political cost and military or economic cost: political cost is not fungible. States that widen wars often have aims distinct from the initial combatants and, so too, are their costs separate. States may render military or financial aid, but political cost is borne alone.

While the actual political cost of a venture cannot be known with certainty beforehand, estimates of political cost can be and generally are made based on recent history. Political cost is directly attributable to the decisiveness of warfare; the more decisive warfare is, the higher the political cost that ensues. It is only when warfare is decisive that states can threaten to dismember or eliminate an opposing great power. In that sense, eras can be categorized as having either low or high political cost, based on the reasonable understanding of contemporary decision-makers as to their worst possible outcome. Of course, a state's leaders may be mistaken in their assessment. Social or technological factors may affect warfare in ways unanticipated by decision-makers. Or, more rarely, leaders may anticipate a change that does not occur. Overall, however, decisions are based on recent experience. When errors are made, more often than not they are due to a failure to appreciate change.

Low Political Cost: Limited War

Despite almost continual and widespread warfare, many historians have referred to eighteenth-century Europe as an era of limited war. Although recent historians have drawn attention to the fact that these wars hardly seemed limited to active participants,[11] they were limited in one important respect: political cost. With the notable exception of Poland – both a small power and 'political mess',[12] and thus thrice partitioned – individually these wars did not change the political map of Europe in any significant way.[13] States could enter wars, particularly as auxiliaries, with little or no fear of being destroyed, in search of gains, albeit also small, at the peace talks.

This willingness of states to join as auxiliaries is partly due to what Paul Schroeder refers to as the rules of compensations and indemnities, which 'regularly helped make eighteenth-century alliances . . . into power political instruments . . . normally intended for expansion and acquisitions as well as mutual security'.[14] But this willingness to enter conflicts is less a product of the rules and norms of eighteenth-century politics, as Schroeder contends,[15] than it is the nature of armed force in the eighteenth century.

European warfare in the eighteenth century was dominated by a strategy of attrition.[16] Armies were far too costly and difficult to replace for battle to be risked lightly.[17] Even when battles were fought, they were usually indecisive, due in large part to the nature of eighteenth-century battle, which often left the victor almost as badly damaged as the loser and thus unable to undertake the pursuit necessary to destroy the enemy.[18] Thus the defeated party was able to successfully withdraw and regroup without being pursued and destroyed in detail.

The Change to Total War

The French Revolutionary and Napoleonic Wars brought a fundamental change to European warfare. France, which had been
declining steadily in military power since 1700, not only was reinvig-
orated, but profoundly changed the nature of warfare. The *'levée en
masse* gave France . . . a seemingly inexhaustible reservoir of manpower'.[19] Of even greater importance, '[t]he political and social
limitations on warfare were burst asunder by the enormous growth in
the power of the state. Against a background of defeat and economic
chaos, France opted for total war.'[20] All of the components of total war
were present before Napoleon's first successful campaign:[21] the agricultural revolution produced a sizable surplus which freed up more
and better-quality manpower; a divisional system was already in place
to organize these larger armies; increased trade brought improved
communications; and state bureaucracies became more efficient at
extracting resources. In Napoleonic France, these gradual changes
were combined in such a way that a strategy of annihilation was now
feasible, although it was not until the Third or even the Fourth
Coalition that this change was fully understood.[22]

There were no major technological developments in the last half
of the eighteenth century that significantly enhanced warfighting
capability.[23] The musket carried by Napoleon's armies differed little
from those carried by Frederick the Great's Prussian forces two generations earlier. Artillery was slightly more mobile, but no more
accurate. The change from limited to unlimited warfare was not technological, but social.

The first change, ushered in by the French Revolution, was the
rise of the citizen soldier.[24] Soldiers now had a stake in the outcome of
battle beyond traditional plunder. Defense of the fatherland as motivation, combined with the increased reach of the revolutionary state,
helped enable mass conscription, the backbone of most nineteenth-
and twentieth-century land power, and with it, improved tactics.

Through the mid-eighteenth century, logistics constrained the
size of the force a commander could use effectively. Beyond a certain
point, it could no longer be fed or moved. The agricultural revolution
lifted these constraints.[25] By the middle of the eighteenth century,
agriculture began to produce a noticeable surplus, which continued to
grow through the last half of the century. As the surplus grew, more
food became available for sale outside of its immediate neighborhood.

Over time, road networks were expanded and improved to facilitate this trade. Additionally, as farming became more efficient, less labor was needed in the countryside. Young men, whether of their own volition or due to displacement, sought employment in the larger towns and cities, thereby increasing demand for foodstuffs and the roads to transport them.

Furthermore, the pool of men available for military service grew.[26] Improved farming techniques sustained a population boom. As mentioned above, greater labor efficiency freed a larger number of men for military service. Thus, the agricultural revolution made mass armies possible. There were more men available, plenty of food to sustain them, and roads to move them.

Why did larger armies change warfare from limited to unlimited? The size of armies changed the incentives from maneuver to battle at all levels: tactics, strategy and logistics. The eighteenth-century commander's main objective was to preserve the army; his army was small, expensive and, above all, hard to replace.[27] A commander only sought battle if the odds were overwhelmingly in his favor. With opposing commanders operating under essentially the same conditions, few battles were fought and little decided. When armies became very large, all the pressures were on commanders to seek battle, quickly and decisively, inflicting military defeats with momentous political consequences.

Large armies changed tactics in several meaningful ways. First, they greatly reduced the importance of fortresses.[28] Instead of being required to lay a lengthy siege to a fortress in order to progress deeper into enemy territory, a commander could now detach a masking force to cover his rear and proceed unhindered.[29] The large influx of recruits and replacements also accelerated the shift from line tactics to column and mixed, especially in France.[30] The shift began before the French Revolution, but was accelerated by necessity. The column was a way to make use of large numbers of raw troops, but was more useful for attack than defense. The shift in emphasis from line to column, while brought about as a way to utilize poorly trained recruits, also gave commanders another reason to seek battle. The easy availability of replacements also reduced concern for the health of individual soldiers. First the French, and later others, dramatically increased the speed with which their armies could move by eliminating tents for the enlisted ranks.[31] By bivouacking in the open, soldiers could make and strike camp more quickly, and the reduction of the baggage train allowed them to cover more ground in a day.

The rapid increase in the size of armies sped the adoption of the divisional and later the corps system. The divisions were marched separately to gain speed[32] (and for logistic reasons which are explained below). A division contained all the elements of a small army, and the divisions were spaced within about a day's march of one another. If one division encountered enemy forces, it could hold out long enough for the rest of the army to be brought up in support. In the hands of a skillful commander such as Napoleon, an encounter battle could be turned to a major and decisive victory. Thus, the sheer size of armies and available recruits reduced the importance of sieges and gave commanders the speed and tactics with which to force a decision by battle.

Strategically, with a large number of able-bodied men available as replacements, losses were easier to replace.[33] While a major defeat could still be devastating, the losses associated with *winning* a battle were no longer prohibitive.[34] The victor of a major battle could still muster sufficient force to pursue his foe, turning a defeat into a rout. Large armies facilitated the occupation of enemy territory, withholding resources from the enemy army and increasing pressure on the enemy government to come to terms – not to mention making victory quite profitable.

The logistics of fielding and supplying such large armies also favored battle over maneuver.[35] The road networks that were developed and improved to transport the surplus of the agricultural revolution increased the speed armies could travel. The density of these networks facilitated the practice of marching divisions separately. This was not only necessary for speed, but for supply. It was never practical for an army to carry all of its supplies, particularly bulky items such as food and fodder, and it became less practical as armies grew. By dividing an army into self-sufficient divisions and assigning them parallel marching routes, each could be assigned its own forage area. For example, each division could be assigned a forage area extending ten miles on its left. Armies of this time period traveled through the countryside like a plague of locusts. If an entire army of 300,000 men or more marched along the same route, there would be nothing remaining for the forces in the rear.

The demands of an army for food and fodder made it impossible to hold one stationary in the field for more than a short time – it simply could not be supplied. Once assembled, an army either had to be used for battle or dispersed into quarters. The large forces of the

Napoleonic Wars could not wage the protracted game of waiting and maneuver that characterized the wars of preceding generations. Thus the logistic demands of such a large force provided an additional incentive for battle.

Naval warfare also changed from limited to unlimited. British naval officers moved away from line tactics to the *mêlée*, which provided more opportunity for a decisive victory. This was not due to an increase in the size of navies comparable to the increase seen in continental armies. On the contrary, the Royal Navy rarely seemed to have enough ships to cover its ever-expanding responsibilities. At many of Britain's greatest naval victories, such as Trafalgar, the Royal Navy was outnumbered.[36] If anything, the need to force a decisive battle may have stemmed from too few resources. The British change in naval tactics made use of the Royal Navy's advantages in seamanship and gunnery. Whereas land tactics changed because of an abundance of untrained manpower, the revolution in naval tactics took advantage of Britain's adversaries' lack of training. There was no tactical change the French Navy could make to compensate for poorly trained seamen and officers – the sailing ships of the age were much too complicated. The Royal Navy saw this and exploited its enemy's weakness.[37]

With large armies available to them, states had the capability to make the shift from limited to unlimited warfare. This shift did not happen instantly, nor was it immediately recognized. The age of total war dawned slowly but was seen by all certainly no later than Prussia's demise in 1806. The technological changes of the nineteenth and twentieth centuries reinforced the high political cost of warfare. But, just as technological and social change produced the shift from limited war to total war, future change may return us to an era of low political cost.

Using Political Cost to Make Predictions

When the political cost of warfare is low, the incentive for predation is high. States can enter other states' conflicts with little risk of annihilation. States will engage in predatory war widening even for minor gains. Conversely, when the political cost is high, states will refrain from predatory war widening, even if the potential gain is large, because, as discussed above, no gain is worth the risk of annihilation. Even if the likelihood of success is the same in both cases, predation will occur when political cost is low; it will not occur when political cost is high.

Balancing behavior is more likely when the political cost of warfare is high, because warfare is more decisive and thus more likely to shift the balance of power fundamentally. While predation and balancing are inversely related to the level of political cost, they do not occur at the same rate. That is to say, war has not spread at a constant rate, caused by predation in the eighteenth century and balancing afterwards. Balancing produces less war widening for three reasons.

First, not every war, decisive or not, threatens an adverse shift in the balance of power. A war between two small powers cannot, by definition, affect more than the regional balance of power. In this instance, the great powers have no need to balance and the other states in the region have other balancing options, including allying with great powers. Even in great power wars, if the opponents are equally matched, the costs the war imposes on the two initial combatants may increase the relative power of their neighboring states. The wisest option for neutrals is to allow the warring states to bleed each other white; at the end of the conflict the neutrals are likely to emerge relatively stronger than they were at the opening of the war, a situation referred to as the 'dilemma of the victor's inheritance'.

Second, the balance of power is a collective good: all states share in it regardless of which state or states maintain it. A state concerned with its relative power position has every incentive to allow other states to pay the costs of maintaining the balance. In other words, when confronted with a rising hegemon, the other great powers have an incentive to wait for other states to balance against the rising power. This is a tendency commonly referred to as buck-passing. As with other sorts of collective goods problems, this situation can result in no action at all, which in this instance means no war widening.

Third, and perhaps most important, states can often balance using other means, whether diplomatic or economic.[38] States may form new alliances against the victor of the war. States may strengthen existing alliances or other relationships. States may seek to strengthen themselves, improving their economies, infrastructures or militaries.

Reversing the propositions, great powers will only widen wars to balance when:

1 the war threatens to adversely shift the balance of power;
2 it appears that no other state can or will balance in their interests; and
3 other means of balancing have been exhausted.

These three conditions can be and have been met simultaneously. But the necessity of fulfilling all three means that, in general, wars occurring in an era of high political cost are less likely to widen than their counterparts when political cost is low.

Yet, even in an era of high political cost, small powers may still widen a war for predatory reasons. As discussed above, small powers rarely balance. But, when great powers widen a war for balancing reasons, they create predatory incentives for small powers. By joining a great power coalition, small powers limit their costs. Ironically, spoils are easier to obtain from great powers that are balancing and do not covet gains for themselves. Moreover, if a great power war descends into a war of attrition, the bargaining position of small powers is enhanced because of the belief that they just might tip the balance.

To summarize, the predation and balancing arguments offer the following predictions for war widening:

- When political cost is low, predation will cause a high level of war widening.
- When political cost is high, wars will be less likely to widen. Great powers that enter the conflict will do so for balancing reasons.
- When great powers widen a war for balancing reasons, they create incentives for predation by smaller states, which will increase the number of combatants.

In a low political cost environment, predation causes almost every war to widen. In a high political cost environment, fewer wars widen. When they do, great powers enter for balancing reasons, although in so doing they may create incentives for small powers to join in for predatory reasons. Thus, while war widening in a high political cost environment is less likely, it may be explosive when it comes.

Summary

War widening is caused by predation and balancing. When the political cost of warfare is low, as was true from 1700 to 1803, states have a high incentive to engage in predation, which makes any war very likely to widen. When the political cost of war is high, as has been the case from 1803 to the present, great powers have little incentive for predatory war widening, but do have an incentive to widen wars for balancing reasons when other options are not available. To complicate

matters, war widening by the great powers for balancing reasons provides predatory incentives for small powers to join wars, even when
the political cost of war is high.

ALTERNATIVE EXPLANATIONS

International relations theory offers several explanations for war
widening, but two figure most prominently in the literature: alliances
and offense dominance. This section briefly outlines these arguments
and discusses some of the weaknesses associated with them.

The first argument contends that alliances are the primary vehicle
for war widening. Alliances, which may be formed for reasons rang-
ing from ideology to deterrence, make war more likely for their
members should a conflict occur involving one of them. Alliances are
sometimes presented as the sole independent variable; at other times
they are used in conjunction with one or more other variables.[39]

The argument itself is quite simple and there is considerable
empirical data to support it, at least for the period after 1815.[40] The
fundamental problem with the alliance argument results from the
nature of alliances themselves. For the scholar who focuses on the
pressures created by the international system, there is good reason to
suspect a colinearity problem; to wit, many of the same systemic variables that produce alliances also produce war widening. From this
perspective, alliances are at best an intervening variable. Alliances
themselves may be defensive or offensive, or both. In other words,
they may be a vehicle for either balancing or predation. There also
can be great flexibility to alliances, even to the point where states rou-
tinely calculate the point at which they expect their allies to defect.
With such great alliance flexibility, it is really meaningless to speak of
alliances as causing war widening.

The most intriguing counter-argument is offense dominance.
Offense dominance has two variants: technology and belief.[41] The
argument is basically the same for each: when statesmen believe that
offense is more effective than a defensive posture, that is, when it is
easier to attack than defend, security becomes scarcer and alliances
widen and tighten.[42] In effect, it provides the independent variable
missing from the alliance argument presented above.

The technology version of the offense dominance argument
holds that certain weapons, through either mobility or vulnerability,

favor offensive military action. The most straightforward criticism of the technology version of the offense dominance argument is that offensive/defensive dominance does not exist.[43] Weapons (and weapons systems), especially conventional, cannot be categorized as either 'offensive' or 'defensive'. For example, the same mobility that leads many theorists to conclude that the tank is an offensive weapon can favor defensive action when incorporated into a mobile defense or defense in depth. Likewise, fortifications, long held out as the ultimate defensive system, can favor the offense when utilized to conserve troop strength for concentration at the point of attack. As critics of a technology-based offense–defense distinction have correctly argued, technology is but one of several factors manipulated by political–military leaders when formulating strategy. Further, geographic variation within a state system is generally significant enough so that even if technology produced an offensive or defensive advantage, it would not be a system-wide characteristic.

The belief version of offense dominance is sometimes referred to as the 'cult of the offensive'.[44] It sidesteps the criticisms outlined above by emphasizing statesmen's *belief* in offense dominance, rather than any real offensive advantage. Even so, problems remain. There is no guarantee that statesmen will perceive the balance, real or imagined, in the same way. Furthermore, any supposed offensive bias can be manifested, not in plans for war initiation, but in plans to retake the offensive *after* the initial assault. The US Army's doctrine, Air–Land Battle, was based on precisely this principle.

Additionally, both versions of the offense dominance argument, technology and belief, rest on the presumption that offense dominance will translate into offensive military doctrine.[45] Barry Posen made the same basic argument about the effects of offensive doctrines to justify his study of their origin.[46] In this study, he concludes that military doctrines are primarily determined by the balance of power. As such, military doctrines are heterogeneous across a state system and cannot be a significant cause of war widening in the manner suggested by the offense dominance argument.[47]

Lastly, as the evidence presented in this study shows, neither the alliance nor the offense dominance argument fits the facts. Alliances can explain only a small proportion of the widening that occurs in some wars and absolutely none of the widening that occurs in other wars. Offense dominance is an even poorer explanation. If one accepts the dubious distinction between offense and defense dominance, the results of this study show the correlation is reversed. To the extent that 'defense dominance' can be related to low political cost, war widening is more likely under defense dominance than offense dominance.

CONCLUSION

Predation is responsible for the largest amount of war widening. Predation by great powers occurs only when political cost is low, enabling states to seek gains without risk of annihilation. Therefore, when political cost is low, all wars have a significant risk of widening. War widening does not disappear, however, when political cost is high. Rather, if the potential outcome of the war threatens to shift the balance of power adversely, and no other means of balancing is available, great powers may join the war. The addition of a great power to balance a war provides strong incentives for small powers to join for predatory reasons. Thus, when political cost is high, fewer wars widen. But those that do widen can do so explosively.

NOTES

1. This follows the same basic assumption as Geoffrey Blainey. See ch. 15, 'The Mystery of Wide Wars', in *The Causes of War*, 3rd edn (New York: The Free Press, 1988).
2. See Stacy B. Haldi, 'The Influence of Logistics on War Widening', *Defense and Security Analysis*, 18, 1 (March 2002), pp. 3–14.
3. This is similar to what Stephen Van Evera calls 'opportunistic expansionism'. See Van Evera, 'Offense, Defense and the Causes of War', *International Security*, 22, 4 (Spring 1998), pp. 5–43. It is also related to Charles Glaser's concept of the 'greedy' state. See Glaser, 'Political Consequences of Military Strategy: Expanding and Refining the Spiral and Deterrence Models', *World Politics*, 44, 4 (July 1992), pp. 497–538.
4. For a cogent argument on states as 'defensive security maximizers', see chs 3 and 4 in Ashley Tellis, 'The Drive to Domination: Toward a Pure Theory of Realist Politics', unpub. dissert., University of Chicago, 1994. For a strong argument that all states want to increase their power, see John J. Mearsheimer, *The Tragedy of Great Power Politics* (New York: W. W. Norton, 2001), p. 33.
5. By focusing on the ability of initial wars to create new situations for other states, this argument follows a line of thought used by Richard Smoke in *War: Controlling Escalation* (Cambridge, MA: Harvard University Press, 1977). However, Smoke focuses much of his argument on escalation as something inadvertent, while this argument views war widening as a deliberate act.

6. See Chapter 4.
7. Hans Delbrück, *History of the Art of War within the Framework of Political History: Vol. 4, The Modern Era*, trans. Walter J. Renfroe, Jr, Contributions in Military History, 39 (Westport, CT: Greenwood Press, 1985 [originally published Berlin, 1920]), p. 296.
8. Randall L. Schweller, 'Bandwagoning for Profit: Bringing the Revisionist State Back In', *International Security*, 19, 1 (Summer 1994), pp. 72–107, see 79.
9. Randall L. Schweller, *Deadly Imbalances: Tripolarity and Hitler's Strategy of World Conquest* (New York: Columbia University Press, 1998), p. 64.
10. For example, Bueno de Mesquita and Randolph Siverson argue that there is a significant difference in the ability of leaders in different regime types to survive wars. See Bruce Bueno de Mesquita and Randolph M. Siverson, 'War and the Survival of Political Leaders: A Comparative Study of Regime Types and Political Accountability', *American Political Science Review*, 89, 4 (December 1995), pp. 841–55.
11. See John Childs, *Armies and Warfare in Europe: 1648–1789* (New York: Holmes & Meier, 1982).
12. According to Childs, 'Seventeenth- and eighteenth-century Poland was a political mess, a country which had failed to modernise its governmental or social structure'. Childs, *Armies and Warfare in Europe*, p. 39. This, in part, helps to explain Poland's demise and why it was so exceptional.
13. This even holds for the Seven Years' War which 'ended without any significant territorial change in Europe and without change in the relationships of the great powers'. Delbrück, *History of the Art of War*, p. 387.
14. Paul W. Schroeder, *The Transformation of European Politics 1768–1848* (Oxford: Clarendon Press, 1994), p. 7.
15. Schroeder, *Transformation of European Politics*, p. vii.
16. For a discussion of the predominance of attrition (versus annihilation) strategy in the eighteenth century, see Delbrück, *History of the Art of War*, ch. 4.
17. Hew Strachan, *European Armies and the Conduct of War* (London: Unwin Hyman, 1983), pp. 15–17; Michael Howard, *War in European History* (Oxford: Oxford University Press, 1976), pp. 70–1.
18. See Childs, *Armies and Warfare in Europe*, p. 70.
19. Strachan, *European Armies and the Conduct of War*, p. 40.
20. Ibid.
21. Ibid., pp. 41–3.
22. Delbrück, *History of the Art of War*, p. 304.
23. Gunther E. Rothenberg, *The Art of Warfare in the Age of Napoleon* (Bloomington, IN: Indiana University Press, 1978), p. 28.
24. Jeremy Black, *European Warfare 1660–1815* (New Haven, CT: Yale University Press, 1994), p. 168; Delbrück, *History of the Art of War*, p. 407; Strachan, *European Armies and the Conduct of War*, p. 40.
25. For a cogent discussion of the role of the agricultural revolution on military force, see Strachan, *European Armies and the Conduct of War*, pp. 41–54.
26. William McNeill credits the population rise to a drop in the rate of infectious diseases. See William H. McNeill, *The Pursuit of Power: Technology, Armed Force and Society since AD 1000* (Chicago, IL: University of Chicago Press, 1982), pp. 185, 200. I think, however, it has as much or more to do with the greatly improved nutrition of the population because of the agricultural revolution. People who are well-fed are better able to withstand infections that can be lethal in those suffering from malnutrition.

27. This is what Delbrück refers to as a 'strategy of attrition'. See Delbrück, *History of the Art of War*, p. 296.
28. Delbrück, *History of the Art of War*, pp. 409, 423.
29. Martin Van Creveld, *Supplying War: Logistics from Wallenstein to Patton* (Cambridge: Cambridge University Press, 1977), p. 42.
30. Delbrück, *History of the Art of War*, pp. 398–400. However, this was not true in the British Army, which, due to its small size and long-service troops, was able to maintain the intensive training and discipline necessary for line tactics to be effective. When French attacking columns met British (and British-trained Portuguese) lines, the result usually favored the British.
31. Rothenberg, *The Art of Warfare in the Age of Napoleon*, p. 36.
32. Russell F. Weigley, *The Age of Battles: The Quest for Decisive Warfare from Breitenfeld to Waterloo* (Bloomington, IN: Indiana University Press, 1991), pp. 264–5.
33. Rothenberg, *The Art of Warfare in the Age of Napoleon*, p. 36. But in the campaign of 1812, however, Napoleon lost too many men and was forced to call up recruit classes early. With population growth foundering due to so many men in the army, Napoleon was hard-pressed to find enough men to take the field in 1813 and 1814, a fact which contributed significantly to his final defeat.
34. Delbrück, *History of the Art of War*, pp. 296, 304.
35. On military logistics under Napoleon, see Van Creveld, *Supplying War*, ch 2.
36. Paul M. Kennedy, *The Rise and Fall of British Naval Mastery* (London: The Ashfield Press, 1976), pp. 125–6.
37. Ibid., pp. 126, 128.
38. This is essentially what happened during the Wars of German Unification. No single conflict threatened to overturn the balance of power decisively. Furthermore, in a loose, multipolar environment, the states threatened by the increase in Prussian/German power had other means to balance, both through alliances and internal development. See Jack Levy, 'Big Wars, Little Wars, and Theory Construction', *International Interactions*, 16, 2 (1990), pp. 215–24, see 218.
39. For example, see Randolph M. Siverson and Harvey Starr, *The Diffusion of War: A Study of Opportunity and Willingness* (Ann Arbor, MI: University of Michigan Press, 1991).
40. See Jack Levy, *War in the Modern Great Power System, 1495–1975* (Lexington, KY: University Press of Kentucky, 1983), p. 153. See also Ido Oren, 'The War Proneness of Alliances', *JCR*, 34, 2 (1990), pp. 208–23, in which Oren concludes: 'the larger the alliance, the larger the average number of wars that each of its members experience.' See also Michael F. Altfeld and Bruce Bueno de Mesquita, 'Choosing Sides in Wars', *International Studies Quarterly*, 23, 11 (March 1979), pp. 87–112. Alliances are an integral component of the utility measurement used in this model.
41. Van Evera divides the two into 'real' and 'perceptual'; Van Evera, 'Offense, Defense and the Causes of War', p. 6.
42. See Robert Jervis, 'Cooperation under the Security Dilemma', *World Politics*, 30, 2 (January 1978), pp. 167–214.
43. For an excellent refutation of the offense dominance argument, see Jonathan Shimshoni, 'Technology, Military Advantage and World War I: A Case for Military Entrepreneurship', *International Security*, 15, 3 (Winter 1990/91), pp. 187–215. For a theoretical and empirical critique, see Jack S. Levy, 'The Offensive/Defensive Balance of Military Technology: A Theoretical and Historical Analysis', *International Studies Quarterly*, 28 (1984), pp. 219–38; and Kier A. Lieber, 'Grasping the Technological Peace: The Offense–Defense

Balance and International Security', *International Security*, 25, 1 (Summer 2000), pp. 71–104.

44. See Stephen Van Evera, 'The Cult of the Offensive and the Origins of the First World War', *International Security*, 9, 1 (Summer 1984), pp. 58–107.

45. An offensive strategy can utilize defensive tactics and vice versa. For example, General Longstreet is quoted as saying: 'I then accepted his proposition to make a campaign into Pennsylvania, provided it should be offensive in strategy but defensive in tactics, forcing the Federal army to give us battle when we were in a strong position and ready to receive them.' Shelby Foote, *The Civil War: A Narrative: Fredericksburg to Meridian* (New York: Random House, 1963), p. 2:436.

46. Barry R. Posen, *The Sources of Military Doctrine: France, Britain and Germany between the World Wars* (Ithaca, NY: Cornell University Press, 1984).

47. Posen's conclusion as to the cause of war widening appears somewhat contradictory in nature. On the one hand, he attributes war widening to ineffectual balancing (*Sources of Military Doctrine*, p. 29). On the other hand, he states that balancing will be quick and intense when offensive military doctrines are prevalent (p. 66). Perhaps, contrary to the usual offense dominance argument, Posen is suggesting that war widening is less likely when the offense dominates. His position on the war widening question is unclear because he does not directly address the issue. However, if this interpretation of his position is correct, then it is in keeping with the position of this thesis.

3

The Seven Years' War
(1756–63)

> Past facts are good to store the imagination, and the memory; they furnish a
> repository of ideas, whence a supply of materials may be obtained; but which
> wought to be purified by passing through the strainer of the judgment.
> *Frederick the Great*

The Seven Years' War is misnamed; it was only a seven-year war on the
Continent. In truth, it began a year or two earlier as a colonial war
between Britain and France. This war ultimately provided Austria with
the tools it had been seeking since the peace of Aix-la-Chapelle (1748)
to build an offensive coalition to attack Prussia. This continental war
would not have occurred at this time if the colonial war were not being
waged. The Seven Years' War shows how predatory war widening can
turn a war on the periphery into a world war.

The Seven Years' War was chosen as a case study for two reasons.
First, as a colonial war which became a continental war, it differs significantly from the other general wars usually studied, such as World War I
and World War II. Second, it has been described as a 'balancing' war in
an era this theory predicts should be dominated by predatory war
widening.

The Seven Years' War makes three important points about war
widening in an era of low political cost. First, most war widening is the
result of predation: Austria, Russia and Sweden joined the war for the
express purpose of partitioning Prussia among themselves and, as the case
shows, this was not because Prussia was any immediate threat. That they
ultimately failed is due in part to the limited nature of eighteenth-
century warfare, not their intentions. Second, alliances did not cause this
war to widen in the way such an argument generally contemplates.
Rather, the colonial war caused a dramatic shift in alliances: the
Diplomatic Revolution, created for the purpose of fighting the Seven

Years' War. Alliances did not cause war widening; war widening caused alliances. Austria had attempted to change the traditional alliance pattern since 1749, but only the existence of the Anglo-French colonial war enabled it to do so. Finally, perceptions of any offensive or defensive balance played no part in decisions to enter this war.

This chapter proceeds with a brief review of the war widening theory and what it predicts about the Seven Years' War. It then discusses the Seven Years' War with a very brief overview of the war itself, its origins and the Diplomatic Revolution it spawned. Each state that entered is then discussed separately to uncover its reason for entering the conflict given the circumstances it faced. A similar discussion follows for those states that could have, but did not, join the war. After this presentation of the Seven Years' War, the competing theories of war widening are assessed in light of the information provided about the case. Finally, a concluding section assesses how well this theory explains the case.

THEORETICAL PREDICTIONS

Predation

The theory of war widening presented in this study asserts that, when the political cost of warfare is low, neutrals widen wars for predatory purposes. That is, they seize an opportunity for gain either by attacking another neutral while the other states are occupied with their own war or by joining against an initial combatant. The 1750s is certainly a period where states perceived the political cost of warfare to be low. The previous conflict, the War of the Austrian Succession, had been concluded at Aix-la-Chapelle in 1748, essentially because of exhaustion on all sides. Although the war had been fought with utmost vigor, the *political costs* of the conflict were minimal. Austria lost Silesia to Prussia. Otherwise, the conflict did little to resolve any of the outstanding issues involved, and the combatants retired behind their frontiers to prepare for the next war. Therefore, the instances of war widening in the Seven Years' War should result from predation. Simply put, states should be taking the opportunity provided by the Anglo-French colonial war to seize coveted territory and expand while France and Britain are preoccupied with their own conflict.

Balancing

Balancing logic only dictates that states enter an ongoing conflict when that conflict threatens their interests or threatens to shift the balance of power adversely. As the Anglo-French war was primarily a colonial and naval war, the only states threatened by this conflict were Spain and, to a much lesser extent, Holland. Overwhelming British victory in the colonial war eventually prompted Spain to ally with France to balance Britain, but the action was too late to be effective and Britain was left the virtually undisputed master of the colonial world.

The war widening theory presented in this thesis predicts that predation should be a strong motivating factor for war widening. It predicts very little war widening for balancing reasons. However, due to predation, the overall level of widening should be high.

THE SEVEN YEARS' WAR: AN OVERVIEW

Anglo-French colonial rivalry in America and India gradually intensified until, by January 1753, war seemed inevitable. Bloodletting began in India in 1752 and America in 1754. In 1755, the British navy captured two French ships. As a result, France broke relations in July. Nevertheless, the war remained undeclared while France and Britain searched for allies because neither wanted to be accused of starting a war in Europe.[2] This changed on 10 May 1756 when Britain received news of the 18 April French attack on Minorca and declared war on France.

It was this act which set about the events known as the Diplomatic Revolution and enabled the Seven Years' War to engulf the Continent. The 'Old System' consisted of two camps: Britain, Austria, Holland, Russia and Sardinia against France, Spain, Prussia, Sweden, Turkey and Sicily. This arrangement, however, worked against any expansionist aims of Austria and Russia, particularly any attempt to partition Prussia. As discussed more fully below, Austrian policy from 1749 onward was to retake Silesia and partition Prussia between itself and Russia. This could not be done under the Old System. Austrian attempts to break the Franco-Prussian alliance during the interwar period were unsuccessful, and Austria was unwilling to go to war against Prussia without France. The status quo not only prevented Austria (and Russia) from dividing up Prussia, Britain was also able to use it to prevent Russia from attacking Sweden in the 1750 crisis. The war in the colonies changed everything.

The Anglo-French war meant that Britain had to worry about defending Hanover and the Low Countries. Traditionally, Britain had done so through the agreements for barrier defense with Austria and the Low Countries. Essentially, Austria (and Holland) refused to fulfill the terms of the Barrier Treaty, forcing Britain to search Europe for another Continental ally to assist in defending Hanover. Britain first signed a treaty with Russia, which in turn frightened Frederick into signing the Treaty of Westminster on 16 January 1756. This defensive treaty between Britain and Prussia led to a breach in the earlier Anglo-Russian treaty and, most importantly, threatened France with isolation. Austria used Westminster to increase pressure on France for an Austro-French treaty, by threatening to join forces with Britain. This led to the first Treaty of Versailles on 1 May 1756, and the Diplomatic Revolution was complete. The stage was set for the Austro-Russian partition of Prussia.

The major events of the war are relatively straightforward. With Russian and Austrian troops mobilizing, Frederick the Great of Prussia sent an ultimatum to Austria demanding an explanation. With none forthcoming, Frederick attacked Saxony, an Austrian ally, on 29 August 1756. The campaign season quickly came to an end. In 1757, Austria, Russia, Sweden and France began their campaigns against Prussia and the British/Hanoverian Army of Observation. Prussia succeeded in holding off the seemingly overwhelming might of its enemies through 1761. Much of this success was due to the military genius of Frederick the Great. British subsidies also contributed to Prussia's survival. But, as much as Prussia succeeded, the coalition also failed: poor roads and supply difficulties prevented them from concentrating against Frederick and following up victories. In short, they were hindered by the limits of eighteenth-century warfare. Even so, by the end of 1761, Prussia appeared, finally, to be on the brink of defeat.

January 1762 produced a dramatic turn of events. Britain declared war against Spain, which implied a weakening of the British commitment to Germany as forces were drawn off to defend Portugal. However, on 5 January the Czarina Elizabeth died and was succeeded by Peter III, who immediately began negotiations with Prussia, which led to the 15 May Treaty of St Petersburg. By this treaty, Russia restored all occupied areas to Prussia and loaned Frederick one division to use against Austria. Sweden, following Russia's lead, made peace with Prussia by signing the 22 May Treaty of Hamburg. Prussia's fortunes rose further with an Anglo-Prussian victory over France in the 24 June Battle of Wilhelmstal. On 9 July, Peter III was deposed by his wife

Catherine. Russia, however, honored the peace except for withdrawing its Prussian division. At peace with Russia and Sweden, Frederick was able to inflict a series of defeats on Austria and France, leading to an armistice in November and finally peace with the Treaty of Hubertusburg on 16 February 1763. Thus the war ended because, while Frederick may have been near the brink of defeat in 1762, the allies were equally exhausted.[3] It was clear to all that Prussia could not be defeated.[4]

TO JOIN?

Each state involved in the Seven Years' War entered for different reasons and faced different circumstances and is therefore discussed individually. The logical starting point is with the instigator of the Diplomatic Revolution: Austria.

Austria

Austrian policy in the interwar period sought to recover Silesia from Prussia. In order to do this both cheaply and effectively, it needed to build an overwhelming offensive coalition. To that end, Austria maintained close relations with Russia, which also had designs against Prussia. Austria also wooed France, while keeping its lines to its British ally open until a new relationship with France was secure, which would free it to attack Prussia.

In March 1749, Empress Maria Theresa asked her ministers for an assessment of Austrian foreign policy. All of her ministers argued that Austria should continue to pursue the Old System except one: Kaunitz. Kaunitz argued that Prussia, now in possession of Silesia, was Austria's most dangerous enemy,[5] and threatened Austrian hegemony in the Empire. Past French success had shown the futility of attempting to defend the Austrian Netherlands, which at any rate benefitted Britain more than Austria. Austria's maritime allies were of no value in recovering Silesia. They were both unwilling to wage war on Prussia and unable to render meaningful assistance. In order to wage a successful war on Prussia there was only one solution: an alliance with France. This would serve two purposes. It would deny Prussia a powerful ally and, additionally, the close Franco-Turkish relationship would restrain Turkey from attacking Austria on the flank.[6]

Kaunitz's ideas found a receptive audience in Maria Theresa. The Empress was determined to recover Silesia from Prussia. The loss of Silesia was more than a blow to Habsburg prestige; the loss of its German-speaking inhabitants increased the weight of the Slav element in the Empire, historically a source of difficulty for Vienna. Further, many in Vienna felt the loss of Silesia was in part because of Britain, not just British pressure at the peace negotiations but, more importantly, the drain on Austrian troops to fulfill the Anglo-Austro-Dutch Barrier Treaty.[7] Maria Theresa immediately set about putting Kaunitz's ideas into effect and he was returned to France as Austrian ambassador.[8]

Meanwhile Maria Theresa had signed the 1746 Treaty of Two Empresses with Elizabeth of Russia. This Austro-Russian treaty was outwardly a defensive and friendship treaty between the two powers. However, it contained secret articles for the partition of Prussia, to which another article for mutual defense against Turkey was added later. Russia was wholly in support of Austria's designs against Prussia, a topic that dominated Austro-Russian relations.[9] Austria and Russia could not carry out their plans alone, however, for two reasons. First, so long as the Franco-Prussian treaty held, France threatened to come to Prussia's aid. Second, both Austria and Russia were notoriously short of mobilization funds. Both factors derailed an Austro-Russian move against Prussia in 1753; France threatened to assist Prussia and Britain refused, despite poor relations with Prussia, to pay Russia the subsidies it requested.[10]

Austria's diplomatic approaches to France in the interwar period were unsuccessful. Austria made it clear to French envoys from 1750 through 1753 that it desired an alliance. Although Kaunitz was well-received at Versailles, France was unwilling to give up its Prussian alliance so long as Austria was allied with Britain. France was receptive to a rapprochement with Austria, but would commit no further.[11]

Austria, however, could not or would not abandon the Old System without a ready substitute. Accordingly, Austria kept both irons in the fire. In 1750, Austria invited Britain to accede to the Treaty of Two Empresses. Britain declined because of the provisions against Prussia.[12] Austria dragged out the negotiations with Britain for the defense of the Low Countries. Kaunitz (Austrian Foreign Minister from 13 May 1753) repeatedly stressed to the British that an Anglo-Russian subsidy agreement was a prerequisite for Austrian defense of Hanover and the Low Countries, forcing Britain to reopen negotiations with Russia in 1755.[13] While Anglo-Russian negotiations were proceeding well, Austria nevertheless stiffened its negotiating position on the Low Countries, signaling that the Old System was dead.

Ironically, the collapse of Anglo-Austrian negotiations for barrier defense gave an even greater impetus to the Anglo-Russian negotiations which, by subsidizing Russia's forces in the anticipated war against Prussia, served Austria almost as well as a treaty with France. On 15 September 1755, Britain and Russia signed a treaty calling for 55,000 Russian troops and 50 galleys along the coast.[14] The Anglo-Russian treaty also specifically provided that Russia was 'privileged to plunder the enemy's lands'.[15] Although the treaty only referred to a 'common enemy', at the time it was negotiated, that enemy was obviously Prussia. Austria received a minor setback, however, when the Anglo-Russian treaty frightened Frederick into signing the Treaty of Westminster with Britain on 16 January 1756. Although defensive in nature, the Anglo-Prussian treaty led Elizabeth to repudiate her treaty with Britain.

Although the Treaty of Westminster meant that war against Prussia could no longer be financed by Britain, it also caused a break in Franco-Prussian relations. It was the opening Austria had anticipated. Sudden fear of isolation made France more receptive to Austrian proposals. Kaunitz warned that Britain would try to have Russia sign on to Westminster, making Prussia the arbiter of Europe. France had no relations with Russia during the interwar period and had no way of knowing what transpired in St Petersburg. Other French allies were also Prussian allies, and it was not clear initially where they would side. Despite the bad feelings left by Westminster, France had no wish to see Prussia dismembered. Nevertheless, when Austria threatened to go over to Britain unless there was an Austro-French alliance, France succumbed and signed the first Treaty of Versailles on 1 May 1756.[16]

The first Treaty of Versailles was primarily a defensive treaty, guaranteeing mutual neutrality. Kaunitz had already informed the Czarina that France was ready for an offensive coalition. When a defensive alliance was all he could get, he had to urgently request that Elizabeth halt her military preparations.[17] The treaty did, however, have a secret article where Austria pledged to help France were France attacked by any *ally* (Prussia) of Britain.[18] At the time it was signed, the colonial and naval war was actually going well for France, and France had no desire to be drawn into a costly Continental war (any more than Britain). Russia, as Austria's ally, was invited to adhere to the first Treaty of Versailles, but France and Russia could not come to an agreement. However, further Austro-French negotiations led to the second Treaty of Versailles of 1

April 1757, which was kept secret from Russia. It provided that parts of Prussia were to be surrendered to Austria, Sweden and Saxony and, *once Austria had recovered Silesia*, part of Belgium was to be ceded to France. Austria was to be compensated for Belgium in Italy, in addition to large French subsidies to prosecute the war.[19]

The Anglo-French naval and colonial war provided Austria with the opportunity it had been seeking to attack Prussia. By refusing to honor the Barrier treaties, Austria forced Britain to look for new allies to defend Hanover. As long as France and Prussia were allies, Prussia was the main threat to Hanover, and any British Continental alliance would be directed against Prussia, with British gold subsidizing Austrian war aims. By signing the Treaty of Westminster with Prussia, Britain actually freed France for an alliance with Austria, and the last piece in Austria's plan against Prussia had fallen into place. Frederick's attack into Saxony, although causing Austria strategic difficulties, was a benefit diplomatically by activating the defensive provisions of the first Treaty of Versailles.

Russia

Russian foreign policy leading up to and including the Seven Years' War was conditioned by three factors. The first was the presumption by many foreign courts, particularly the British, that Russian foreign policy was for sale – that the Russian army was a mercenary force available to the highest bidder.[20] Although bribery figured prominently at St Petersburg, Russia clearly and consistently pursued Russian interests and used this general misconception to dupe other states into paying it to pursue its own policies.[21] Second, there was the issue of Elizabeth's frail health. Not only did it frequently delay policy decisions, but the ordinary apprehension of regime change was exacerbated in the Russian case by the policy views of the so-called Young Court, which were antithetical to those of Elizabeth.[22] Last, Elizabeth's Russia was expansionist but wary of costs and ultimately very patient.

Russian expansion was not only directed south, toward Turkey, but also north and west, toward Sweden and Poland. Russia used both military and political means. In 1749–50, Russia assembled an army in Finland, attempting to take advantage of the Swedish king's illness. Russia was forced to back down, however, by a combined Franco-Prussian deterrent and a lack of support from Britain.[23] Thereafter, Russia confined its activities in Sweden to supporting, both financially and diplomatically, the now out-of-power Caps party.[24] Russian activity in Poland was similarly restricted to support of the pro-Russian faction in the Diet.

Russia's activities in Poland, Sweden and Turkey brought it into direct conflict with France. Sweden and Turkey were French client states. France had historically been active in Polish politics and French interest in Poland was reawakened in the 1750s.[25] Following the War of Austrian Succession, Franco-Russian affairs were so bad that there were no relations, diplomatic or commercial, between them at all.[26]

Anglo-Russian relations were generally good. There was a friendship treaty between the two powers dating from 1742 along with commercial treaties that were periodically renewed. Russia took advantage of Britain's concern over Hanover to strengthen the relationship. These negotiations ultimately resulted in the Anglo-Russian subsidy treaty. With Austrian armies behind it and British gold paying its way, Russia was ready to move on Sweden, Turkey and Poland.[27]

In October 1755, the Russian Council declared that Russia would assist any power attacking Prussia.[28] As already mentioned, Russia and Austria were signatories to the 1746 Treaty of Two Empresses. Although the wording of the treaty was defensive, it was clearly designed to return Silesia to Austria. An important provision of this treaty was that it could also be invoked by any Prussian move toward Poland.[29] While much has been made of the Czarina's hatred for Frederick, it was in Poland where Russian interests lay, and Russian designs against Prussia were to seize east Prussia, threaten Poland with encirclement, and force Poland to concede Courland and agree to a 'border rectification'.[30] In essence, Russia would move the state of Poland further west at Prussia's expense.

Russia was determined to partition Prussia as a means of gaining Polish territory. The British subsidy treaty, despite the recent coolness in Anglo-Austrian relations, would have allowed Russia to pursue all of its foreign-policy goals while being paid to do it, including fulfilling the Treaty of Two Empresses. Russia would have been able to move against France's allies, Prussia, Sweden[31] and Turkey. When Russia learned of the Anglo-Prussian Treaty of Westminster in February 1756, Elizabeth informed Britain that their treaty was only good against Prussia and could not be directed against France. British influence at St Petersburg collapsed.[32]

Russia continued the troop build-up on the border, determined to move against Prussia even without British assistance. On 25 March 1756, the Russian Council agreed to treat with Austria for an offensive alliance against Prussia, promising 80,000 Russian troops for the effort.[33] Austria, while eager for war, tried to prevent Russia from moving too hastily. Kaunitz did not want to go to war without France. While Austria was negotiating an offensive treaty with Russia, Vienna was also negotiating a defensive treaty with France. If Russia had made the first move, France might not have participated. Russia and Austria concluded their agreement, the Treaty of St Petersburg, on 2 February 1757, operationalizing the 1746 Treaty of Two Empresses, and inviting Sweden, France and Denmark to join their coalition for the partition of Prussia.[34]

While Russia and Austria were close allies, and France and Austria were allies, France and Russia were not allied at the outbreak of the Seven Years' War and pursued different and somewhat antagonistic policies. France eventually acceded to the Treaty of St Petersburg on 19 April 1757, only after Louis XV had a secret article against Turkey removed. France initially tried to shield its client states from the effects of its shift in policy. Over French protestations, Russia insisted on marching through Poland, which left a Russian army in Poland should there be an election for king, a situation which Augustus's health indicated might be possible. By 1758, France was forced to abandon Poland and leave that kingdom to its fate.[35] Likewise, the wartime alliance left Russia in a win/win situation in Sweden; if Swedish forces were successful they would assist Russia, if unsuccessful they would blame France.

Moreover, Russia never made any move to, nor did it intend to, help France against Britain. Russia was never at war with Britain.[36] Despite Britain's loss of influence at St Petersburg following the Treaty of Westminster, Britain and Russia retained close commercial ties.[37] Russia refused France's request for Russian assistance in invading Scotland. Further, Russia actively obstructed French peace efforts in 1759, refusing to discuss peace until Russian territorial gains in Prussia were guaranteed – something Britain would not agree to.

On 5 January 1762, Elizabeth died and was succeeded by her adopted son, Peter III. Peter had already made it clear that he was pro-Prussian, pro-British and anti-Austrian. His long-range strategy envisioned a new system of Russian alliances based on close ties with Prussia, Britain and Sweden. By 8 January 1762, Peter had instructed his commanders to halt their advance and agree to an armistice if Prussia proposed one.[38] Secret Russo-Prussian negotiations began immediately. On 23 March, Peter proposed to guarantee Silesia, restore all Prussian territory under Russian control, and negotiate an offensive–defensive alliance. Russia sought Prussian help against Denmark to regain Holstein, a desire

Frederick tried to bridle. By May the Russo-Prussian agreement was made, and Peter loaned Frederick 15,000 troops to use against Austria. This remarkable reversal in Russian policy is sometimes referred to as the 'Miracle of the House of Brandenburg'.

Why did Peter III commit Russia to this about-face in foreign policy? It is certainly rational for Russia to switch from a pro-Austrian to a pro-Prussian policy stance from a geopolitical standpoint, but abruptly withdrawing from conquered territory and loaning a division to a former enemy to use against a former ally is highly unusual. Part of the explanation appears to be personal. Peter had 'an overwhelming admiration of Frederick II and all things Prussian'.[39] Peter would rather have Prussia's help in regaining his hereditary Schleswig-Holstein from Denmark than use Prussian territory to trade for part of Poland. In other ways, Peter's shift was not as severe as it seemed. He reverted to the strong anti-French position Russia had held before the war, and remained pro-British.[40] Secondly, the war had been costly to Russia and was a continuing drain on both men and money. There were clearly cheaper ways to gain Polish territory, as the later partitions demonstrate. While Frederick was nearly exhausted by this point, so were all of the other combatants, and they had still failed to crush Prussia.[41]

In July, Catherine overthrew her husband and became the new czarina. Despite rumors that she would rejoin Russia's former allies, Catherine honored the Russo-Prussian peace. She did, however, recall the division loaned to Frederick – but not before he used it successfully against Austria. Russia entered the war for significant territorial changes. Russia achieved little in the war with the exception of completely destroying French influence in Poland and greatly reducing it in Sweden. Russia's minimal gains were not at the expense of Prussia, but of its erstwhile partner, France.

Prussia

Despite friction in their relationship, France and Prussia were still allied by a subsidy treaty that was due to expire in 1756. Because of an extensive network of spies, Frederick was well aware of Austro-Russian designs against him. He further knew that a principal factor restraining Russia in 1749–50 and again in 1753 was the Franco-Prussian alliance. Nevertheless, he entered into the Treaty of Westminster with France's enemy, Britain, and invaded Saxony, activating the Treaty of Versailles. Why?

Prussia did not want war in 1756. Frederick was occupied strengthening Prussia and incorporating Silesia.[42] As the colonial war between France and Britain gained momentum, Prussia's position became more and more tenuous. Frederick believed that despite initial setbacks, Britain, with its overwhelming naval strength, would ultimately get the best of France and that France would have to attack Hanover in order to have something with which to barter back its lost colonies. France would certainly demand Prussia's assistance in any invasion of Hanover, which would precipitate an Austro-Russian attack on his exposed frontier. Lastly, Frederick did not believe that France would be either willing or able to offer Prussia much meaningful support in dealing with Austria and Russia, partly because of what he perceived to be French inefficiencies, and partly as revenge for Frederick's double desertion of France in the last war. In July 1755, Frederick attempted to preserve Prussian neutrality by urging France to occupy the Low Countries instead of Hanover, which would both provide collateral for the French against Britain, and presumably also tie down Austrian forces in its defense. But Paris ignored his request.[43]

Meanwhile, Britain had resumed subsidy negotiations with Russia in November 1754. This was especially dangerous to Prussia because a British subsidy would relieve Russia's chronic shortage of mobilization funds.[44] Although despised by his uncle, King George II, Frederick nevertheless proposed a meeting through the Duke of Brunswick. At first George refused.[45] However, by 12 August, Britain began making overtures to Prussia. Frederick initially responded with an offer to mediate.[46] On 31 August 1755, Frederick learned of the Anglo-Russian subsidy treaty.[47] Convinced that an attack on Hanover would result in an attack by Russia, Frederick began negotiating with Britain in earnest. These negotiations led to the Anglo-Prussian Treaty of Westminster, dated 16 January 1756.[48]

The Treaty of Westminster was a limited treaty. The parties agreed only to neutrality and to warn their own allies not to attack the other.[49] It did not technically violate the Anglo-Russian agreement, nor was it directed against France. However, the Treaty of Westminster infuriated France and Russia. Both Frederick and the British believed that Britain would be able to use its influence to restrain Russia (and hopefully redirect Russian efforts against France), and further, that Austria would not move without Russia.[50] In short, they believed that the Treaty of Westminster would prevent the Anglo-French war from spreading to the Continent. They were mistaken. Fear of isolation drove France into

Austria's arms, and Russia, not to be denied, repudiated the British treaty and began negotiations with Austria for an offensive treaty against Prussia.

Soon it was very clear to Frederick that the Treaty of Westminster had failed to preserve Prussian neutrality. Russia continued its force build-up on the border. By March, news had reached him of French negotiations at St Petersburg, where the previous October Russia had declared itself willing to support any state willing to attack Prussia.[51] Reports reached Prussia through Frederick's extensive spy network that Austria, France and Russia intended to attack in the spring of 1757.[52] Although aware that both the Treaty of Two Empresses (1746) and the first Treaty of Versailles (1756) required that Prussia be the aggressor, Frederick decided to strike first and invade Saxony.

Frederick had to balance the diplomatic costs of being labeled the aggressor against the strategic benefits of invading Saxony, and chose the latter for several reasons. First of all, despite the defensive wording of the two treaties, refraining from action would not guarantee Prussia peace. Not only may treaties be renegotiated from defensive to offensive, but deciding that a certain state is the aggressor is often just a matter of declaring it so. Second, Prussia's only hope of survival was to defeat its enemies in detail. Frederick was quite certain that Russia would not be prepared to attack until spring 1757.[53] Therefore, an attack against Saxony would both eliminate Saxon troops from the next campaign[54] and, if successful, provide breathing room against Austria, perhaps even allowing for a few successful engagements against Austria before the armies were forced into winter quarters.

The most important reason for the attack on Saxony, however, was logistical. First of all, Prussia extracted almost twice as much money from Saxony as it received from its British subsidy, in addition to recruits, fodder and food.[55] Second, it was important for operational reasons to secure the Elbe river, which ran through Saxony like a highway connecting Bohemia and Prussia. Control of the Elbe was crucial.[56] Certain that he would be attacked the following year, Frederick chose to preempt his enemies. His victim, Saxony, was chosen for logistical reasons.

Sweden

Sweden had only two policy choices in the Seven Years' War: predation or neutrality; balancing was not an option. This was not simply because of Sweden's small size; rather, it was due to the Franco-Russian rapprochement and later French accession to the Treaty of St Petersburg. On 29 May 1747, Sweden had signed a defensive alliance with Prussia to which France acceded.[57] This defensive alliance was aimed at Russia. The Diplomatic Revolution rendered this moot – at least for the time being. Although it is possible that Sweden could have honored its treaty with Prussia, this most likely would have resulted in a policy of neutrality.[58]

Sweden did not join the war immediately. As it became increasingly likely that the war would come to the Continent, Sweden concluded a convention with Denmark to protect their commerce from any power seeking to control the Baltic.[59] However, upon the conclusion of the Treaty of St Petersburg (2 February 1757), Sweden was invited to join the alliance in exchange for the Prussian territory of Pomerania.

On 21 March, Sweden signed a convention with France and Austria where, in exchange for 20,000 Swedish troops, Sweden was to receive a French subsidy in addition to Pomerania. There was a secret article to the treaty stipulating that Sweden would also get part of east Prussia. France wanted Swedish gains to offset any Russian gains in the area.[60] Russia adhered to the Swedish treaty in November 1757; Russia and Sweden planned joint naval actions in the Baltic.

Despite Swedish action in Pomerania and the Baltic, Britain still attempted to detach Sweden from France. Britain appointed a new minister to Sweden with instructions to threaten Sweden with Prussian revenge should France and Austria lose.[61] This action failed, for in 1758 Frederick was losing in the east, which raised Sweden's Baltic hopes.[62] Sweden, however, was only interested in gains in the Baltic; it refused France's request for troops to assist in an invasion of Scotland.[63]

By 1762, however, Sweden was desperate for peace. Although it still held on to some small sections of Pomerania, it had no hope of retaining them once Russia had pulled out of the war. Furthermore, the costs of the war were exorbitant and the French subsidies were grossly inadequate. The pro-French Hat party was reduced to the final humiliation of begging Queen Louisa Ulrika, Frederick's sister, to sue for peace, which was signed on the basis of 'no annexations' in May.[64]

Spain

Spain was the only state to join the Seven Years' War for balancing reasons, and did not do so until the war was almost over. Following the peace of Aix-la-Chapelle, Spain maintained close relations with France, but also normalized relations with Britain. Madrid continued to maintain good relations with both states through not only the colonial phase of the conflict, but well after it spread to the Continent. It was only after Britain had greatly shifted the colonial balance of power that, alarmed its colonies would be at the mercy of the British, Spain allied with France. It was too late.

King Ferdinand VI was determined that, after Aix-la-Chapelle, Spain should maintain a policy of neutrality and concentrate on internal development and building up the fleet.[65] Despite Spain's naval build-up, relations with Britain were good, including a convention in 1750, which settled several of their outstanding trade disputes.[66] Although Spain was still closely allied with France, Britain was assured of Spanish neutrality when Britain officially declared war in 1756.[67]

Spain declined several inducements to join the war. In August 1757, Britain instructed its ambassador to offer Gibraltar to Spain in exchange for Spanish assistance in recapturing Minorca. Spain refused.[68] The following year, France and Austria appealed to Spain as co-religionists and offered it Minorca. Although British success in America was beginning to alarm the Spanish government, it remained neutral.[69]

In August 1759, Ferdinand died and was succeeded by his half-brother, Don Carlos. After Carlos succeeded to the Spanish throne as Charles III, his agent informed Britain that Spain was uneasy with British gains in America and that Britain was 'upsetting the equilibrium long since established between British and French interests, a thing Spain could not view with indifference'.[70] Spain followed up with an offer to mediate in December. But Britain was unreceptive and Spain was rebuffed.

Given British intransigence and the threatening nature of Britain's overwhelming gains in America, Charles III was receptive to French approaches in 1761. However, Spain was militarily unprepared for war.[71] Charles III decided that, if his demands were once more refused, Spain would join France. Britain did refuse the demands Spain put forth on behalf of France and Austria, and countered by proposing even harsher terms.[72] Charles III then signed the first of two treaties with France, which together comprise the Family Compact. The first treaty, signed on 15 August 1761, was a defensive alliance; the second was an offensive alliance, signed in February 1762. Although France pledged Minorca and Gibraltar to Spain, it is clear by Spain's previous refusal of the territory as well as Spanish diplomacy, that checking British imperialism was the main motivation. By the Family Compact, Charles III committed Spain to declaring war on Britain on 1 May 1762.[73]

Believing war with Spain inevitable, owing both to rumors of the Family Compact (which was secret) and to the sharp decline in Anglo-Spanish diplomatic relations, Britain pledged itself to defend Portugal and declared war on Spain in January 1762. Unfortunately for Spain, the Family Compact came too late. Spain was initially successful in Portugal, but the arrival of British forces pushed it back.[74] Instead of redressing the balance of power and rescuing France, Spain only joined the war in time to share in French losses.

OR NOT TO JOIN?

Denmark

Denmark signed a subsidy treaty with France in 1742, which was renewed in 1754. Danish foreign policy was predicated on good relations with France for two reasons. First, Denmark wanted to balance against Russia; France was Russia's most powerful adversary. Second, Copenhagen wanted better relations with its historic rival, Sweden, a French ally. Although Denmark was pro-French, it was not anti-British. Both sides sought Danish assistance, but Denmark remained neutral.

France and its allies tried to enlist Danish aid in prosecution of the war, but were largely unsuccessful, despite French subsidies. Denmark concluded a defensive pact with Sweden in July 1756 to protect its Baltic commerce.[75] Denmark was invited to join the Treaty of St Petersburg and was offered territorial compensation; it was likewise invited to join the 1757 conventions between France and Sweden. Denmark refused.[76] Denmark had no desire to assist its rivals, Russia and Sweden, become more powerful. By 4 May 1758, France did succeed in concluding a new subsidy agreement with Denmark whereby Denmark would station 24,000 troops in Holstein. This was a defensive move both to prevent a possible retreat into Holstein by the British forces and also to ward off any possible attacks by Prussia or, for that matter, Russia. Otherwise, Denmark trusted in France to help it settle the Holstein question with Russia.[77]

Despite Denmark's close ties with France, relations with Britain were good and London tried to enlist Danish aid in the war on several occasions. Britain and Denmark had mutually guaranteed each other's possessions, including the potentially controversial Danish accession of Schleswig in 1720.[78] As early as 1754, Britain tried to make a subsidy treaty with Denmark, but Denmark contended that anything more than a treaty for the direct defense of Hanover would be inconsistent with its obligations to France, and Britain had to remain satisfied with the Danish king's friendship and neutrality.[79] Britain continued to try for treaties with Denmark, stressing first the dangers of the Treaty of Versailles and later Russian successes and possible annexation of East Prussia. By 1759, the fear of Russia was increasing Danish interest in an alliance with Britain and Prussia, but it remained allied with France because France assured it that there would be peace soon and it would assist Denmark in its dealings with Russia.[80]

Denmark's position took a turn for the worse in 1762. On 5 January, Czarina Elizabeth died and was succeeded by Peter III. Although French influence at St Petersburg was virtually non-existent before Peter took the throne, his expulsion of all Frenchmen on 7 January was certain to dash any remaining hope that France would be able to provide Denmark with diplomatic assistance against Russia.[81] To make matters worse, it was known that Peter harbored a great hatred for Denmark and he refused to accept Denmark's 1720 accession of Schleswig and Denmark's 1749 agreement with Sweden.[82] Although the withdrawal of Russian forces from east Prussia gave Denmark some momentary breathing space, the Russo-Prussian rapprochement boded ill for Denmark. Frederick dropped his alliance negotiations with Copenhagen and formed close ties with Russia – ties that were widely believed to include a Russo-Prussian attack on Denmark. Denmark responded to this new situation by invoking its 1720 treaty with Britain, but London, concerned about preserving good relations with Russia and needing all of its available manpower to defend Portugal, only promised Denmark neutrality. It is entirely likely that without Catherine's *coup d'état* in July, Denmark would have been attacked by Russia.[83]

Denmark could not be tempted by any of the gains offered it. Nor could Britain and Prussia frighten Denmark into joining them to balance against its primary adversaries, Sweden and Russia. This is partly because Russian and Swedish gains were a long-term threat, and also because Denmark hoped that their common ally, France, would be able to successfully press Denmark's cause at St Petersburg. In this, as in its other dealings with Russia, France failed. Denmark's situation became acute when Peter III ascended the throne, only to be relieved again when Catherine took over. Except for that close call, Denmark came out of the war in relatively better shape than when it began. While Denmark did not gain anything directly, Russia remained behind its frontiers and Sweden had been humiliated.

Holland

Dutch policy was largely unaffected by the Diplomatic Revolution. Instead, it was conditioned by the Anglo-French conflict itself. Holland was pro-French in trade policy and pro-British in security policy. By treaty obligations, the Dutch were British allies; they had no existing treaties with France, not even commercial, except as guarantors of Aix-la-Chapelle. Why, then, did they abrogate their treaty with Britain?

The Dutch decision not to honor its treaty commitment to Britain was because of two factors. First, it became increasingly apparent, both from events in the War of Austrian Succession and the later collapse of Anglo-Dutch and Anglo-Austrian discussions for barrier defense, that defending the Low Countries was disproportionately difficult.[84] Once Anglo-Dutch negotiations for implementation of the Barrier Treaty broke down in the autumn of 1754, the Dutch pulled their troops in from the barrier defenses because they were untenable alone.[85] Simply put, they were unable to balance against France without a strong British and Austrian presence.

Second, and related to the first, the more remote the likelihood that the barrier would be defended, the less likely France was to invade.[86] France guaranteed the Low Countries on condition that the United Provinces remained neutral. France coupled this diplomatic 'carrot' with a military 'stick': 40,000 troops in Flanders.[87] Britain withdrew its request for the 8,000 troops the Dutch owed under treaty so as not to embarrass the Dutch.[88] Holland declared neutrality on 25 May 1756 and indicated a desire not to withdraw from existing treaties.[89] Despite British attempts to frighten Holland with the prospect of a Franco-Austrian exchange of Belgium, the Dutch were unmoved in their neutral policy.

The nature of Dutch neutrality is worth examining. It was not an armed neutrality like Denmark, although they did provide armed escorts for some merchants. Furthermore, they refused to join the defensive pact formed by Denmark and Sweden. Rather, they followed a policy of equal concession, which, while an accepted norm in neutral behavior, is especially important in the Dutch case. This policy gave the appearance of being pro-French, in that France had greater need of Dutch concessions than Britain or Prussia, especially neutral merchantmen. However, there is a reasonable probability that a policy of equal concession, instead of a policy of equal refusal, saved the Dutch from a French attack. Holland was an important transit route for both east–west and north–south shipment, and virtually essential for warfighting in northern Germany. During the course of the war, both sides shipped stores through Holland with great regularity.[90] Given the ease with which France could have attacked the Dutch, and given the importance of Holland in French prosecution of the war in Germany, it may well be that this policy of equal concession, while creating some friction with Britain, staved off a French attack for logistical reasons.[91]

Summary

Three states – Sweden, Russia and Austria – entered the Seven Years' War for predatory reasons. Although Sweden and Russia made no pretenses about their aggressive designs, Pomerania and east Prussia/Poland respectively, Kaunitz did frame his anti-Prussian foreign policy in terms of Prussia being Austria's 'greatest threat'. That is using the term 'threat' loosely and any claims that Austria was balancing against Prussia by forming an offensive coalition to dismember it should be discounted for several reasons. First of all, Silesia had already been ceded to Prussia, so, in the strictest sense, any attempt to capture Prussian territory can be deemed predation. Second, in the years between Aix-la-Chapelle and 1756, as Austria was forming its coalition, Frederick was making no threatening moves against Austria. In fact, he seemed quite satisfied with the Silesian acquisition. If anything, Russian designs on Poland were a greater threat to Austria. To exaggerate the Prussian 'threat' to Austria and therefore claim that Austria was balancing is to render the latter term so broad as to encompass virtually all state behavior.

On the other hand, a true example of balancing behavior can be seen in Spain, which spurned earlier predatory inducements and only allied with France when British military gains combined with British diplomatic intransigence directly threatened Spanish security. Prussia, anticipating attack, preempted by attacking Saxony. As a party to the Austro-Russian plans, Saxony would have been yet another predator had it not been a victim instead. Two states courted by the belligerents remained out of the conflict. Denmark followed a policy of armed neutrality because the Diplomatic Revolution denied it a primary balancing ally and there were no spoils to acquire. Holland staved off a possible attack for logistic reasons by adopting a neutral position of equal concession.

COMPETING THEORIES

Alliances

The alliance argument holds that alliances made for deterrence purposes cause wars to widen once they break out because additional states enter the conflict in fulfillment of their prewar alliance commitments. In the case of the Seven Years' War, this argument predicts a coalition of France, Prussia, Sweden and Spain against Britain, Austria, the United Provinces and perhaps Russia. The Seven Years' War does not conform to this argument. Instead, the war was fought by a coalition of France, Austria, Russia, Sweden and Spain against Britain and Prussia. The initial Anglo-French war opened an opportunity to create new alliances which in turn widened the war.

The prewar alliance pattern deterred Austrian and Russian aggression, most obviously in 1750 and 1753. Austria was not willing to move against Prussia unless France was a party, and Austrian diplomacy prior to the Treaty of Westminster was unable to secure French complicity. It was the outbreak of the Anglo-French war, which precipitated the Diplomatic Revolution, which in turn permitted Austria and Russia to implement their plans for the partition of Prussia. While alliances are an important part of the story of the Seven Years' War, these alliances were *offensive* alliances created for the express purpose of widening the war; they were not defensive alliances activated by the war.

In addition to the new alliances created by the Diplomatic Revolution, other ante bellum alliances, which could have widened the war, did not do so. Despite a close allliance with France, Spain did not enter the war until late. Despite subsidy treaties with France, Denmark remained neutral. Likewise, the Dutch stayed out of the conflict despite a treaty commitment to Britain.

The Seven Years' War clearly shows that alliances did not cause the conflict to widen. States did not honor their prewar alliance commitments. Instead, Austria used the initial Anglo-French war to create new alliances for the express purpose of widening the war.

Offense Dominance

Another competing explanation of war widening is offense dominance. According to this argument, when offense is stronger than defense, or when decision-makers believe the offense is dominant, alliances widen and tighten. Wars are more likely to widen because states find it imperative to strike first in crises if they have no faith in their ability to defend themselves. Further, they must come to the swift and immediate aid of their allies or risk finding themselves isolated as allies are quickly defeated.

The widening of the Seven Years' War had absolutely nothing to do with a belief, real or imagined, in offense dominance or, for that matter, defense dominance. Austria, Russia and Sweden (and France) did believe that they could defeat Prussia quickly and easily. This belief was not, however, conditioned on any belief in the superiority of the offense – rather, they believed that it would be impossible for Prussia to stand up to such a preponderance of force. Moreover, if there were a pervasive belief in offense dominance, Spain would have entered the war much earlier. Spain should have feared the possibility of just such a British colonial victory. Yet Spain did not enter the war until six years after it had officially begun.

CONCLUSION

The theory of war widening developed in this study makes two predictions about the Seven Years' War based on its outbreak in the pre-1815 time period. First, because the political cost to warfare was low, there should be a large amount of war widening. Second, predation should be the primary motivation behind that widening. States could risk joining wars for gain because the *political* costs if they lost would be minimal. (Despite the ferocity of the previous war, Austria was the only state to lose any significant territory, and never faced the possibility of annihilation.) The examination of the Seven Years' War substantiates both of these predictions.

Austria, Sweden and Russia joined this war for the express purpose of partitioning Prussia. Each state wanted gains and saw the war as an opportunity to seize them at Prussian (and French) expense.[92] The simplest version of the story of the Seven Years' War is that Russia and Austria used the Anglo-French war as an opportunity to prey on Prussia while France was occupied with Britain, which is precisely what the theory predicts.

The only state to balance in this war was Spain. Spain was the only state whose interests were directly threatened by the Anglo-French war. Even then, Spain waited to act until it was too late. This is in part also because of the low political cost of warfare; Spain did not anticipate such an overwhelming British victory in North America. In fact, France was largely successful against Britain at the beginning of the war. By the time Spain was able to act, it was too late.

While the theory of war widening presented in this thesis was substantiated, an examination of the Seven Years' War casts doubt on alternative explanations. Alliances were an important factor, but in almost the reverse of what is usually suggested by such an argument. Offense dominance played absolutely no role in the widening of this war. To the contrary, the mid-eighteenth century should, if anything, be considered defense dominant. Therefore, if offense/defense dominance plays any role in war widening, it, too, is the reverse of what the argument suggests.

The Seven Years' War also reinforces the identification of the eighteenth century as one where the political cost of warfare was limited. Prussia survived intact despite fighting a hostile coalition that included three great powers. Britain's victory over France was colonial; at no time was France threatened with annihilation. Unlike World War I, which temporarily removed Russia, and permanently removed Austria as great powers, and World War II, which created a new, bipolar international system, the effects of the Seven Years' War were felt only on the periphery, where the war began.

The Seven Years' War is an enlightening example of how a war on the periphery can spread to the heart of Europe. It clearly shows how states can use the existence of one war to further their predatory ambitions. It also shows that alternative explanations do not adequately account for these facts.

NOTES

1. See R. Ernest Dupuy and Trevor N. Dupuy, *The Encyclopedia of Military History: From 3500 BC to the Present*, 2nd rev edn (New York: Harper & Row, 1986), p. 667.
2. O. A. Sherrard, *Lord Chatham: Pitt and the Seven Years' War* (London: The Bodley Head, 1955), pp. 60–1.
3. Austria had to reduce its army by 20,000 because of lack of funds. See F. J. P. Veale, *Frederick the Great: His Life and Place in History* (London: Hamish Hamilton, 1912), p. 220.

4. R. B. Mowat, *Europe 1715–1815* (New York: Longmans, Green, 1929), p. 101.

5. The question of whether Austrian designs against Prussia should be considered balancing or predation is considered at the end of this section.

6. Le Duc de Broglie, *L'Alliance Autrichienne* (Paris: Calmann Levy, 1897), pp. 13–18; Evan Charteris, *William Augustus Duke of Cumberland and the Seven Years' War* (London: Hutchinson, 1925), pp. 9–12; Charles W. Ingrao, 'Habsburg Strategy and Geopolitics during the Eighteenth Century', in Gunther E. Rothenberg, Béla K. Kiràly and Peter E. Sugar, eds, *East Central European Society and War in the Pre-Revolutionary Eighteenth Century*, East European Monographs, 122 (Boulder, CO: Social Science Monographs, 1982), pp. 59–63; L. Jay Oliva, *Misalliance: A Study of French Policy in Russia during the Seven Years' War* (New York: New York University Press, 1964), p. 2; Sherrard, *Lord Chatham*, p. 44; Karl W. Schweizer, *Frederick the Great, William Pitt and Lord Bute: The Anglo-Prussian Alliance, 1756–1763* (New York: Garland, 1991), pp. 3–4.

7. Arthur Hassall, *The Balance of Power: 1715–1789*, Vol. VI, in *Periods of European History*, ed. Arthur Hassall (New York: Macmillan, 1907), p. 211.

8. Broglie, *L'Alliance Autrichienne*, pp. 19–20. Kaunitz did not actually arrive in France until October 1750 because Versailles delayed sending an ambassador to Austria. Franz A. J. Szabo, *Kaunitz and Enlightened Absolutism 1753–1780* (Cambridge: Cambridge University Press, 1994), p. 19.

9. Hassall, *The Balance of Power*, pp. 207–8, 223–4.

10. Ibid.

11. Ibid.

12. Charteris, *William Augustus Duke of Cumberland and the Seven Years' War*, p. 86; Schweizer, *Frederick the Great, William Pitt and Lord Bute*, pp. 6–7.

13. Charteris, *William Augustus Duke of Cumberland and the Seven Years' War*, pp. 156–7; Carl William Eldon, 'England's Subsidy Policy towards the Continent during the Seven Years' War', unpub. dissert., University of Pennsylvania, 1938, pp. 11–12.

14. Sherrard, *Lord Chatham*, p. 65.

15. Eldon, 'England's Subsidy Policy towards the Continent during the Seven Years' War', p. 39.

16. Broglie, *L'Alliance Autrichienne*, 331–50.

17. Veale, *Frederick the Great*, p. 180.

18. Charteris, *William Augustus Duke of Cumberland and the Seven Years' War*, p. 201.

19. Hassall, *The Balance of Power*, p. 239; Charteris, *William Augustus Duke of Cumberland and the Seven Years' War*, p. 251.

20. See Eldon, 'England's Subsidy Policy towards the Continent during the Seven Years' War', pp. 73–4.

21. As the late Chicago Mayor Harold Washington is reputed to have said: 'Take their money but give me your vote.'

22. It was well known that Elizabeth's heir, Peter, was anti-Austrian and pro-Prussian.

23. Hassall, *The Balance of Power*, p. 224; John Entick, *The General History of the Late War* (London: Edward Silly & John Millan, 1793), p. 1:39.

24. Michael Roberts, *The Age of Liberty: Sweden 1719–1772* (Cambridge: Cambridge University Press, 1986), p. 119.

25. See Duc de Broglie, *The King's Secret: Being the Secret Correspondence of Louis XV with his Diplomatic Agents from 1752 to 1774* (London: Cassell, Peter & Galpin, 1879).

26. Oliva, *Misalliance*, pp. 4–7.

27. Ibid., p. 19.

28. Hassall, *The Balance of Power*, p. 235.

29. Entick, *The General History of the Late War*, p. 262.

30. Oliva, *Misalliance*, p. 32.

31. Provisions for Anglo-Russian cooperation in the Baltic would have facilitated this move greatly.
32. Schweizer, *Frederick the Great, William Pitt and Lord Bute*, p. 18–19.
33. Eldon, 'England's Subsidy Policy towards the Continent during the Seven Years' War', pp. 31–2; Oliva, *Misalliance*, p. 64.
34. Eldon, 'England's Subsidy Policy towards the Continent during the Seven Years' War', p. 79.
35. France suggested moving Russian troops by boat to Danzig. Oliva, *Misalliance War*, pp. 47–9, 103.
36. Hassall, *The Balance of Power*, p. 263.
37. Despite Frederick's repeated entreaties, Britain would not send any naval assistance to the Baltic, where the Russian fleet was raiding the Prussian coast. Britain pleaded that it was too short of ships. The truth was more probably, as Schweizer has contended, Britain did not want to jeopardize the Anglo-Russian commercial treaty which was up for renewal at the end of 1757. Schweizer, *Frederick the Great, William Pitt and Lord Bute*, p. 57. See also Oliva, *Misalliance*, p. 133.
38. Entick, *The General History of the Late War*, pp. 199, 254.
39. Schweizer, *Frederick the Great, William Pitt and Lord Bute*, p. 199.
40. Although, had Russia and Prussia gone to war against Denmark, as surely would have happened without the July coup, this would have put an inordinate strain on Anglo-Russian relations.
41. Hassall, *The Balance of Power*, p. 274.
42. Eldon, 'England's Subsidy Policy towards the Continent during the Seven Years' War', p. 60. Christopher Duffy points out that there have been some allegations that Prussia had aggressive designs on Saxony and therefore wanted war for purposes of aggrandizement. Duffy himself refrains from making any definitive judgment, stating that 'Ultimately the "guilt" for the Seven Years' War is one of those intractable questions which depend on how widely we draw the boundaries of our inquiry'. Christopher Duffy, *The Military Life of Frederick the Great* (New York: Atheneum, 1986), p. 86.
43. Hassall, *The Balance of Power*, pp. 231–2; Eldon, 'England's Subsidy Policy towards the Continent during the Seven Years' War', p. 60.
44. Schweizer, *Frederick the Great, William Pitt and Lord Bute*, p. 16.
45. Charteris, *William Augustus Duke of Cumberland and the Seven Years' War*, p. 159.
46. Ibid., pp. 178–80.
47. The first version was signed on 9 August and was later revised.
48. Eldon, 'England's Subsidy Policy towards the Continent during the Seven Years' War', p. 60.
49. Sherrard, *Lord Chatham*, pp. 66–7.
50. Ibid., p. 67.
51. Hassall, *The Balance of Power*, p. 235.
52. Duffy, *The Military Life of Frederick the Great*, p. 86.
53. This was in part due to the lack of a British subsidy, which Britain refused to pay once Russia made it clear the treaty could not be used against France. Frederick was so certain that Russia would be unable to attack in 1756 that he sent 10,000 troops to Hanover with the understanding that they were to be returned in time for the 1757 campaign. See Sherrard, *Lord Chatham*, p. 129.
54. Saxony was a party to the Treaty of Two Empresses although Augustus had refrained from any provocative action.
55. Duffy, *The Military Life of Frederick the Great*, p. 109–10.
56. For a detailed discussion of the logistical reasons prompting Prussia's attack on Saxony, see Stacy B. Haldi, 'War Widening', unpub. dissert., University of Chicago, 2000, ch. 7.

57. Hassall, *The Balance of Power*, p. 224.
58. Queen Ulrika, who was Frederick II's sister, attempted a royalist revolution in 1756, but was unsuccessful. Roberts, *The Age of Liberty*, p. 124. Had this been successful, Sweden could have adhered to the 1747 treaty and refused to wage war against Prussia. In this sense, Swedish policy could have more closely resembled that of Denmark.
59. Eldon, 'England's Subsidy Policy towards the Continent during the Seven Years' War', p. 81.
60. Oliva, *Misalliance*, p. 75.
61. Eldon, 'England's Subsidy Policy towards the Continent during the Seven Years' War', p. 98.
62. Alice Clare Carter, *The Dutch Republic in Europe and the Seven Years' War* (London: Macmillan, 1971), p. 72.
63. Oliva, *Misalliance*, pp. 138–40. As both Sweden and Russia had refused to assist France in an invasion of Scotland, France had to abort any large-scale invasion plans, and ended up with a small raid on Ireland, which was easily defeated by Britain once the troops re-embarked.
64. Schweizer, *Frederick the Great, William Pitt and Lord Bute*, p. 271; Roberts, *The Age of Liberty*, pp. 125–6; R. Nisbet Bain, *Gustavus III and his Contemporaries, 1746–1792: An Overlooked Chapter of Eighteenth-century History* (London: Kegan Paul, Trübner, 1894), p. 1:30.
65. Apparently he was successful: 'When Ferdinand VI died in 1759, Spain was once more a prosperous nation, with a powerful fleet, and three millions sterling in the treasury.' Louis Bertrand and Charles Petrie, *The History of Spain*, 2nd edn (New York: Macmillan, 1952), p. 292.
66. Entick, *The General History of the Late War*, pp. 2–7.
67. Sherrard, *Lord Chatham*, p. 111.
68. Sherrard, *Lord Chatham*, pp. 232–34; Schweizer, *Frederick the Great, William Pitt and Lord Bute*, p. 62.
69. Hassall, *The Balance of Power*, p. 248.
70. Sherrard, *Lord Chatham*, p. 328.
71. Ibid., p. 409.
72. Oliva, *Misalliance*, p. 185.
73. Sherrard, *Lord Chatham*, p. 415; Hassall, *The Balance of Power*, p. 272; Charles E. Chapman, *A History of Spain: Founded on the Historia de España y de la Civilización Española of Rafael Altamira* (New York: The Free Press, 1918), pp. 383, 385–6.
74. Britain and Spain historically tended to 'resolve' their conflicts in Portugal.
75. Carter, *The Dutch Republic in Europe and the Seven Years' War*, p. 70.
76. Hassall, *The Balance of Power*, pp. 243–5.
77. Eldon, 'England's Subsidy Policy towards the Continent during the Seven Years' War', p. 112.
78. Ibid., pp. 25–6.
79. Ibid., pp. 26–8.
80. Ibid., pp. 125–31.
81. Oliva, *Misalliance*, p. 192.
82. Oliva, *Misalliance*, p. 114.
83. Schweizer, *Frederick the Great, William Pitt and Lord Bute*, pp. 270, 285.
84. Carter, *The Dutch Republic in Europe and the Seven Years' War*, pp. 2, 9–11.
85. Ibid., pp. 32–3.
86. Ibid., p. 34.
87. Entick, *The General History of the Late War*, p. 259.
88. This also freed Britain from an obligation to honor the Dutch naval treaty, which

allowed the principal of 'free goods, free ships' and could only have benefitted France. At any rate, the Dutch refused the British demands on 19 February. Eldon, 'England's Subsidy Policy towards the Continent during the Seven Years' War', p. 66.

89. Carter, *The Dutch Republic in Europe and the Seven Years' War*, pp. 66–7.
90. Ibid., pp. 69, 91–7.
91. Most of the Dutch friction with Britain arose over Dutch shipping of French goods, which reduced the effectiveness of the British blockade. This led to the British Law of War of 1756, by which neutrals could not trade in areas they were prohibited from in times of peace (for example, French West Indies). This was accepted by the Dutch who refused convoys to such merchants. See Carter, *The Dutch Republic in Europe and the Seven Years' War*, p. 104.
92. If their intended victim had not preempted them with an attack on Saxony, the following year would most likely have seen an attack by these states, accompanied by Saxony, on Prussia, which would have increased the amount of predation.

4

The French Revolutionary and Napoleonic Wars

> Europe and you, Sire, will never come to terms. When you have made peace,
> it has been nothing more than a truce. To you, success and failure are equally
> strong motives for war. This time the whole of Europe will fight against you.
>
> *Metternich to Napoleon, 1813*[1]

When the French Revolutionary and Napoleonic Wars began, France
was a radical, disorganized state. During two decades of warfare it
transformed itself into an empire more powerful than any since the
Roman Empire. The wars ended with the dismantling of the French
Empire, but not a return to the status quo ante. The French
Revolutionary and Napoleonic Wars had fundamentally changed the
nature of warfare and, with it, the goals and calculations of statesmen.

The French Revolutionary and Napoleonic Wars are included as a
case study for two primary reasons. The first is duration and scope. A
period of warfare which lasted virtually uninterrupted for two
decades, raged across much of the world, and changed the face of
Europe cannot be overlooked. The second and most important reason
is that these wars marked the transition from a period of limited warfare to one of total war, both in means and objectives. The theory
presented in this study identifies this transition as the key to understanding the relative likelihood of predation and balancing behavior,
and thus the expected cause and amount of war widening in a given
era. Understanding what precipitated the change from limited to
unlimited warfare and how this change affected state decision-making
is central to establishing and understanding the theory of war widening put forth in this book.

The scope of the French Revolutionary and Napoleonic Wars is
too great to be competently covered in one chapter. Instead, this chapter focuses on the beginning and the end – the First Coalition and the

War of Liberation, respectively. This approach highlights the changes in warfare and state behavior which in truth happened gradually over a generation.

This historical study reveals that the First Coalition was largely predatory. It was motivated by the perceived weakness of France and the desire to reap gains both directly at her expense and, most importantly, in other areas as the opportunity arose. The final coalition differed drastically from the first. It was primarily a balancing coalition, formed as a reaction to French hegemony in Europe. This difference is due to a fundamental change in warfare, in which limited wars for limited gains were replaced with unlimited wars for the greatest prize of all: control of Europe.

This chapter begins with a brief discussion of the war widening theory and how it relates to the case, followed by an examination of the changes in warfare that so fundamentally altered both its costs and results. It then proceeds to the First Coalition and the War of Liberation. After the presentation, the two competing theories, offense dominance and alliances, are measured against this case. Finally, the war widening and competing theories are assessed against each other with reference to this case.

THEORETICAL PREDICTIONS

This war widening theory posits that states enter ongoing conflicts for either predation or balancing. Predation and balancing are to a large extent inversely related; when the cost of warfare is low, the incentives for predation are high and balancing low; when the cost of warfare is high, the incentives for balancing are high and predation low. This does not mean, however, that they cancel each other out. The gains from predation accrue to the individual, whereas the gains from balancing are collective. Therefore, states are more likely to enter wars for predatory reasons and attempt to 'pass the buck' when balancing incentives predominate. Thus, across a period of time, predation causes a greater overall level of war widening than balancing.

Predation

When states fight wars for gain, we refer to the behavior as predation. This behavior is most likely when the political cost of warfare is low;

that is, war carries with it little risk of annihilation. The French Revolution occurred in just such an environment. Even the Seven Years' War, the most costly of that century, failed to make any major changes to the map of Europe.[2] Therefore, the French Revolution was a powerful temptation for other European states to aggrandize themselves. Revolutionary France proved more resilient than anticipated. As time wore on, the costs rose, gains seemed elusive, and incentives for predation diminished accordingly.

Balancing

Entering conflicts to prevent a current or potential adversary from becoming strong enough to endanger one, to preserve the so-called balance of power, is referred to as balancing. When Napoleon emerged as the political and military leader of France, the victories that helped propel him there were still within eighteenth-century norms. His peace with Austria did not remove the Habsburgs from the great power arena; his reorganization of Germany was ominous but not unprecedented. However, the dismantling of Prussia after Jena and Auerstädt made it clear for all to see that world politics, and especially warfare, had become a high-stakes, winner-take-all enterprise. Thus, after Napoleon made such an example of Prussia, the great powers should enter wars primarily for balancing reasons.

The predictions the theory makes about this case can be summarized as follows:

1 Low political cost raised the incentives for predation at the outbreak of war and should account for most of the war widening.
2 High political cost lowered the incentives for predation but raised the incentives for balancing by the War of Liberation which should account for the war widening during that conflict.
3 Because predation should produce more war widening than balancing, the widening should be greater during the First Coalition than the War of Liberation.

FIRST COALITION (1792–97)

At first glance, the First Coalition might seem to be outside the scope of this study, if it were construed as the intervention of outside powers in a revolution/civil war. That is not the case. French domestic politics were relevant only insofar as they created a perception of vulnerability. The First Coalition originated with Austria and Prussia, and grew to include Britain, Holland, Sardinia, Naples, Rome, Tuscany, Portugal, Spain and the Holy Roman Empire.[3] Russia was conspicuously absent.

That is not to say that the French Revolution was not important. It was critical but not for its ideological content. The revolution did two very important things. First, it eliminated, or appeared to eliminate, France as a great power for the immediate future.[4] The French navy had mutinied; more than half of the French officer corps had emigrated; what remained of the army was poorly armed.[5] French insolvency had precipitated the calling of the Estates General; the revolution made a bad economic situation worse. To any rational observer, the revolution had debilitated France. French impotence, even prior to the revolution, was demonstrated by its inability to back up its allies. France had to stand aside as Prussia crushed the pro-French Patriot party in Holland in 1787.[6] Again in 1790, France had to deny its Spanish ally assistance against Britain over the Nootka Sound incident.[7] The French Revolution created a power vacuum.

The French Revolution also threw European alliance politics into disarray. European politics for the past half-century were structured on a Franco-Austrian alliance. The alliance had not been terribly beneficial to the parties, but French impotence left Austria with a useless ally. The Austrophobia of the French Revolution was not due to ideological incompatibility; it reflected a belief, originating before the revolution and crossing social strata, that the Austrian alliance was responsible for France's declining great power status.[8] Ultimately, the French Revolution stripped Austria of any ally at all.

Austria faced isolation at a time when the situation in eastern Europe was particularly volatile. The most recent Russo-Turkish war strained Austro-Russian relations. Poland rebelled against Russia and the prospect of a Polish partition loomed. Prussia, meanwhile, was frustrated at its inability to reap any gains from the recent Turkish war. Instability in Poland and a power vacuum in France led to the Austro-Prussian alliance, the seed of the First Coalition and the French Revolutionary War.

France declared war against Austria on 20 April 1792. France and Austria ended hostilities with the Treaty of Campo Formio on 17 October 1797. In the intervening years, Prussia, Britain, Sardinia, Spain, Portugal, Holland, Tuscany, Rome and the Holy Roman

Empire joined the conflict. Britain remained at war with France and served as the basis for the Second Coalition.

TO JOIN?

Prussia

Why would Prussia join Austria in a war against France? The answer is simple: territorial aggrandizement. Despite what Prussian advisers believed to be a propitious international situation, Prussia had failed to reap any benefit from the recent Turkish war (1787–90) and resulting international instability.[9] Forced to demobilize by London,[10] Berlin started to rethink Prussia's international alliances, with a view to gaining greater independence from the 'perfidious Albion'. Berlin sent feelers to Austria early in 1791.[11] Although Prussia's primary expansion target lay to the east, Berlin was not averse to acquiring territory in the west should it prove expedient.

Ideology was clearly not Prussia's main motive in pursuing action against France. Prussia engaged in talks with France but broke them off when Berlin concluded the French price was too high. Meanwhile, Prussia pursued Austria with an eye to both the east and the west. Frederick William met Emperor Leopold at Pillnitz in August 1791. Publicly, the Pillnitz Declaration announced that they were ready to intervene in France should the other states ask them to do so. Privately, however, Pillnitz dealt with Poland, committing both parties to support a member of the Saxon ruling family for the Polish throne.[12] On the face of it, this agreement was a setback for Prussian interests, but it further separated Austria from Russia and France.

In negotiations leading up to a formal alliance, Prussia laid out demands for compensation. Berlin demanded Jülich and Berg, whose present ruler, along with Austria, would be compensated out of the French territory of Alsace and Lorraine. Prussia cemented this new relationship with Austria in an alliance of 7 February 1792. Within that same month Prussia expanded its war aims, to include compensations from Poland as well.[13]

Prussia believed that France would fall within two months.[14] From the Prussian perspective it appeared to be a win/win situation. Prussia gained an alliance with Austria, freeing Berlin from dependence on Britain. Prussia gained territory for little or no effort. If France resisted, Prussia could claim even more territory.

In the 1790s, Prussia sought expansion. Failing in the east, Prussia made a marriage of convenience and joined forces with Austria to gain territory at French expense. Fortunately for France, opportunities arose in the east just as Prussia's efforts in the west were becoming more difficult, and Berlin's attention again shifted toward Poland.

Britain

Great Britain was content to watch France self-destruct. Anything that weakened France, or distracted Britain's traditional rival, was a benefit to Britain. At the outset, all of the events in France seemed to point in that direction, particularly the naval mutinies. So long as this was the case, London pointedly refrained from actions hostile to France. But there was one action England could not tolerate: French annexation of Belgium.

Ideology did not cause the British entry into the war. The French Revolution was initially welcomed in London. Britain declined to join the Pillnitz Declaration and kept Hanover out of the initial anti-French coalition.[15] In May 1792, London officially announced Britain's determination to remain neutral in the Austro-French war.[16] The executions of Louis XVI and Marie Antoinette provided the public justification for war with France, but the real reason was French expansion into the Low Countries.[17]

Britain had recently demonstrated its intent to preserve Belgium and Holland. First, its pressured its ally, Prussia, to intervene in Holland on behalf of the pro-British Stadtholder in 1787. Second, it helped Austria recover Belgium at the 1791 Convention of Reichenbach. Even so, the French march on Belgium in 1792 did not cause undue angst in London because it was widely believed that France was too weak to hold Belgium. France was sure to be beaten back by Austria and Prussia, an assessment verified by immediate events. Britain could stay out of the events on the Continent and trust that Austria, serving its own interests, would also preserve those of the island.

This changed with the French victory at Valmy on 20 September 1792.[18] After Valmy, the Prussian forces withdrew into Germany. Valmy was followed on 6 November by the Battle of Jemappes, in which France defeated Austria. France captured Brussels a week later and besieged Antwerp. On 19 November, Paris issued the First Propaganda Decree, promising 'aid and friendship for all peoples who wished to attain liberty'.[19] The decree was designed to reassure pro-French parties within Belgium and was not a call for universal revolution, a point on which the French Foreign Minister tried to reassure London.[20] Nevertheless, it indicated that France had no intention of returning the Low Countries, or at minimum would maintain considerable influence there. This was unacceptable to Great Britain. On 24 January 1793, the British Prime Minister ordered the French envoy home, precluding any further negotiations.[21]

French control of Belgium also threatened Holland. As dangerous as French control of Belgium could be, French control of Holland was worse. France demanded Holland open the Scheldt river to navigation, which had been reserved to the Dutch by treaty in 1788.[22] From a security standpoint, 'the Netherlands contained the best ports and estuaries for hiding and sheltering invasion barges'.[23] Additionally, the Dutch had a considerable navy and colonies.[24] London traditionally feared that France could create an amalgamated navy, and thus overcome Britain's 'wooden walls'.[25] As things turned out, the French did ultimately capture the Dutch navy in January 1795. When the new Batavian republic declared war against Great Britain, it added 15 ships of the line and 30 smaller vessels to the French navy. This was not just a gain for the French navy, but a loss to the British, because the Dutch navy had previously been at the virtual disposal of the Royal Navy.[26]

France declared war against Britain. Nevertheless, Paris was correct in the assessment that French control of Belgium made a British war inevitable, a position emphasized by the British expulsion of their envoy. The younger Pitt was resolved to uphold English rights and protect British interests. According to one historian, 'Pitt was compelled to stand by the provisions of the treaty to assist Holland. War then became inevitable'.[27] London's intolerance of a French-controlled Belgium was not due to ideology; it mattered not whether Belgium was in the hands of a French monarchy or a French republic. Although France declared war against Britain, it can reasonably be assumed that had it not, Britain would have declared war against France for balancing reasons.[28]

Holland

When France declared war on Britain, it also declared war on Holland. In this case, France also believed it was acting preemptively. Holland would not tolerate French control of Belgium. The threat posed to the Dutch was both strategic and ideological. In addition to the obvious threat posed by a common border with France, as opposed to the buffer provided by a Habsburg Belgium, the French republic threatened Holland's internal stability. The House of Orange had a very tenuous hold on the government. In 1787 William had needed British and Prussian help to maintain his position as Stadtholder. The Dutch republicans had sought French assistance in the past and now France was ready to give it.

However, the same logic can point toward Dutch neutrality. Calling up levies and raising taxes generally exacerbates internal problems. The Dutch army was too small to have any material effect on the conflict. Left to his own devices, perhaps the best policy for the Stadtholder would have been to do nothing and hope that the major powers would contain France without his participation.

Holland, however, was not free to chart its own course. William of Orange was indebted to the British for his position at home. If the British were going to fight on the Continent, they needed landing bases which would have to be provided by the Dutch. Even had William been willing to stand up to the British (which he was not), the threat of war with Britain carried costs almost as large as war with France. The British navy could cut off Holland's trade with its own colonies, devastating the Dutch economy and quite possibly costing Holland its overseas empire. Like many small states over the next two decades, Holland was caught between the proverbial rock and a hard place. Had France not declared war on 1 February 1793, it is likely that Holland would have declared against France shortly thereafter.

Italy

Italy, of course, was not a single state in the 1790s. It was comprised of Sardinia–Piedmont, Genoa, Venice, Modena, Tuscany, the Papal States and Sicily–Naples. Of these, Sardinia, the Papal States, Tuscany and Modena joined the First Coalition.[29] As the largest of these states, we will focus our discussion on Sardinia.

Caught between Austria and France, the King of Sardinia at first made an appeal for neutrality among the Italian states, but this was ignored.[30] France appealed to Sardinia, offering Lombardy as an inducement.[31] But before the Battle of Valmy (15 September 1792), it must have seemed incredible that republican France would be able to fulfill such a promise. Sardinia joined with Austria in the First

Coalition. Drawn by the lure of compensations and subsidies, Sardinia sent 50,000 troops against France in exchange for British subsidies. Defeated, Sardinia made peace with France in 1796.[32]

Spain

Spanish behavior in this period is disjointed because of several ministerial changes. The one constant, however, is a concern over the preservation of and possible addition to its colonial empire. While there was genuine concern over the fate of the French monarchy, particularly since both monarchies were of the House of Bourbon, ideology was not the driving force behind Spanish actions. Spain and France were allies at the outbreak of the French Revolution, bound together by their common enmity for Britain.[33] Despite the reactionary character of the Spanish monarchy, the revolution itself did not immediately end their friendship. War finally came on 7 March 1794 – again, because France declared it.

On 4 September 1792, Madrid announced Spain would join the Austro-Prussian coalition. This decision was fueled in part by indignation at the fall of the French monarchy, but also by the prospect of making some easy colonial gains at French expense. However, Spain was not prepared for war and was slow to mobilize. The French victory at Valmy dissipated 'the chance of cheap participation in some easy spoils of victory'.[34] Spain then returned to a policy of neutrality.

Spain had hoped to mediate on France's behalf as a means of securing French support for Spanish colonial ambitions.[35] On the other hand, Spain also spent considerable money and effort trying to preserve the life of Louis XVI.[36] These policies were not mutually exclusive if understood in the same light as Austrian policy toward France: securing a then-grateful ally.

What probably had greater effect on Spanish behavior was the shift in British policy. As Britain became more hostile toward France, London approached Spain for an alliance. At the same time, France hardened its stance after its victories at Valmy and Jemappes. Now Paris would accept Spanish neutrality only if Madrid renounced the Bourbon claim to the throne.[37] The choice Spain faced in early 1793 was whether to accept humiliating French conditions or join forces with Austria, Prussia and Britain, and gain some of France's colonial territories. Spain therefore broke off talks with France.[38]

While Spanish policy was erratic, French policy was not. Spanish attempts to interfere on behalf of King Louis greatly angered the Convention.[39] After beheading the king (21 January 1793), France declared war on Spain on 7 March 1793.[40] Paris believed war with Spain was inevitable and that France was acting preemptively.[41] This is probably true. Spain was ready to go to war with France in 1793, not for Louis XVI, but to get a share of France's overseas colonies as compensation.

Portugal

After France went to war against Spain, Paris sent an envoy to Lisbon to seek Portuguese neutrality in the conflict. The Portuguese government expelled him.[42] Portugal entered the war against France.

The French Revolutionary War interrupted Anglo-French trade. This improved the market for Portuguese wines and thereby improved Portugal's trade balance.[43] Trade linked Portugal to the British cause.

Ideology linked Portugal to the Spanish cause. Although Spain and Portugal had a stormy relationship, Lisbon shared Madrid's horror at the excesses of the French Revolution. On her accession, Queen Maria had removed the anti-clerical, dictatorial minister Pombal and tried to restore order.[44] The French Revolution was a threat to that delicate stability.

In July 1793, Portugal formed an alliance with Britain and Spain. Portugal sent 6,000 troops to fight with the Spaniards in compliance with the treaty provisions.[45] Portugal continued to fight even after Spain came to terms with France. French attempts to break the Anglo-Portuguese alliance failed until just before Britain herself came to terms with the Treaty of Amiens.[46]

OR NOT TO JOIN?

Russia

Russia was conspicuous by its absence. Russia did not join the First Coalition because it was more concerned with events closer to home. Russia had to finish a war with Turkey and Sweden, and put down a rebellion in Poland.

The Ottoman Empire declared war on Russia on 19 August 1787. Russia received tepid support from Austria at the outset, and Austria withdrew from the war in 1791. Sweden, meanwhile, had seized the opportunity to attack Russia, and Britain and Prussia threatened to intervene on behalf of the Turks. Not to be swayed, Catherine ignored the threats and successfully prosecuted the war. The Turks were forced to make significant territorial concessions by the Treaty of Jassy of 9 January 1792.[47]

The Treaty of Jassy freed Catherine to crush the new regime in Poland.[48] Russia invaded Poland in July 1792. Catherine conducted secret talks with both Prussia and Austria on the fate of Poland. In January 1793, Russia reached a partition agreement with Prussia.[49] The Poles, however, were not through fighting yet. They staged an insurrection in March 1794. Catherine then decided to completely dismember Poland. However, rather than strengthen Prussia, she approached Austria, hoping for Habsburg approval of a more comprehensive plan that included the dismemberment of the Ottoman Empire. Austria and Russia signed a treaty for the Third Partition of Poland on 3 January 1795. It included a secret alliance against Prussia specific to the Polish issue. Frederick William refused to accept the treaty and the Third Partition was not finalized until 1796.[50] When it was done, Russia had moved west to the Niemen.

Russia was the most ideologically opposed to the French Revolution of any of the great powers. Catherine's rhetoric against the French Revolution was vitriolic. Russia, however, made no attempt to form a coalition against France in the early stages of the revolution, nor did it assist the Austro-Prussian coalition once it was formed. Instead of assisting the cause of absolutism in western Europe, Russia busily enlarged itself at the expense of two historical French allies, Turkey and Poland.

Sweden

Traditionally, France had been Sweden's great power ally, a counterweight to Russian support for Denmark. The power vacuum in western Europe, caused by the perception of French weakness because of the revolution, left Sweden in a position similar to Austria. Sweden faced diplomatic isolation and needed a new ally. Gustav III could either resurrect one from the ashes in Paris, find a new one, or do both.

As a small power, Sweden's primary concern was with the balance of power in its own region, the Baltic. Sweden had conflicts with Russia over Finland, and with Denmark over Norway.[51] Denmark was allied with Russia to deter Swedish aggression toward Norway. Sweden had treaties with France, including a defensive and subsidy treaty concluded in 1784, to balance the Russian relationship with Denmark.[52] Of the other powers, Great Britain and Prussia also had interests in the area, primarily keeping the Baltic open to trade and preventing domination of the waters by any one power, which usually meant Russia.

Sweden entered the Russo-Turkish War in 1788 in an attempt to use Russian preoccupation to win back parts of Finland that Sweden had lost in previous wars. Having fought Russia to a standstill, Sweden made peace with Russia on the basis of the status quo ante bellum, which was concluded on 14 August 1790 at Värälä.[53] Almost as soon as the peace with Russia was signed, Gustav tried to lead Sweden in an abrupt change of policy by trying to persuade his former foe, Empress Catherine, to join him in action against revolutionary France. At the same time, Sweden was intriguing within France. It was a Swedish agent, Axel Fersen, who led Louis XVI and Marie Antoinette out of Paris.[54] Had they made it to safety, it would have been quite a coup. Gustav also tried to build a coalition against France under his own leadership. The most Gustav was able to get was a subsidy treaty and defensive alliance with Russia signed in October 1791.[55]

Gustav's change in policy can be understood from both a power politics and an ideological perspective. Internationally, Sweden's position was similar to that of Austria. It had lost its main great power ally and was isolated. Sweden had also lost French subsidies which Stockholm needed to keep the government and military running. By forming a coalition to restore the Bourbons, with himself at the head of course, Gustav could accomplish two objectives. First, he could break Sweden's diplomatic isolation. Second, if the plan was successful, he would succor an ally that would presumably show its gratitude with generous subsidies much needed by the Swedish treasury.[56]

Gustav's machinations ended when he was assassinated in March 1792 and his brother took over as regent.[57] War between France, Austria and Prussia broke out shortly thereafter, but Sweden remained on the sidelines.[58]

France sent a diplomatic agent to Stockholm in May; he began secret discussions pertaining to an alliance.[59] Although the new

Swedish regime was sympathetic toward the French constitutional monarchy, at this time it was more concerned with maintaining itself than with international affairs.[60] Negotiations continued on and off until September 1795, when Sweden concluded a defensive alliance with France. By this treaty, France provided Sweden with a subsidy to assist Sweden in defending its maritime rights.[61]

The Franco-Swedish treaty did not come about solely because of ideological sympathy. By the time it was signed, the French king had been guillotined and France had become much more radical, appalling to all but the most dedicated republicans. Rather, Prussia and Spain had already made peace with France which, along with the successes of French arms, made France an attractive ally. Also, British maritime policy had become hostile to neutrals. In response, Sweden and Denmark formed an Armed Neutrality Convention in March 1794 against the British.[62]

Sweden entered the period as a French ally, but defected when France appeared to be too weak to be an effective great power sponsor. Sweden tried both restoring Louis and allying with its traditional foe, Russia. When France proved to be a great power yet, Sweden returned to the historical pattern of Franco-Swedish alliance. All France asked in exchange for subsidies was that Sweden defend its maritime rights.

Summary

Almost all of the widening of the French Revolutionary War was technically caused by France: Paris declared war on many of the states that joined the conflict. Yet France believed it was acting preemptively, and in hindsight it appears the French assessment at the time was accurate. What motivated these states to war against France? Greed.

In most cases, it was desire for French territory, either on the Continent or colonial possessions. Such was the case with Spain and Sardinia. In the Prussian case, it was free-floating greed – east or west did not matter so much as what was readily available. Portuguese behavior was less overtly greedy, being primarily economic. Moreover, Lisbon's policy was over-determined, because both economics and ideology brought it into the anti-French coalition.

There were two notable exceptions to this motivation for war: Britain and Holland. French domination of Belgium was a grave security threat to these states, one which they determined to oppose. Once at war, however, Britain was not averse to snapping up vulnerable

French colonies, but this opportunity alone was not sufficient to drive Britain to war.

The predatory nature of the anti-French coalition led it to its own demise. Bickering over the spoils, whether from France or in Poland, led to political divisions among the allies. Divergent aims necessarily produced divergent military strategies. This uncoordinated and generally lackluster effort on the part of the allied forces was met with extraordinary effort by France. France was able to defeat the smaller powers such as Holland and Sardinia outright. Paris raised the costs of the war, facilitating separate peaces with Prussia (1795) and Spain (1796). Finally, French force of arms, under the leadership of Napoleon Bonaparte, forced Austria to sign the Treaty of Campo Formio (17 October 1797). The predatory states were out of the war; France's initial enemy was defeated. But France retained control of the Low Countries and thus remained at war with the lone remaining balancer: Great Britain.

THE WAR OF LIBERATION

Napoleon invaded Russia in June 1812. Alexander did not come to terms when Moscow was occupied and Napoleon was forced to retreat, losing most of his army in the process. The participation of Russia, the weakness of France, and the lessons of recent history helped the states of Europe form an anti-French coalition that was sufficiently durable to overcome the rivalries, jealousies, opposing interests and defeats which had doomed previous efforts.

How did the War of Liberation differ from the French Revolutionary War? The obvious answer is that this time the allies won and France lost. Many would argue that Napoleon lost through the destruction of the Imperial Army on its retreat from Moscow.[63] But the allies had France on the ropes in the early years and failed to follow through. Moreover, Napoleon was not yet defeated and would go on to win more battles. No, the real difference between the War of Liberation and those fought two decades earlier was the nature of the anti-French coalition. This time the coalition included all major powers, was more cohesive, and willing to pay a higher price for Napoleon's defeat. Napoleon's defeat of the Third Coalition at the Battle of Austerlitz on 2 December 1805 led to the severe Peace of Pressburg, in which Austria lost its Venetian and German territories.[64] The following year, Napoleon's victories at Jena and Auerstädt reduced Prussia to a shadow of its former self. According to one author,

> These events had no parallel in earlier wars. The magnitude of the opposing armies was merely unusual; but the speed and sweep of French operations were unique, as was the emperor's handling of diplomacy and force to destroy within a matter of months the traditional checks and balances on the Continent.[65]

The coalition which defeated Napoleon was different because it was a balancing coalition.

TO JOIN?

Prussia

In 1811, Prussia was but a shadow of its glorious self under Frederick the Great. Carved down to a rump of its pre-Jena boundaries, its army reduced to 42,000 men[66] and still garrisoned by French soldiers, Prussia was understandably fearful of the outcome of the impending Franco-Russian conflict. While many Prussian reformers and nationalists believed joining Russia was the only way to regain true Prussian independence, should the gamble fail Napoleon would certainly wipe Prussia off the map. Neutrality was not an option; Prussia stood directly between the belligerents.

Berlin was squeezed by both Paris and Moscow as the war clouds gathered. In an earlier time, Berlin would have been able to turn this to Prussian advantage, but in 1811–12 Prussia was too weak and was treated with contempt, particularly by Napoleon. Britain shipped arms to Prussia in 1811 in the hope that Prussia would join with Russia.[67] In fact, Scharnhorst signed a treaty with Russia on Prussia's behalf in St Petersburg on 18 October 1811. But Russia promised Prussia only six divisions in the opening weeks of war. King Frederick William III believed that Prussia would be crushed unless Austria was also willing to join Prussia and Russia. Despite a top-secret trip by Scharnhorst to Vienna, Austria refused Prussia's overture.[68]

Meanwhile, Napoleon coerced Prussia into signing an offensive/defensive alliance on 24 February 1812, which opened virtually all of Prussia to French occupation, and gave Napoleon Prussian troops for his anticipated invasion of Russia. Frederick William tried to avert Alexander's wrath by sending a secret envoy with assurances of friendship. But the only saving grace of the arrangement was that the Prussian forces remained a separate contingent under a Prussian general.[69]

The Prussian General Yorck von Wartenburg played a pivotal role at this juncture. During the attack on Russia he avoided committing his corps. After Napoleon's reversal, he sent an officer to King Frederick William III for instructions in light of the new situation. He was given no definite orders, but apparently told to 'act according to circumstances'.[70] When word came from Russia that it would fight until Prussia recovered its 1806 position, Yorck, on his own initiative, signed the Convention of Tauroggen on 30 December 1812. He neutralized his army, agreeing to a two-month armistice with Russia.[71]

Frederick William did not repudiate Tauroggen. At the beginning of February, Prussia called for volunteers and called up the reserves. Prussia signed a secret offensive/defensive alliance with Russia, the Treaty of Kalisch (26 February 1813), which promised to restore Prussia to its 1806 boundaries.[72] Frederick William tried to keep the Russo-Prussian treaty secret until the French had withdrawn from Prussia, but word leaked out, so Prussia declared war on France on 27 March.[73]

Even with the reserves, Prussia was at first able to field only 65,675 officers and men. However, the reformers' goal of creating the nation-in-arms seemed achieved when, by the end of the year, Prussia had 280,000 men under arms, roughly 6 per cent of the total population.[74] Prussia was once again a force to be reckoned with.

Prussia fought both to regain its independence and to recover lost territory. Frederick William acceded to Napoleon's demands under duress, not because he hoped to profit by the war with Russia, but for fear of France – a stark contrast to Prussian behavior in the First Coalition. Prussia's about-face reflected what its policy would have been had Russia promised it greater support at the outset. That Prussia wanted to be rid of French garrisons and regain its independence is clearly balancing behavior. Prussia's desire to regain its 1806 boundaries would on the face of it seem predatory. However, because the territory had been lost for only six years, all things considered, Prussian actions in the War of Liberation can best be understood as balancing. Prussia's tremendous war effort speaks volumes for the seriousness of its intent.

Austria

Austria's primary concern following its defeat in 1809 was self-preservation, which Vienna believed dictated caution in all things. It was within French power to depose the Habsburgs and fully dismember what remained of the Empire, a notion Napoleon was known to have considered. Therefore, 'they accepted that another mistake would be fatal'.[75] Metternich made every effort to keep the peace with France and allow Austria to recover, both from its military losses and from the impact of the indemnities it agreed to pay to France under the Peace of Schonbrunn.[76]

When in 1811 war between Russia and France seemed imminent, Austria made it clear to both Prussia and Russia that it would not join them against France.[77] Austria knew that Russia would have to fight defensively at the outset, and not be able to assist Austria. Neither Prussia nor Britain would be able to shield Austria from Napoleon's wrath. Moreover, Metternich believed that Napoleon would reconstitute the Kingdom of Poland after he defeated Russia and that if Austria wanted compensations for territory that would be given to Poland, it would receive consideration only as Napoleon's ally.[78]

Austria was not as weak as Prussia and was able to negotiate with France on better terms. The agreement, signed on 14 March 1812, gave Austria territory in Silesia, Illyria and elsewhere in exchange for one corps of 60,000 men.[79] Vienna sought this territory in anticipation of the elevation of Poland from the Duchy of Warsaw, and the Austrian territory which would be taken to make it a reality. Austria retained command over its own corps. Additionally, the Imperial Army marched to the north, so that Austria was not occupied by French forces.

Austrian policy was not so Francophile as to burn bridges with Russia. Vienna's messages to the Czar indicated that Austria would pursue the war with less than full vigor and stressed the advantages of the Austro-French agreement, which preserved Austria to fight another day. Russia withdrew its forces from the Austrian border to the mutual benefit of both parties.[80] But this should not be interpreted as evidence that Austria was truly pro-Russian and merely unable to act on its true sympathies, although this was the impression intended for the Czar.

Emperor Francis and Metternich were pro-Austrian. They believed that an independent center could be revived. Unlike Francophiles or Russophiles at court who saw either France or Russia as Austria's primary threat, Metternich viewed them *both* as threats which needed to be balanced against each other. Russia's recent Ottoman War for the Danubian Principalities was as much a threat to Austrian long-term interests as Napoleon's actions in Germany. Supplanting French domination in Europe with Russian would leave Austria in an equally bad, if not worse, position. Austrian mediation efforts during the armistice and after must be understood in this context.

In November 1812, when it was clear Napoleon's war against Russia was not succeeding, Metternich attempted to negotiate peace between Russia and France while maneuvering Austria into a neutral position. He feared another Franco-Russian agreement like Tilsit, which would buy peace at other states' expense.[81] After the Prussian armistice with Russia, Prussia approached Austria for an alliance; again Austria refused.[82] Metternich was striving for peace and neutrality, hence the refusal.[83] On 7 January 1813, Napoleon authorized the Austrian negotiations. Although still bound by its treaty with France, 'Austria had won de facto independence'.[84] In keeping with its drive toward neutrality, Austria reached an armistice with Russia on 30 January 1813, withdrew its forces into Bohemia and began to enlarge its army. In April, Napoleon demanded full military support from Austria under their treaty. Metternich rejected the demand and made it clear that Austria was an independent mediator.[85] Metternich was able to use Austrian strength to turn the combatants' war-weariness into an armistice, signed at Pleiswitz in June.[86]

Both sides used the armistice to rebuild.[87] For Metternich, it was a last-ditch effort at peace. Considering British peace conditions too extreme, Metternich tried armed mediation. If Napoleon did not agree to his more moderate peace proposal, Austria would join the allies. Napoleon did not negotiate in good faith, so Austria declared war on 12 August 1813.[88] Austria's war aims were, like Britain's, a balance of power on the Continent, but differed in that Austria wanted to preserve strong German states so that they would look neither to Russia nor France for their protection, and saving the German sovereigns was one of Metternich's primary diplomatic goals. Further, Metternich repeatedly worked to prevent the total destruction of France, so that it might remain as a counterweight against Russia. In this, Metternich eventually reached a meeting of the minds with his British counterpart, Castlereagh. This in large part explains the allies' decision to restore the Bourbons.[89]

Austria's primary goal was self-preservation. As a central power, both France and Russia were threats. Austrian policy was very cautious, not only because it feared Napoleon, but because it also feared Alexander. Austria was not only balancing against France, it was balancing against Russia too.

Britain

Britain, of course, had been at war with France since 1803. While Napoleon fought in Russia, British forces fought against France in the Peninsula. Beginning in May 1811, the British government began a policy to retrain and equip Portuguese troops under Wellington. Slowly the British amassed a formidable presence on the Continent for the first time in the war. In May 1811, British and Portuguese forces drove France out of Portugal.[90] In June 1813, while Austria was undecided and many Russians counseled against further advancement, Wellington soundly defeated Joseph Bonaparte at Vittoria, sending the French forces back across the Pyrenees.[91]

Despite an enhanced position on the ground, London never had any illusions about defeating Napoleon without the rest of Europe. British diplomats worked tirelessly at building a formidable coalition against France, resolving not only many of its own disputes with other powers, such as Russia, but also doing what it could to ease disputes and form alliances between other states.[92] British diplomacy received a severe test in January 1814. Metternich was worried lest Austria exchange French domination for Russian.[93] The Austrian minister became so concerned over some of Tsar Alexander's reorganization schemes that he ordered the Austrian forces to halt operations. A visit with Castlereagh allayed his fears, resulting in what amounted to a Prussian, Austrian and English defensive alliance against Russia.[94]

Nevertheless, the coalition was still held together by a series of narrowly construed agreements and bilateral treaties. There was no guarantee that British objectives would be incorporated into a future peace. Of even greater importance from the British perspective was to strengthen the alliance and extend it even after the peace. For British statesmen, 'France was the disturber of the European equilibrium, and if France was restrained everyone else would be happy'.[95] This was not a vision shared by other European statesmen. The allies were still bickering over the future of France in February, when Napoleon fought a series of victorious battles, forcing the allied headquarters to retreat 50 miles. With Napoleon more intransigent than ever,

Castlereagh, the British Foreign Secretary, was able to achieve his major goal: the Treaty of Chaumont, signed on 9 March 1814. By this treaty, the four 'major' powers – Britain, Russia, Austria and Prussia – guaranteed each others' possessions against French aggression in a defensive alliance which extended 20 years beyond the conclusion of the war. This treaty was acceded to by the 'lesser' powers – Spain, Portugal, Holland and Sweden[96] – and was in effect for Napoleon's return, the Hundred Days.

Reflecting the British world-view, Article 16 of the treaty, stipulating the 20-year term of the alliance, states its purpose as 'maintaining the balance in Europe'.[97] By the treaty, London gained a significant role in determining the balance without sacrificing any role to European powers in naval matters.[98] This is because Britain had shown that it could stay at war with Napoleon without the Continental powers while they, after suffering French depredations for so long, needed British subsidies to the tune of £5 million annually, per the treaty.[99] And this time Britain had a Continental army of its own.

British money and materiel were necessary for the other European powers to fight against Napoleon. These bought Britain a stronger voice in alliance politics than it might otherwise have had. By failing to negotiate seriously, both during the armistice and after, Napoleon gave credence to the British position that Europe would not be at peace as long as he ruled France. British diplomats worked tirelessly at building an alliance system, which they believed would not only defeat Napoleon, but would preserve peace on the Continent by assuring a 'balance' among the powers. After 20 years of war, British decision-makers believed such a balance was the only way to ensure peace and prosperity.

Spain and Portugal

By 1812, Spain and Portugal had very little independence in their foreign policy. The Portuguese Court had been relocated to South America; the Spanish Court was imprisoned by Napoleon, leaving disparate and often conflicting regional juntas. The objectives of both states were the same: to regain their independence and as much of their former colonies as possible. In this pursuit, both were already at war with France and bound tightly to Great Britain.

Of the two, Portugal had the least independence. Its army had been entirely incorporated into Wellington's forces in the Peninsula.

Portugal went with Britain, literally and figuratively. Spain's position was more confusing – even chaotic. In the aftermath of the uprisings and defeat of Spain's regular forces, provincial juntas had assumed local control. Most paid some degree of homage to the royal family, but bickered among themselves and had to be dealt with individually by London. Most of the regular Spanish forces were eventually defeated by France. Some units survived and operated with Wellington. However, these forces were not British-trained or led. The Spanish guerrillas were crucial to the Peninsular Campaign, but formed no coherent diplomatic force. Nevertheless, under British auspices, Spain signed a treaty with Russia on 20 July 1812, as part of British efforts to build a new anti-French coalition.[100] This alliance helped thwart Napoleon's attempt to form a separate peace with Spain in 1813.[101] Spain acceded to the Treaty of Chaumont, which in the first secret article guaranteed Spain its ancient limits under King Ferdinand VII.

Spain and Portugal were fighting against France for their very existence as sovereign states. Their only leverage with the other European powers came through Britain. Nevertheless, they welcomed the addition of the other states as a means to finally defeat Napoleon and guarantee their territory – even survival.

Other German States

The Germany of 1812 was Napoleon's creation. It had been reorganized into the Confederation of the Rhine and tightly bound to France. After his new alliance with Austria was cemented by his marriage to Marie Louise, Napoleon stopped dealing with the Rheinbund,[102] thus stripping them of what little leverage collective bargaining had bought them. The two largest of the German states were Saxony and Bavaria. Both states owed most of their position to Napoleon. Both were bound to France by treaty and required to provide forces for the Imperial army.[103] And both pursued very similar policies.

Early in 1811, Napoleon ordered the Rheinbund states to prepare their armies for war. This was obeyed without protest. Saxony and Bavaria provided their required contingents for the 1812 campaign. They stuck with Napoleon after the retreat from Moscow, even after Prussia and Austria neutralized their forces and Prussia went over to the Russians. Prussia's alliance with Russia gave both states, but especially Saxony, an even stronger incentive to cling to France, because

Russia and Prussia wanted to redistribute Saxon territory. In fact, Russia and Prussia wanted Saxony to continue resistance to the allies for that very reason.[104] Napoleon was still strong enough to compel the German states to deliver at least part of the 1813 conscript class Napoleon demanded on his return to Paris.[105]

But Austria wanted a neutralized Germany, a policy the German states were able to turn to their advantage. In April, Prussian forces forced the King of Saxony to flee. He was able to seek refuge in Vienna where he negotiated a treaty pledging Austrian protection against Prussian annexation.[106] Likewise, when faced with threats by a Prussian envoy, Bavaria declared neutrality on 25 April 1813 and began discussions with Austria shortly thereafter.[107] These negotiations were repudiated by both Saxony and Bavaria after Napoleon's battlefield victories in May.

Despite their defection in May, Vienna remained open to the German sovereigns even after Austria declared war in August. In October 1813, with the war going nominally in the allies' favor, Bavaria joined Austria with 36,000 men, for a territorial guarante.[108] Following the Battle of Nations (16–19 October 1813), Napoleon had to fight through Bavarian forces at Hanau on 29 October.[109] Saxony stayed with France, but the Saxon corps deserted during the Battle of the Nations.[110] Saxony, on the losing side, occupied, with its army in shambles, had no bargaining power and fell under Russian control.[111]

Saxony and Bavaria both did what they believed necessary to survive. Having benefitted immensely because of Napoleon in the past, too weak to defy him had they wanted to, they readily acquiesced to their treaty obligations. Bavaria was able to successfully switch sides, ensuring its survival. Saxony was not, because it had acquired much of the territory Prussia had lost. The German states were brought into the war through alliance commitments that were honored, as much or more from self-preservation at this point, than hope of gain. What successful changing of sides occurred was clearly motivated by self-preservation.

Sweden

In the years leading up to 1812, Sweden faced severe difficulties. Through warfare, its trade and finances were crippled and it had been forced to cede Finland to Russia in 1809. Domestically, it was also divided, which ultimately led to the election of the French Marshal

Bernadotte as Crown Prince in August 1810.[112] Yet Sweden was not without a role yet to play on the world stage, and the Franco-Russian conflict which erupted in 1812 provided just such an opportunity.

Bernadotte, now Crown Prince Karl Johan, took control of Swedish politics in March 1811, following the King's stroke, ruling on the King's behalf until his own accession to the Swedish throne in 1818.[113] Instead of being Napoleon's satrap, as expected, or following traditional Swedish foreign policy, Karl Johan devised what became known as the 'Policy of 1812': accept the loss of Finland and seek Norway as compensation. Finland would be difficult to conquer and retain, whereas Norway would be easier to acquire and 'ensure Sweden's security within natural frontiers'.[114] The policy shift was sensible, but enacting it would require excellent timing.

In November 1811, Napoleon sent an ultimatum to Sweden, demanding Sweden declare war against Britain. Under the circumstances, Sweden had to accede, although both Sweden and Britain treated the war as a formality and did not undertake active hostilities.[115] Meanwhile, relations with Russia continued to improve.[116] By the beginning of 1812, Russia was exploring the possibility of a Swedish alliance. Sweden's move toward Russia was given a push when, in January 1812, Napoleon occupied Swedish Pomerania and sent its garrison to France as prisoners of war.[117] Three months later, on 5 April, a Russo-Swedish alliance was concluded at St Petersburg. Alexander promised to provide 15–20,000 troops plus naval forces to assist Bernadotte in obtaining Norway – only *after* which Sweden would use the Russo-Swedish force to mount a diversion against France in northern Germany.[118]

Bernadotte kept the April 1812 treaty secret and did not immediately sever relations with France. Napoleon offered Sweden assistance in recapturing Finland but could make no offer regarding Norway, which was Danish territory. Believing that Norway was superior to Finland, and perhaps having a lower assessment of France's long-term survivability than others, Bernadotte believed the Russian offer was best – although he used the French approaches to strengthen his negotiating position.[119]

Bernadotte strengthened Sweden's diplomatic position by signing a peace with Britain in June 1812.[120] The British promised Sweden £500,000 in material aid, but would not pay so long as Norway was Sweden's first object. But, without cash, the Swedish army was unprepared for any object.[121] Moreover, Bernadotte did not want to irrevocably commit himself until the outcome of the war was clear.[122]

By early 1813, London relented. Believing that Sweden could tip the balance, Britain promised Sweden £1 million, Guadeloupe and diplomatic and naval support in the acquisition of Norway. All this in exchange for a 30,000-man Swedish force, which Britain had to accept might attack Danish Jutland before northern Germany.[123]

Sweden began landing its troops in northern Germany, but the process was slow, both because of Sweden's financial difficulties and Russo-Swedish tensions. By the arrival of the armistice, Sweden had contributed nothing worthy of compensations and could even lose territory if Tilsit were any indicator.[124]

It was Marshal Bernadotte who saved Swedish ambitions. Respected by the allies for his battlefield experience and inside knowledge of Napoleonic strategy, he was invited to Trachtenberg in July to consider strategy. The plan adopted, of which Bernadotte (Karl Johan) claimed much of the credit, gave him control of the northern of the three allied armies.[125] While the allies were debating whether to cross the Rhine after the Battle of the Nations, Bernadotte seized his opportunity and invaded Holstein. As Denmark's military situation declined, it was finally forced to sign the Peace of Kiel with Sweden on 14 January 1814. Sweden received all of Norway in exchange for Swedish Pomerania and Rügen, and Denmark came over to the allies. Thereupon Bernadotte rejoined the allies and resumed the offensive.[126]

Despite the provocation involving the garrison of Swedish Pomerania, the evidence overwhelmingly supports a conclusion that Swedish participation in the allied coalition was predatory. The argument that Norway would make Sweden more defensible is fatuous. It would not help against any state but Britain; what Anglo-Swedish conflict did exist in the past largely revolved around the rights of neutral shippers; the acquisition of Norway would do little to improve Sweden's naval position versus the victor of Trafalgar. No, Sweden wanted to expand and Norway was the most attractive target. The War of Liberation provided the opportunity.

Denmark

Denmark tried to remain neutral during the earlier years of the Napoleonic Wars for both security and economic reasons. Denmark was increasingly exposed to Napoleon's armies in Europe, while its fleet and far-flung provinces, especially Norway, were vulnerable to the British fleet. Denmark attempted to profit by wartime commerce but, following the Franco-Russian extension of the Continental System in the 1807 Treaty of Tilsit, this became increasingly difficult. Finally, Denmark declared war on Britain on 17 August 1807, the same day Britain moved against Copenhagen. Copenhagen surrendered the Danish fleet to Britain on 7 September. A Franco-Danish alliance was concluded on 31 October, after which Denmark remained a firm French ally until forced to change sides by Bernadotte with the Peace of Kiel (14 January 1814).[127] Denmark went to war against Russia with Napoleon in 1812. Why?

Recent history had made it clear that neither Britain nor France would tolerate Danish neutrality. However, with the loss of the Danish fleet, the Anglo-Danish war had degenerated into a *guerre de course*. The war was destroying the Danish economy, but otherwise Britain had made no direct threat to Danish security.[128] Napoleon, meanwhile, could easily crush Denmark with the Imperial Army. Denmark's 1807 alliance with France had been made out of fear of France, fueled by anger at Britain. The new alliance Denmark signed on 3 March 1812 gave Napoleon a force of 10,000 men.[129] It was concluded fully a month before the first *secret* Swedish–Russian treaty, so it is unlikely that fear of Swedish designs played a major role. Rather, it is more likely that this agreement was prompted much like the first: Napoleon demanded – Denmark had little option and acquiesced.

In March 1813, Russia approached Denmark, hinting that Denmark would be able to preserve Norway if Frederick VI joined the allies. Copenhagen sent envoys to London and St Petersburg but, on word of the Anglo-Swedish agreement, Russia backed away from its proposals, instead offering Denmark only compensations in Germany or Holland.[130] How seriously Denmark took this Russian approach or whether it would have switched sides had it not meant the loss of Norway is uncertain. But Napoleon's situation in early 1813 was not nearly so grim as to induce Copenhagen to abandon France and Norway. Instead, on 10 June 1813, Denmark concluded a new alliance with France in which Denmark increased its contribution to 12,500 men.[131] This agreement was clearly in Denmark's security interests: only with Napoleon's victory could Denmark retain Norway. Norway was a high priority in Copenhagen. Even after military reversals forced Denmark to cede Norway to Sweden in the Treaty of Kiel, Frederick and the Crown Prince tried to subvert the treaty by fostering a Norwegian independence movement, which Sweden had to put down with force.[132]

Denmark's adherence to its treaty with France in 1812 was probably motivated as much by fear of Napoleon as friendship or common interests with France. But the new Franco-Danish treaty of 1813 was clearly a Danish attempt to preserve its own territory. Swedish avarice ensured that Denmark had to balance against the allied coalition, not against France.

The United States of America

The entry of the United States into the war in 1812 had little impact on Continental operations. Nor was it calculated to affect the outcome of that conflict. The War of 1812 was an independent conflict, brought about by the effects of the Anglo-French war, but entirely separate from it.

Throughout most of the war, the United States reaped the rewards and suffered the pitfalls of neutrality. Initially, US trade prospered from the war and with it the American economy.[133] Further, it was recognized that it was only the threat of renewed war that induced Napoleon to sell the Louisiana territory to the United States.[134] Maintaining that neutrality had been difficult. As a minor power far from the center of the conflict, American interests were not taken seriously. French attempts to meddle in American domestic politics led to a rupture in relations in January 1797, followed by an undeclared naval war the next year. Britain offered the United States naval support; the United States declined in order to avoid becoming part of the Continental conflict.[135] The matter was settled in 1800, and Franco-American relations were smooth until Napoleon realized that the United States would not join him against Britain, not even for Florida, after which relations again soured.[136] The United States signed the Jay Treaty with Britain in 1794, which resolved some outstanding issues. However, it did not resolve the impressment issue. President Adams ignored impressment, but Jefferson and Madison did not.[137] Impressment was a major contributor to the outbreak of Anglo-American hostilities in 1812.

As the Anglo-French economic war heated up, relations between the United States and both powers declined rapidly. Locked in their life-and-death struggle, both France and Britain viewed American complaints through the lens of their war. Each believed in the formulation: 'If you're not with us, you're against us.' Britain felt Jefferson was a Francophile, while Napoleon believed the United States served

British interests. What neither combatant troubled to consider was that the United States, like the other small neutrals, had its own distinct interests. If anything, American policy at this time could be expressed as 'a pox on both your houses'. Jefferson and Madison believed that the best outcome from the United States' perspective would be if France and Britain destroyed each other.[138]

The reason the United States went to war against Britain, rather than France or both together,[139] is simple, although the politics that brought about the declaration of war are too convoluted to relate here: namely proximity. After the British victory at Trafalgar, France could only damage US interests when American ships reached Europe. The British Navy, however, was omnipresent. It maintained a blockade along the eastern seaboard, stopping and searching US vessels for contraband and impressing sailors: 15,000 men between 1793 and 1812.[140] The British also commandeered supplies from coastal towns. In addition to special outrages such as the *Chesapeake* incident, any American could look across a harbor and see daily insult to his flag.[141]

The British were also present on land. They still maintained a significant presence in Canada and the northwest, with attendant border disputes. More to the point from the American perspective, British agents had contact with Native American tribes. Americans in the south and west believed the British were intriguing with the Native Americans. In reality, Tecumseh and his followers had their own agenda. But he was able to trade the British desire for goodwill in the event of war into arms to prosecute the war.[142]

Despite a common enemy, the United States and France were not allies, nor did they coordinate war plans. Madison feared becoming another French satellite and being compelled to acquiesce in the transfer of Canada to a victorious France.[143] The American invasion of Canada was not just the only way to strike at Britain, but also reflected the desire to rid North America of European interference and thus assure the United States future security.[144]

The United States was alone among weak neutral states to enter the conflict without a great power alliance. Perhaps this is due to the great distance separating the United States from the main war in Europe. But judging from the behavior of states such as Denmark and Prussia, who could have faulted the United States for bandwagoning with, in this case, Great Britain?[145] The audacity of a country as little prepared as the United States in declaring war against Britain is startling even two centuries later. For some, 1812 was a second war for independence and credibility as an independent power;[146] for others war could not be worse than the current situation.[147]

The United States believed both France and Great Britain were threats to its security and independence. Unlike Denmark and Portugal, American distance from the heart of the conflict allowed it to remain neutral longer, and finally to declare war on one without an alliance with the other. That the USA declared war against Britain in 1812 is because Britain was the most immediate threat, but it did nothing to soften the American perception of Napoleonic France.

Summary

The states that entered the War of Liberation did so for balancing reasons, with the exception of Sweden. Not all, however, were balancing against France. Denmark was balancing against Sweden, while Saxony and Bavaria were balancing against Prussia. Meanwhile, the United States was balancing against the growth in British naval power.

Why Did This Coalition Succeed?

Most significantly, it took a balancing coalition to defeat France. The First Coalition had France all but defeated. But, instead of finishing the job, the states bickered among themselves over the division of the spoils. These divisions manifested themselves on the battlefield and allowed France precious time to recover. Additionally, the First Coalition was not prepared to pay a high price for defeating France. Revolutionary France did not have to defeat its enemies to win, it merely had to raise the cost of the war. By 1812, Napoleonic France had to be crushed for the anti-French coalition to be victorious. This required a greater commitment from the allies, which only balancing could provide. In the words of Clausewitz: 'Only in recent times did the extreme danger emanating from Bonaparte, or his own unlimited driving power, force people to act in a natural manner.'[148] As evidence, we can look at their treaties, their war aims and their cohesion.

The treaties that formed the diplomatic basis of the final allied coalition initially were not very different from those of the first. They were an assortment of bilateral agreements focused on specific concerns of individual parties, such as restoring Prussia to its old boundaries, and not about ways to create a more lasting peace. But finally, with the Treaty of Chaumont in 1814, the allies concluded the general alliance that had been absent from all of the previous coalitions.

The war aims of this coalition were not as predatory as those of the early alliances. Russia and Austria were to receive very little, especially when compared to their huge outlays in blood and treasure. Britain was not receiving anything it did not already possess. The main predator was Sweden, which was to gain Norway, and was still strong enough to bargain independently. Most of the territory taken from France, instead of being incorporated into the great powers, was being restored to the smaller powers that had been eliminated (Sardinia) or, in the case of the Low Countries, new powers were being created. One cannot say that these war aims were predatory because these territorial changes were not directly benefitting the great powers, and the small powers that received the benefit had no leverage whatsoever. These changes were being made to create a buffer zone around France in an effort to ensure the future peace.[149]

The allies showed much greater solidarity than they had ever done in the past. This is not to gloss over their differences, for there were many and the allies quarreled among themselves at least as much as they had ever done.[150] But this time they all shared at least two goals: defeat France and restore a balance on the Continent to create a lasting peace. The disagreements among the allies revolved around how best to achieve the latter. In an essay entitled, 'Problems of Coalition Warfare: The Military Alliance against Napoleon, 1813–1814', Gordon Craig outlined all of the difficulties faced by the allies: principally differing war aims, civil–military conflict, disagreements among commanders. But, in drawing lessons for modern alliances, Craig concluded:

> The pressure exerted by the mere knowledge that Bonaparte was still at large, reinforced as it was by his sudden and dreadful appearances, was enough to hold the alliance together in moments of crisis and eventually to persuade it to consolidate its resources in such a way that victory became possible.[151]

Napoleon hoped to exacerbate these disagreements and break up the coalition as he had so successfully done in the past, but this time he failed.[152] This alliance survived and succeeded because it was balancing against the supreme threat; the First Coalition disintegrated over spoils.

The allies' greater cohesiveness was made manifest in their war plans. During the armistice of Pleiswitz, the allies reached a common strategic plan – a stark contrast to previous coalitions.[153] With the notable exception of Bernadotte's descent on Denmark, the allies' efforts were coordinated toward the common goal of defeating Napoleon. Squabbles among the generals and diplomats remained but, unlike the previous coalitions, the differences were not fatal.[154] The allied armies were better coordinated and Napoleon was unable to defeat them in detail as he had done so successfully in the past.

Lastly, the allies were willing to pay a high price to defeat Napoleon. The allied armies were no better, and perhaps worse than they had been in earlier years. They had no commanding genius to lead them. What they had was endurance. They suffered heavy losses but maintained order. Defeat in one battle did not end the war. Napoleon won some brilliant victories in 1814, but the allies did not break. They retreated when they were forced to but, instead of suing for peace as they had done so often in the past, they regrouped and resumed the offensive until, finally, France was defeated.[155]

CASE CONCLUSION

This case was chosen because it encompasses the transition from limited to total war. According to the war widening thesis developed in this project, limited war, involving limited political costs, occasions predatory behavior; total war, with its high attendant costs, discourages predatory behavior and prompts balancing behavior. The question of whether the associated cost of warfare produces predation or balancing incentives is important because it affects the overall level of war widening. When balancing predominates, there should be less war widening because not all wars affect the balance of power, and because the balance of power is a collective good, there is an inclination to 'pass the buck'. Consequently, the war widening theory makes three predictions in this case:

1 War widening in the French Revolutionary War will be due to predation.
2 War widening in the War of Liberation will be due to balancing.
3 There will be more war widening in the French Revolutionary War than the War of Liberation.

The case presented clearly establishes that most of the widening of the French Revolutionary War was due to predation. France was

believed to have been weakened by the revolution, and was seen as
easy prey. By the same token, when France proved it could still fight,
the First Coalition began to disintegrate. Britain and Holland were
the exceptions, balancing against French possession of Belgium. But
their interests were not shared by the other powers and thus not sufficient to hold the First Coalition together. The evidence supports the
proposition that war widening in the French Revolutionary War will
be due to predation.

The case also establishes that the overwhelming bulk of widening
in the War of Liberation was prompted by balancing considerations.
The lone predator was Sweden. The great powers were all balancing
against Napoleonic France and French hegemony. Smaller powers,
concerned more with regional interests, were balancing against
regional threats, in some cases against the allies. Thus Denmark
remained with France because of fear of Sweden, and the United
States fought against Great Britain. Thus, the evidence supports the
second prediction that the widening of the War of Liberation will be
due to balancing.

The case does not support the third prediction, that there will be
more widening in the First Coalition than the War of Liberation. To
the contrary, there are more states involved in the War of Liberation
than the First Coalition. This can be explained by the fact that everyone knew this war would determine the balance of power and that the
states involved also knew that 'buckpassing' had contributed to the
failure of past coalitions. So, while the case clearly does not meet the
theoretical prediction, it can be explained within the parameters of
the war widening theory.

Moreover, the failure to form comprehensive coalitions in the
years preceding the Wars of Liberation is entirely consistent with the
theory's predictions. The difficulties inherent in forming a balancing
coalition suppressed war widening even after it became clear that
France was a hegemonic threat. Even if that realization is dated as late
as 1806, fully six years of war continued before the explosive widening that comprised the War of Liberation. This case confirmed that
the early widening was caused by predation and that the later widening was caused by balancing. The theory was contradicted by the
greater level of war widening in the War of Liberation than the First
Coalition, but upheld by the low level of widening in the five years
leading up to 1812.

COMPETING THEORIES

This explanation of war widening contrasts itself against two competing theories: offense dominance and alliances. The theoretical merits
of these arguments are debated in Chapter 2. This section limits itself
to examining how well these arguments explain the war widening that
occurred in the French Revolutionary and Napoleonic Wars.

Offense Dominance

Offense dominance can be defined as obtaining when 'it is easier to
destroy the other's army and take its territory than it is to defend
one's own'.[156] Ostensibly, offense dominance exacerbates the security
dilemma producing more frequent wars with more participants.[157]
There are two variants to the offense dominance argument. The first
is a straightforward technological one, that certain weaponry and
other technology can favor either defensive or offensive action. The
second version is ideological: whether or not technology favors
offense or defense is immaterial, what matters is what decision-
makers believe a future war will look like.

The period preceding the French Revolution has commonly been
known as one of limited war in Europe. There were no major technological innovations in warfare either leading up to or during the period covered by the French Revolutionary and Napoleonic Wars.
Artillery was made lighter and thus somewhat more mobile, but it was
not a dramatic improvement. Therefore, there is no technological reason to expect a shift from a 'defense dominant' to an 'offense dominant' world, thus explaining the tremendous amount of war widening
in the period.

There were, however, social factors that changed the nature of
warfare, making it more mobile and more decisive – arguably more
offense dominant.[158] However, the underlying social, economic and
organizational changes did not really begin to make themselves felt
on the battlefield until after France declared the *levée en masse* in 1793,
fully a year after the allied invasion of France, and two years after the
Declaration of Pillnitz. The armies that entered the First Coalition
were eighteenth-century forces and the changes that made warfare so
much more decisive were not fully realized until harnessed by
Napoleon.[159]

Offense dominance can explain the widening of the War of
Liberation, but not the First Coalition. Nor can offense dominance

explain why the wars of the intervening years widened so little. Napoleon had illustrated the effectiveness of the offensive in warfare, yet he was generally able to face his enemies singly or in pairs. It was the failure of a comprehensive anti-French coalition to form that aided the growth of the French Empire. Rather than confirming the offense dominance argument, the evidence of this case tends to reverse the causality. It appears that, if offense dominance plays any role, it *inhibits* war widening.

The ideological variant of the offense dominance argument skirts this whole issue by arguing that the state of military technology in and of itself is irrelevant; what decision-makers believe about their world matters. In his influential article, 'The Cult of the Offensive and the Origins of the First World War',[160] Stephen Van Evera argues that a *belief* that the offense was much stronger than the defense caused World War I. Was there a 'cult of the offensive' in this case, which could explain much of the widening in the French Revolutionary and Napoleonic Wars?

There is considerable evidence that revolutionary France was infected by a cult of the offensive. The French Assembly believed that revolutionary ideology gave French forces an advantage, both by strengthening themselves and weakening their corrupt enemies. While not every French leader necessarily believed this argument, rhetoric along these lines was a powerful tool used to convince many members to go along with an offensive French foreign policy. It was France that declared war against Austria, Britain, Spain, Portugal and the others. At first blush, it would seem that a cult of the offensive played a large role in causing so much widening of the French Revolutionary War.

But the case examination reveals that, not only did the members of the French Assembly *believe* they were acting preemptively when they declared war on the other European states, they were *in fact* acting to preempt. A cult of the offensive may have led France to believe that being the first to declare war conferred some advantage, but the facts of the case indicate that the other states would have entered the conflict in any event. Were these other states prompted by a belief in the superiority of the offense? Whether you believe that the allies had predatory motives, as argued in this chapter, or that they feared the spread of revolutionary ideology, the allies clearly believed that defeating France would be easy. This was not because offense was easier than defense in general, but because the French Revolution had disrupted the French state and weakened its armed forces.

A similar point can be made regarding the War of Liberation. It is certainly true that Napoleon favored the offensive, but Napoleon's strategy is only relevant in that it failed against Russia. Nowhere is there evidence that a belief in the strength of the offensive contributed to the formation of the final coalition. To the contrary, the Czar was advised by his military *not* to assume the offensive and pursue Napoleon.[161] Likewise, it was Bernadotte's assessment that an offensive to retake Finland would be too difficult that paved the way for a Russo-Swedish rapprochement and Sweden's entry into a coalition against France. The strategy adopted by the allies at Trachtenberg was quite conservative, bordering on defensive.

In both instances there is evidence that a belief in the superiority of the offense existed – in revolutionary France. There is no evidence that such a belief prompted the behavior of the other states. So, while evidence can be found for the existence of a cult of the offensive, it did not cause the widening of this conflict.

Alliances

The alliance argument holds that alliances cause wars to widen; two-party wars are more likely to spread the wider and tighter the prewar alliance systems are. The alliance argument suffers, as is discussed in Chapter 2, from the fact that it is at best an intervening variable; an independent variable is necessary to explain how alliances occur and why they tighten. The offense dominance argument purports to do this, but its failure does not alone end the viability of the alliance argument. There may be other or even multiple causes for alliance formation rather than offense dominance, such as economics, ideology or the old classic, balancing. The validity of the alliance argument can, however, be assessed on the evidence, which in this case is mixed.

Alliances played virtually no role in widening the First Coalition. France fought without allies, fighting against its principal ally of the previous half-century, Austria. The alliances that formed the First Coalition were formed expressly for the purpose of prosecuting the war. While Britain used its Dutch alliance as an excuse to join the war, British interests dictated it join whether or not the alliance was in effect. Generally, agreements were arrived at between the parties *after* they entered the conflict. Alliances cannot logically be claimed to have had any causal effect on the nature or number of states entering the Wars of the French Revolution.

Alliances did play a small role in the War of Liberation. Napoleon was able to bring his allies along for the attack against Russia. Most of these alliances proved fragile, however. Prussia and Austria defected early. Bavaria went over to the allies later. Denmark stayed true to Napoleon until military defeat forced it to change sides. But the great power alliance necessary to bring about victory – Great Britain, Austria, Russia and Prussia – was not formed until after the war began, as were some of the agreements between the allies and smaller powers such as Sweden. The antecedent alliances involving Britain, Spain and Portugal did have the effect of combining the Peninsular War with the War of Liberation, but of course did not increase the number of combatants Napoleon faced. What these agreements did do was allow Britain to press for Spanish and Portuguese interests in negotiations with the other powers – interests Russia, Austria and Prussia were initially inclined to ignore.

The amount of widening attributable to alliances is restricted to the states Napoleon was able to retain from his 1812 attack on Russia – Bavaria, Saxony and Denmark. Alliances cannot be said to have played any causal role in the First Coalition. Based on the evidence of this case, it can be stated that any link between alliances and war widening is tenuous, if it exists at all.

While alliances cannot tell us much about the war widening in this case, the case can tell us something about alliances. The purpose for which the alliance is formed contributes significantly to the durability of the alliance. While both the First Coalition and the alliance that was the basis for the War of Liberation were both formed after hostilities began, the former was very fragile while the latter formed the basis for the Concert of Europe. This would indicate that balancing alliances are much more durable than predatory alliances.

CONCLUSION

The French Revolutionary and Napoleonic Wars are important because they encompass the transition from limited to total war. The period shows us the shift from predation to balancing as causes of war widening. The First Coalition was brought about and widened as a result of a predatory coalition that aimed at taking advantage of a supposedly weak and disorganized French state. In the intervening years, as the shift to total war became apparent, the coalitions grew smaller and war widening was less prevalent. The period culminated in the largest coalition, driven by balancing considerations, which finally brought about Napoleon's defeat and the end of the French Empire.

The competing explanations – offense dominance and alliances – do a poor job of explaining this period. It can be argued that there was a shift from defense to offense dominance that would explain the widening which occurred during the War of Liberation. However, it does not explain the widening of the First Coalition, nor does it explain the decreasing amount of widening in the intervening years. Likewise, alliances can explain a small amount of the widening in the War of Liberation, but virtually none of the widening in the rest of the case. Clearly, then, these arguments fail to explain why the French Revolutionary and Napoleonic Wars widened.

The war widening theory presented here does a reasonably good job of explaining the widening that happened during this period. It explains the reasons for the widening: predation during limited war and balancing during total war. Where the war widening theory fails in its prediction is the large amount of widening occurring in the War of Liberation. It was argued that balancing produces less war widening than predation because (1) not all wars threaten the balance of power; (2) states have other means of balancing; and (3) states 'pass the buck' when they can. The circumstances surrounding the War of Liberation do not fall into any of those categories. It was clear to all after Napoleon's disastrous retreat from Moscow that this war was likely to change the balance of power. All other balancing options had been exhausted long before. Moreover, all of Europe had been living with the consequences of their failure to contribute and coordinate their actions: the French Empire. The colossal widening of the War of Liberation is less a failure of the war widening theory than it is the exception that proves the rule.

NOTES

1. Quoted in Emil Ludwig, *Napoleon*, trans. Eden and Cedar Paul (New York: Boni & Liveright, 1926), p. 440.
2. Hans Delbrück, *History of the Art of War within the Framework of Political History: Vol. 4, The Modern Era*, trans. Walter J. Renfroe, Jr, Contributions in Military History, 39 (Westport, CT: Greenwood Press, 1985), p. 387.
3. Lucius Hudson Holt and Alexander Wheeler Chilton, *A Brief History of Europe from 1789 to 1815* (New York: Macmillan), p. 156.
4. Gunther E. Rothenberg, *The Art of Warfare in the Age of Napoleon* (Bloomington,

IN: Indiana University Press, 1978), p. 31; R. B. Mowat, *The Diplomacy of Napoleon* (London: Edward Arnold, 1924), p. 8; T. C. W. Blanning, *The Origins of the French Revolutionary War* (London: Longman, 1986), pp. 115–16.

5. William H. McNeill, *The Pursuit of Power: Technology, Armed Force, and Society since AD 1000* (Chicago, IL: University of Chicago Press, 1982), pp. 188–91.

6. Blanning, *The Origins of the French Revolutionary War*, p. 50.

7. Ibid., p. 61.

8. Ibid., pp. 44–5. See also Simon Schama, *Citizens: A Chronicle of the French Revolution* (New York: Alfred A. Knopf, 1989), p. 592.

9. Blanning, *The Origins of the French Revolutionary War*, pp. 52–5.

10. Holt and Chilton, *A Brief History of Europe from 1789 to 1815*, pp. 138–9.

11. Blanning, *The Origins of the French Revolutionary War*, pp. 54–5.

12. Steven T. Ross, *European Diplomatic History 1789–1815: France against Europe* (Garden City, New York: Anchor Books, 1969), p. 38.

13. Blanning, *The Origins of the French Revolutionary War*, pp. 114–15.

14. Ibid., p. 116.

15. Ibid., p. 133.

16. Duff Cooper, *Talleyrand* (New York: Fromm International Publishing, 1986), p. 57. See also Blanning, *The Origins of the French Revolutionary War*, p. 134.

17. Ross, *European Diplomatic History 1789–1815*, p. 66.

18. Blanning, *The Origins of the French Revolutionary War*, pp. 135–6.

19. Ross, *European Diplomatic History 1789–1815*, p. 61.

20. Ibid., p. 62.

21. Ibid., p. 66.

22. Holt and Chilton, *A Brief History of Europe from 1789 to 1815*, p. 155.

23. Daniel A. Baugh, 'Great Britain's "Blue Water" Policy, 1689–1815', *International History Review*, 10 (1988), pp. 33–58, see 47.

24. Among the Dutch colonies were the Cape of Good Hope and Ceylon, which were on the sea routes to India. See Blanning, *The Origins of the French Revolutionary War*, p. 138.

25. Baugh, 'Great Britain's "Blue Water" Policy', p. 50.

26. Russell F. Weigley, *The Age of Battles: The Quest for Decisive Warfare from Breitenfeld to Waterloo* (Bloomington, IN: Indiana University Press, 1991), p. 297.

27. Holt and Chilton, *A Brief History of Europe from 1789 to 1815*, p. 155.

28. See Paul W. Schroeder, *The Transformation of European Politics 1763–1848* (Oxford: Clarendon Press, 1994), pp. 113–14. The evidence against Britain's defensive aims in joining the First Coalition consists largely of Britain's sustained war effort in the West Indies. According to Schroeder, 'British leaders did not expect victories there to bring France down, only to help pay for the war and make it popular, and exhaust and demoralize the enemy'. Schroeder, *The Transformation of European Politics 1763–1848*, p. 127. Once Holland was defeated, Britain could only bring force to bear against French colonies.

29. Weigley, *The Age of Battles*, p. 288.

30. Joseph Marie, Comte de Maistre, *Memoires Politiques et Correspondance Diplomatique de Joseph de Maistre*, Albert Blanc, ed., 3rd edn (Paris: M. Levy, 1864), p. 19.

31. Maistre, *Memoirs Politiques et Correspondance Diplomatique de Joseph de Maistre*, p. 19.

32. Schroeder, *The Transformation of European Politics 1763–1848*, pp. 127, 153, 161.
33. Spain appealed for help against Britain during the Nootka Sound Incident, but the anticipated assistance was partially curtailed by the National Assembly. See Jeremy Black, *European Warfare: 1660–1815* (New Haven, CT: Yale University Press, 1994), p. 169.
34. Blanning, *The Origins of the French Revolutionary War*, p. 161.
35. Weigley, *The Age of Battles*, p. 288.
36. Holt and Chilton, *A Brief History of Europe from 1789 to 1815*, p. 151.
37. Blanning, *The Origins of the French Revolutionary War*, p. 161.
38. Ross, *European Diplomatic History 1789–1815*, p. 66.
39. Holt and Chilton, *A Brief History of Europe from 1789 to 1815*, p. 151.
40. Blanning, *The Origins of the French Revolutionary War*, p. 162.
41. Weigley, *The Age of Battles*, p. 288.
42. H. V. Livermore, *A New History of Portugal*, 2nd edn (London: Cambridge University Press, 1976), p. 245.
43. Ibid., p. 243.
44. Ibid., p. 239.
45. Ibid., p. 245. According to Holt and Chilton, the number was 5,000; *A Brief History of Europe from 1789 to 1815*.
46. Livermore, *A New History of Portugal*, pp. 245–6.
47. Alan W. Fisher, *Russian Annexation of the Crimea: 1771–1783* (Cambridge: Cambridge University Press, 1970), pp. 56–7, 154–6.
48. Poland was particularly vulnerable because of a combination of relative weakness and geographic location.
49. Ross, *European Diplomatic History 1789–1815*, pp. 51, 58.
50. Ibid., p. 97.
51. Russian northern expansion had led to the Russian acquisition of part of Finland. Denmark controlled Norway, which Sweden coveted.
52. H. Arnold Barton, *Scandinavia in the Revolutionary Era, 1760–1815* (Minneapolis, MN: University of Minnesota Press, 1986), p. 133.
53. Barton, *Scandinavia in the Revolutionary Era*, p. 191.
54. Ibid., p. 193.
55. Ibid., p. 194.
56. Ibid., p. 195.
57. Ibid., pp. 200–2.
58. Except for Swedish Pomerania, which was a member of the Holy Roman Empire, and was involved to the limited extent of financial contributions. Barton, *Scandinavia in the Revolutionary Era*, p. 226.
59. Ibid.
60. Ibid., pp. 204, 226.
61. Ibid., p. 226.
62. Ibid., p. 227.
63. 270,000 Imperial troops died, 200,000 were captured, 1,000 cannon and 200,000 horses were lost. See Ross, *European Diplomatic History 1789–1815*, p. 325.
64. Mowat, *The Diplomacy of Napoleon*, pp. 150–1.
65. Peter Paret, 'Napoleon and the Revolution in War', ch. 5 in Peter Paret, ed., *Makers of Modern Strategy from Machiavelli to the Nuclear Age* (Princeton, NJ:

Princeton University Press, 1986), p. 123.

66. Weigley, *The Age of Battles*, p. 461.

67. Rory Muir, *Britain and the Defeat of Napoleon, 1807–1815* (New Haven, CT: Yale University Press, 1996), pp. 188–9.

68. Curtis Cate, *The War of Two Emperors: The Duel between Napoleon and Alexander, Russia 1812* (New York: Random House, 1985), pp. 60–2.

69. Cate, *The War of Two Emperors*, p. 63; Jacques Godechot, Beatrice F. Hyslop and David L. Dowd, *The Napoleonic Era in Europe* (New York: Holt, Rinehart & Winston, 1971), p. 192.

70. Mowat, *The Diplomacy of Napoleon*, p. 269.

71. Ibid., pp. 269–79; Ross, *European Diplomatic History 1789–1815*, p. 326; Godechot, Hyslop and Dowd, *The Napoleonic Era in Europe*, p. 195.

72. Mowat, *The Diplomacy of Napoleon*, p. 273; Ross, *European Diplomatic History 1789–1815*, p. 327.

73. Weigley, *The Age of Battles*, p. 456.

74. Ibid., pp. 461–2.

75. Muir, *Britain and the Defeat of Napoleon*, p. 176.

76. Enno E. Kraehe, *Metternich's German Policy: Volume I: The Contest with Napoleon, 1799–1814* (Princeton, NJ: Princeton University Press, 1963), pp. 119–24. Austria agreed to the debilitating Peace of Schonbrunn in the fear that one more defeat would have 'the inevitable consequence of the obliteration of Austria from the map of Europe'. See F. Loraine Petre, *Napoleon and the Archduke Charles: A History of the Franco-Austrian Campaign in the Valley of the Danube in 1809* (London: Greenhill Books, 1991), p. 407.

77. Muir, *Britain and the Defeat of Napoleon*, pp. 182–3.

78. Kraehe, *Metternich's German Policy*, pp. 137–8.

79. Ibid., pp. 141–3; Muir, *Britain and the Defeat of Napoleon*, p. 191; Mowat, *The Diplomacy of Napoleon*, p. 255.

80. Kraehe, *Metternich's German Policy*, p. 147; Godechot, Hyslop and Dowd, *The Napoleonic Era in Europe*, p. 192.

81. Kraehe, *Metternich's German Policy*, pp. 152–3.

82. Ibid., p. 155.

83. Mowat, *The Diplomacy of Napoleon*, p. 276.

84. Kraehe, *Metternich's German Policy*, 153.

85. Godechot, Hyslop and Dowd, *The Napoleonic Era in Europe*, p. 195; Ross, *European Diplomatic History 1789–1815*, p. 329; Mowat, *The Diplomacy of Napoleon*, p. 275; Kraehe, *Metternich's German Policy*, p. 169.

86. Kraehe, *Metternich's German Policy*, p. 173.

87. See Emile Dard, *Napoleon and Talleyrand*, trans. Christopher R. Turner (London: D. Appleton-Century, 1937), p. 286.

88. Mowat, *The Diplomacy of Napoleon*, pp. 278–80; Kraehe, *Metternich's German Policy*, pp. 178–84.

89. Kraehe, *Metternich's German Policy*, pp. 259–60; Muir, *Britain and the Defeat of Napoleon*, pp. 282, 292–3, 296, 315–17.

90. Muir, *Britain and the Defeat of Napoleon*, pp. 150–3.

91. Paul M. Kennedy, *The Rise and Fall of the Great Powers: Economic Change and Military Conflict from 1500 to 2000* (New York: Random House, 1987), p. 136.

92. Muir, *Britain and the Defeat of Napoleon*, pp. 223, 226, 257, 280. British diplomacy, backed up by the Royal Navy, was instrumental in preventing the Ottoman Empire from agreeing to Napoleon's request for an alliance in 1812. See Vernon J. Puryear, *Napoleon and the Dardanelles* (Berkeley, CA: University of California Press, 1951), pp. 393–4.

93. Ross, *European Diplomatic History 1789–1815*, p. 329.

94. Ibid., pp. 341–8.

95. Muir, *Britain and the Defeat of Napoleon*, p. 295.

96. Ibid., p. 320.

97. 'Le présent Traité d'alliance défensive ayant pour but de maintenir l'équilibre en Europe ...' Traité de Chaumont, reprinted in B. Mourot, ed., *La Diplomatie et La Guerre 1814: Le Traité de Chaumont-en-Bassigny* (Colombey-les-deux-Eglises: St Martin, 1988).

98. Britain did, however, disgorge many of its wartime colonial conquests, except those considered strategically important.

99. Article 3, Treaty of Chaumont. British subsidies were not limited to silver. In 1813, 'Britain exported to Russia, Prussia and Sweden, 218 cannon, 124,000 muskets and 18 million rounds of ball cartridge'. C. A. Bayly, *Imperial Meridian: The British Empire and the World 1780–1830* (London: Longman, 1989), p. 130.

100. Mowat, *The Diplomacy of Napoleon*, p. 268.

101. Ibid., p. 285.

102. Kraehe, *Metternich's German Policy*, p. 130.

103. The Imperial Army Napoleon took into Russia was only about half-French. The remainder was supplied by French allies, including Saxony and Bavaria. See Weigley, *The Age of Battles*, p. 455.

104. Kraehe, *Metternich's German Policy*, p. 158.

105. Weigley, *The Age of Battles*, p. 455.

106. Kraehe, *Metternich's German Policy*, p. 169.

107. Ibid., pp. 170–1.

108. Ibid., p. 211; Muir, *Britain and the Defeat of Napoleon*, p. 288.

109. Mowat, *The Diplomacy of Napoleon*, p. 282.

110. R. Ernest Dupuy and Travor N. Dupuy, *The Encyclopedia of Military History: From 3500 BC to the Present*, 2nd revd edn (New York: Harper & Row, 1986), p. 761. These defections may have been prompted by a belief that Napoleon was using them to bear the brunt of the fighting. See J. P. Riley, *Napoleon and the World War of 1813: Lessons in Coalition Warfighting* (London: Frank Cass, 2000), pp. 163–200.

111. Kraehe, *Metternich's German Policy*, p. 244.

112. Barton, *Scandinavia in the Revolutionary Era*, pp. 299–313.

113. Ibid., p. 316.

114. Ibid., p. 317.

115. Ibid., p. 319; Muir, *Britain and the Defeat of Napoleon*, p. 220; Alfred W. Crosby, Jr, *America, Russia, Hemp, and Napoleon: American Trade with Russia and the Baltic, 1783–1812* (Columbus, OH: Ohio State University Press, 1965), pp. 205–6.

116. Barton, *Scandinavia in the Revolutionary Era*, p. 302.

117. Ibid., p. 320.

118. Ibid.
119. Ibid., pp. 317, 320; Ross, *European Diplomatic History 1789–1815*, pp. 309–10; Holt and Chilton, *A Brief History of Europe from 1789 to 1815*, pp. 286–7.
120. Barton, *Scandinavia in the Revolutionary Era*, p. 320.
121. Muir, *Britain and the Defeat of Napoleon*, p. 223.
122. Barton, *Scandinavia in the Revolutionary Era*, p. 321.
123. Ibid., p. 322; Muir, *Britain and the Defeat of Napoleon*, p. 245.
124. Muir, *Britain and the Defeat of Napoleon*, p. 246.
125. Barton, *Scandinavia in the Revolutionary Era*, p. 323; Rothenberg, *The Art of Warfare in the Age of Napoleon*, p. 56. Credit for the actual plan may properly belong to the Austrian Count Radetzky. See Gordon A. Craig, *War, Politics, and Diplomacy* (New York: Frederick A. Praeger, 1966), p. 28. J. P. Riley contends that allied strategy was developed by General Karl Friedrich von Toll, an adviser to the Russian Czar, assisted by Bernadotte. Riley, *Napoleon and the World War of 1813*, p. 118.
126. Barton, *Scandinavia in the Revolutionary Era*, pp. 336–7; Godechot, Hyslop and Dowd, *The Napoleonic Era in Europe*, p. 213.
127. Barton, *Scandinavia in the Revolutionary Era*, pp. 275–8.
128. Ibid., p. 328; Crosby, *America, Russia, Hemp and Napoleon*, p. 306.
129. Barton, *Scandinavia in the Revolutionary Era*, p. 320.
130. Ibid., p. 322.
131. Ibid., p. 323.
132. Ibid., pp. 348–50.
133. Clifford Egan, *Neither Peace Nor War: Franco-American Relations, 1803–1812* (Baton Rouge, LA: Louisiana State University Press, 1983), p. 6.
134. Egan, *Neither Peace Nor War*, pp. 8–9.
135. The Quasi-War did lead to the creation of a Navy Department, although construction beyond the three frigates authorized in response to the war against the Barbary States was suspended with the conclusion of hostilities. Russell F. Weigley, *The American Way of War: A History of United States Military Strategy and Policy* (Bloomington, IN: Indiana University Press, 1973), pp. 42–3.
136. Henry Blumenthal, *France and the United States: Their Diplomatic Relations, 1789–1914* (Chapel Hill, NC: University of North Carolina Press, 1970), pp. 12–19; Alexander DeConde, *The Quasi-War: The Politics and Diplomacy of the Undeclared War with France 1797–1801* (New York: Charles Scribner's Sons, 1966), *passim*.
137. Egan, *Neither Peace Nor War*, pp. 9–10; Blumenthal, *France and the United States*, p. 13; Reginald Horsman, *The Causes of the War of 1812* (New York: A. S. Barnes, 1962), pp. 22–3.
138. Blumenthal, *France and the United States*, p. 18. Madison, who succeeded Jefferson, served as his Secretary of State. They thought alike on foreign-policy issues, with much of Jefferson's policy actually formulated by Madison. Thus, there was great continuity between the two presidencies. See Egan, *Neither Peace Nor War*, p. 14.
139. Unbelievable as it may seem, it was officially considered. See Blumenthal, *France and the United States*, pp. 23–4.
140. Albert Martin, *1812: The War Nobody Won* (New York: Atheneum, 1985), p. 11.

141. Martin, *1812*, pp. 11–12; Bradford Perkins, *Prologue to War: England and the United States 1805–1812* (Berkeley, CA: University of California Press, 1963), pp. 271–2.

142. Martin, *1812*, pp. 15–19, 143–4, 147; J. C. A. Stagg, *Mr Madison's War: Politics, Diplomacy and Warfare in the Early American Republic, 1783–1830* (Princeton, NJ: Princeton University Press, 1983), pp. 178–87; Perkins, *Prologue to War*, pp. 283–5.

143. Blumenthal, *France and the United States*, pp. 26–7.

144. Weigley, *The American Way of War*, pp. 46–7.

145. This option was periodically raised earlier in the war. See Egan, *Neither Peace Nor War*, p. 50.

146. Perkins, *Prologue to War*, p. 377.

147. Egan, *Neither Peace Nor War*, p. 151.

148. Carl von Clausewitz, *On War*, ed. and trans. Michael Howard and Peter Paret (Princeton, NJ: Princeton University Press, 1976), p. 603.

149. Godechot, Hyslop and Dowd, *The Napoleonic Era in Europe*, p. 213.

150. Ibid., p. 211; Muir, *Britain and the Defeat of Napoleon*, pp. 289–90.

151. Craig, *War, Politics, and Diplomacy*, p. 44.

152. Weigley, *The Age of Battles*, p. 501.

153. Rothenberg, *The Art of Warfare in the Age of Napoleon*, p. 56; Muir, *Britain and the Defeat of Napoleon*, p. 285.

154. For a lively perspective on these squabbles from the Prussian side, see Baron Carl von Müffling, *The Memoirs of Baron von Müffling: A Prussian Officer in the Napoleonic Wars* (London: Greenhill Books, 1997 [orig. pub. 1853]).

155. Muir, *Britain and the Defeat of Napoleon*, pp. 289–90.

156. Robert Jervis, 'Cooperation under the Security Dilemma', *World Politics*, 30, 2 (January 1978), pp. 167–214, see 187.

157. Robert Jervis, 'Offense, Defense, and the Security Dilemma', in *International Politics: Enduring Concepts and Contemporary Issues*, 3rd edn (New York: Harper Collins, 1992), pp. 146–69, see 148.

158. For a discussion of this change, see Ch. 2.

159. Van Evera characterizes the period 1792–1815 as one where 'the offense was fairly strong militarily'. Stephen Van Evera, 'Offense, Defense and the Causes of War', *International Security*, 22, 4 (Spring 1998), p. 26. As this case examination should have made clear, this ignores the fact that the understanding of the new decisiveness in warfare was not realized at the beginning of the period. Napoleon's early victories were fully within eighteenth-century norms.

160. Stephen Van Evera, 'The Cult of the Offensive and the Origins of World War I', *International Security*, 9, 1 (Summer, 1984), pp. 58–107.

161. General Kutusov favored stopping at the Prussian border. Stein advocated liberating Europe. See Holt and Chilton, *A Brief History of Europe from 1789 to 1815*, p. 297.

— 5 —

The Crimean War (1853–56)

Si l'empereur Nicolas ne veut pas la chute de la turquie, il ne croit plus son
existence possible. Le résultat pratique est le même. [If the Emperor does
not wish Turkey to fall, he no longer believes its existence is possible. The
practical result is the same.]

M. Thouvenel to Castelbajac, 2 September 1853[1]

The Crimean War (1853–56) is the expansion of what began as the
ninth Russo-Turkish War. Britain and France entered the war on the
Turkish side late in 1854, eventually followed by Piedmont–Sardinia.
Despite the war's proximity to Europe and the involvement of great
powers, Austria and Prussia did not enter the war – a non-event that
prevented the conflict from becoming a general war. After a year of
siege warfare, the Western powers defeated the Russian forces in the
Crimea and negotiated a settlement before the opening of the 1856
campaign.

The Crimean War was chosen as a case study for four reasons.
First, it occurred during the post-1815 time period, which the theory
indicates had a high political cost to warfare – that is, there should be
less incentive for predation and somewhat more for balancing.
Second, it is the most significant case of war widening in the period
between the French Revolutionary and Napoleonic Wars and World
War I, a century comparatively bereft of such escalation. Third, the
war began as a conflict between a great power and a lesser power, a
type of conflict that has received far less attention in the literature
than those that originate between great powers. Fourth, this was yet
another war closely connected to politics in the Balkans – as much a
hot spot in the nineteenth century as the twentieth.

Most widening that occurred in the Crimean War was predatory.
Of the three states that entered the conflict, only Britain was balanc-

ing; France and Sardinia had predatory motives. What is more note-worthy is that Austria and Prussia found the potential costs of involvement sufficiently high to dissuade them from joining in the war for any predatory motives. At the same time, standard buck-passing logic obviated any need to intervene on balancing grounds; Great Britain was balancing against Russia in other states' stead.

Additionally, several smaller powers with potential predatory interests in the conflict (Greece, Persia and the USA) were easily deterred from entering. Sweden, despite temptations of territorial aggrandizement, was only brought into the allied coalition[2] when convinced that France and Britain would wage a virtually unlimited war against Russia – thus bearing the brunt of the cost. An examination of the Crimean War makes it clear that the higher political cost associated with post-Napoleonic warfare, while not eliminating predatory behavior, certainly had a dampening effect on war widening; it constrained the amount of potential escalation even in the Crimean War, the worst case of war widening in the nineteenth century.

This chapter begins with a brief recapitulation of the war widening theory and what it predicts for this case. This is followed by a very brief history of the Crimean War to orient the reader. Following the synopsis, each instance of widening is discussed by participant: France, Britain and Sardinia. After which the important non-participants are discussed in turn: Austria, Prussia, Sweden, Persia, Greece and the United States. Finally, the chapter shows how competing explanations of war widening fail to adequately explain this case.

THEORETICAL PREDICTIONS

Predation

The theory of war widening presented in this thesis asserts that neutrals widen wars through attacks on initial combatants and other neutrals for predatory purposes. That is, they seize an opportunity for gain while the other states are occupied with their own war. The theory further contends that great powers should only engage in this behavior when the perceived political cost of warfare is low. However, the Crimean War began in 1853, three and a half decades after the close of the Napoleonic Wars. According to this theory, the

Napoleonic Wars ushered in an era of total war, raising the political cost associated with warfare and driving down the incentives for predation. This war-widening theory predicts little or no predatory war widening in this case.

Balancing

As noted above, the Crimean War occurs in a time period where the theory predicts there should be little predation. Therefore, the instances of war widening in the Crimean War should be the result of balancing behavior. Simply put, states should be balancing against perceived Russian aggrandizement at the expense of the Ottoman Empire.

However, balancing logic does not dictate that states should always take action when they perceive a threat. Rather, because there is no absolute gain to be made, it is in any state's interest to let another state pay the cost associated with balancing – that is, 'pass the buck'. States may also balance through alliance formation and by generating more power internally. So, in addition to predicting that the war widening that did occur should be due to balancing considerations, the theory also predicts that the overall level of war widening should be low.

A BRIEF HISTORY OF THE CRIMEAN WAR

What follows is a short description of the major events leading up to and encompassing the Crimean War to give a background to the conflict. While this is a study of war widening, not of the causes of war, this brief overview does include the origins of the war in order to throw light on the environment in which the subsequent states decided whether or not to join the war.

Background

In 1853, Russia and Britain were the only world powers. However, the British were unsure as to where their main threat lay. France and Britain were engaged in a naval armaments race throughout the mid-nineteenth century, including the Crimean War years. Additionally, there was a series of French invasion scares, including one during the

Holy Places Crisis.[3] While France was the primary naval threat, there was a great deal of Russophobia in Britain. Fear of Russia stemmed in large part from Anglo-Russian conflict in Persia and Afghanistan during the 1830s, that in turn threatened the British hold on India.

In the east, the Ottoman Empire had been declining for several decades. The Ottoman Empire was too weak to be considered a great power, but the Sultan still controlled a vast stretch of territory which, among other things, blocked Russian access to the Mediterranean. Russia took advantage of Turkish deterioration to extend its political influence over its Ottoman co-religionists,[4] and territorially into the Crimea, particularly under Catherine's reign. Great Britain, meanwhile, had been gaining influence at Constantinople both economically[5] and politically by sponsoring a Turkish reform movement known as *Tanzimat*. Britain hoped to modernize Turkey and thereby improve its status both as a trading partner and preserving it as a buffer for India, the jewel of its empire.

In central Europe, Austria had also been declining, rocked by the 1848 revolutions, only to be rescued by Russia. Italy continued to be a source of trouble for Austria, agitated by French interference. While Austria was declining, Prussia was gaining strength. Despite some political instability, Prussia was growing stronger economically through its sponsorship of the *Zollverein*.[6]

In the meantime, domestic instability in France allowed Louis Napoleon to take the helm. First elected to office, he staged a coup in December 1852 and was proclaimed Emperor Napoleon III. This touched off a recognition crisis in January 1853, because European leaders were divided over their response, symbolically represented by their decision whether or not to address him as an equal. All the major powers eventually recognized him except Russia.

The Holy Places Crisis

The Crimean War was precipitated by a diplomatic crisis that began in 1850.[7] Essentially, France decided to flex its muscle in support of the rights of Catholics against the Orthodox to access various holy sites in the Levant. This was a convenient marriage of foreign and domestic policy for, in addition to playing well with conservative Catholics in France, it corresponded very well with French policy in support of Pius IX in Italy.

In February 1852, the Ottoman government affirmed Catholic

rights, a political victory for France. Czar Nicholas immediately began to pressure the Ottomans to reverse the policy, and the Ottoman Empire was plunged into a diplomatic struggle between France and Russia, while Austria and Britain attempted to mediate.[8]

The Ottoman Empire and Russia held positions that were inherently incompatible. Russia sought not merely a return to the status quo ante, but to assert its privileges over Orthodox Ottoman subjects in such a way as to completely undermine the Sultan's sovereignty. Thus, mediation attempts failed, and yet another Russo-Turkish war began.

The Ninth Russo-Turkish War

On 2 July 1853 Russian troops occupied the Principalities. Although clearly a belligerent act, Russia declared that it should not be perceived as a declaration of war. Under pressure from the west, the Ottoman Empire held back and did not yet declare war. Negotiations continued amid preparations for war until 4 October, when the Ottoman government (the Porte) ultimately declared war on Russia.

With the declaration of war occurring so close to the end of the campaigning season, diplomats expected only light skirmishing until spring, thus buying additional time for negotiators. But early Ottoman successes both buoyed hopes for victory at the Porte and spurred Russia to greater efforts.[9] On 30 November 1853 the Russian Navy attacked the Ottoman Navy at Sinope in a three-day battle, which became known in Britain as the 'massacre at Sinope', reflecting Russia's overwhelming victory.

The Crimean War

French and British fleets had been in the area (Besika Bay) since June, and were ordered into the Dardanelles in October. Following the Ottoman disaster at Sinope, western ships began escorting Ottoman ships in the Black Sea. On 27 February 1854, Britain and France issued an ultimatum to Russia, demanding evacuation of the Principalities. On 12 March, France, Britain and the Ottoman Empire concluded a military alliance, and on 28 March the western powers declared war on Russia.

Franco-British participation in the war was initially limited to naval attacks in both the Baltic and Black Seas until late summer. By

14 September, France and Britain began landing troops in the Crimea, leading up to the Battle of Alma on 19 September 1854. After the Battle of Alma, the main Russian army withdrew, part into Sevastopol and part into the hinterlands, and the allies laid siege to Sevastopol. Meanwhile, the allies, primarily the British, roamed the Baltic Sea during the summer campaigning season, engaging in commerce raiding and attacking small fortresses. The Russians held out at Sevastopol for a year, until 9 September 1855.

In December 1855, Austria sent an ultimatum to Russia, threatening to join the allies. Facing the possibility of an allied attack on Kronstadt (the fortress on the Baltic Sea, protecting St Petersburg) and Austrian ground forces in the 1856 campaigning season, Russia agreed to negotiate at the Paris peace conference. The treaty ending the Crimean War was ratified by the end of April 1856.

TO JOIN?

France

The French case is by far the most interesting and perhaps puzzling of the Crimean War. It is also the most difficult to decipher because of the dearth of information about Napoleon III's true motivations. Without a record of Napoleon III's thoughts on the matter, one is left to make inferences based on French behavior and policy. Nevertheless, what emerges is the story of how France used the Crimean War to *build* an alliance with Britain as a means to wriggle out of the diplomatic restrictions forced on it by the Concert of Europe, not a story of a country dragged into a war by an existing alliance obligation.

France's primary foreign policy goal was to escape the diplomatic isolation imposed on it by the Holy Alliance following the Napoleonic Wars. This desire became stronger when Louis Napoleon returned to French politics – and acute when he declared himself Emperor Napoleon III on 2 December 1852.[10] In order to accomplish this, France needed an alliance, or at the very least an entente, with one of the major powers. A relationship with Austria was simply out of the question. In addition to being a bulwark of the Holy Alliance, close relations with Austria would frustrate French ambitions in Italy and southern Germany. German competition likewise precluded an alliance with Prussia, which at any rate was not quite powerful enough to end French isolation. By default, therefore, France needed either Britain or Russia.

It was by no means certain that France would choose to ally with Britain. Although Louis Napoleon was an Anglophile,[11] many officials in the new French government believed that Russia was a more natural ally. As a result, there was considerable discussion of a Franco-Russian alliance in the salons of Paris and even in diplomatic circles.[12] Nonetheless, two crises, the recognition crisis in January, and then, of course, the Holy Places Crisis, precluded a Franco-Russian entente in 1853.

To assert that France, and Louis Napoleon in particular, wanted to reconfigure the diplomatic landscape is not to say that Napoleon III precipitated the conflict with Russia in the Holy Places in order to start a war.[13] To the contrary, French diplomatic pressure on the Porte in support of Catholics was initiated by the French Ambassador in 1850 on his own initiative.[14] However, initial success gave Napoleon III a diplomatic victory against Russia in the Near East, along with strengthening the French position in Italy[15] and Napoleon III's relations with conservative Catholics at home. Paris did not intend to provoke a war; moreover, Napoleon III took numerous steps to appease Russia and diffuse the conflict. By May 1853, the new French Ambassador at Constantinople had resolved the central issues of the Holy Places dispute.[16] Nevertheless, Russia remained hostile.

French difficulties with Russia did not guarantee a close relationship with Britain. In order to ease London's fear of growing French naval strength (1853 also saw another invasion scare), Napoleon III emphasized the development and operation of the Mediterranean fleet over the Atlantic Fleet.[17] Nevertheless, France remained the second largest naval power and the two countries continued their naval arms race.

As it became clear that French attempts to reconcile with Russia were bound to fail,[18] France initiated direct and indirect overtures to London in order to secure British support. Verbal overtures were unsuccessful;[19] Napoleon III then tried more direct actions. Of these, perhaps the most important was his decision on 18 or 19 March[20] to send the French fleet to demonstrate at Salamis, in a move calculated to force the British hand. Napoleon III is quoted as saying: 'When we sent our fleet to Salamis, we had only one wish, to draw a cool and hesitant England into an alliance with ourselves.'[21] Essentially, the French move would either force the British to acquiesce in French plans, or abandon British pretensions at Constantinople.

Nevertheless, a decision for a naval demonstration in support of a diplomatic position is not the same as a decision for war and France would not go to war against Russia alone. As of May 1853, France (as well as Britain) was still uncommitted to a war with Russia.[22] The emerging Franco-British entente was still too weak to assure the French that British support would be forthcoming should war be necessary. In June, the French and British sent their fleets to Besika. Although they attempted to coordinate their efforts at Constantinople, they were not working under an alliance agreement. Paris conveyed a willingness to support the Porte with military aid,[23] but this could easily have been limited to a loan of officers and naval escort. On 26 November, a French proposal establishing the status quo as western policy was adopted. Yet, as late as November 1853, Napoleon III had not taken any steps to build up military strength in the theater.[24]

The Ottoman defeat at Sinope forced the French hand. While Sinope did not have nearly the impact on French public opinion that it had in England,[25] it galvanized Napoleon III, who saw it as an opportunity for 'cementing his alliance with England'[26] and determined that his regime could not be militarily humiliated. Nevertheless, as of January, France still refused to send troops to the Crimea.[27] Having solidified the Anglo-French entente (although without an alliance), Napoleon III had in many ways achieved his objectives well short of war. Thus in late January, he made an eleventh-hour peace proposal. Not until February, when it was clear that all peace proposals had failed, did Napoleon III prepare to send French troops from Algeria to the Crimea.[28] On 27 February, France and Britain issued an ultimatum to Russia, which was followed by a French-British-Ottoman alliance on 12 March 1854.

France did not fight the Crimean War to achieve any concrete security objectives. In fact, Napoleon III and others in his government worried that France was fighting to protect British interests in the Near East.[29] French support was critical because Britain, once committed, would have tremendous difficulty fighting the war alone, because it lacked the necessary naval landing vessels and large numbers of soldiers that France could provide. In fact, the lack of concrete security interests in the Crimea, coupled with the importance of

French military strength, afforded Paris a unique position in that it was both indispensable and yet had the greatest flexibility in its bargaining position.[30] France found itself at the center of a major European coalition, its principal foreign policy goal. As the French Ambassador in St Petersburg cautioned in September, France had to be careful to prevent a return to diplomatic isolation when the crisis ended.[31]

What makes French participation so interesting is that it does not fit clearly into either a balancing or a traditional predation mold. While it could be argued that France was balancing against Russian gains made by repressing the revolutions, and certainly against the anticipated gains Russia would make against an unaided Turkey, these gains would come largely at the expense of Austria and Britain. Rather, the evidence indicates that France was attempting to enhance its position in Italy, Germany and Europe as a whole, with these goals mutually reinforcing each other. In order to do this, Napoleon III had to at least weaken the Concert of Europe or, at best, reconfigure the concert with France at its head. In this sense, Paris decided to enter into the Crimean War for predatory reasons, albeit French ambitions were not in the immediate theater.

Great Britain

Britain faced two principal threats: Russia and France. Generally, Britain was deterred from acting against either one for fear that the other would seize the opportunity to attack. The peculiarities of the ninth Russo-Turkish War and the Holy Places Crisis leading up to it placed Britain in a unique situation. While Russia directly threatened British interests in the Near East, Paris' desire to escape diplomatic isolation placed French forces at Britain's disposal rather than at its back. At this moment, Britain was able to weaken one threat without fear of attack from the other.

Relations between London and Constantinople had been gradually growing closer over the two decades preceding the conflict.[32] In 1834, the British began stationing their fleet at Malta. In 1838, Britain and the Porte executed the Convention of Balta Liman, giving Britain an economic stake in the Ottoman Empire. The Straits Convention was signed in 1841 guaranteeing Turkish control of the Straits. British influence at Constantinople continued to grow in the 1840s while its rivals were occupied with domestic upheaval on the Continent. In

1849, the Ottomans tried to interest Britain in a defensive alliance, but these efforts 'became bogged down in British demands for reform and Ottoman wariness of alienating other powers',[33] particularly the Russians, who favored the traditional millet system as the means to exert pressure on behalf of the Ottoman Orthodox.[34]

British security interests required independent Turkish control of the Straits:[35] 'Any other policy would open the way for her rivals to improve their position, adding to the strategic problems of the empire, forcing politically unpopular increases in defense spending.'[36] When the Holy Places Crisis broke, Britain initially supported Russia. Britain favored neither Orthodox nor Catholic, and indeed resented the disruption caused by French meddling. Not being intimately connected to either side, London felt itself to be in a prime position to mediate the conflict. The diplomatic thinking at the time was: 'If the other Great Powers were moderate, Britain could claim the credit. If not, Britain would be in a position to dominate the scene.'[37] Britain gradually shifted from a pro-Russian to a pro-French position. While French actions precipitating the crisis had been troublesome, they were not threatening because France had no plans to partition the Ottoman Empire. Russian actions, meanwhile, soon posed a direct threat to the Ottoman Empire, and thereby to British interests.[38]

In the fall of 1852, Nicholas travelled to Sevastopol, 'evoking shadows of Catherine II's expansionist policies of the 1780s'.[39] At the end of December, Nicholas secretly began to mobilize 100,000 troops.[40] The special Russian mission to Constantinople under Admiral Menshikov in March–May 1853, and its accompanying military display, dramatically heightened British perceptions of the Russian threat. Concern was already aroused by the fact that Nicholas had begun fortifying Sevastopol along with plans for Russia's own 90-gun screw ship when the crisis broke. On 20 February 1853, Nicholas outlined his plans for partition of the Ottoman Empire to British Ambassador Seymour. While under this plan Britain was to receive Crete and Egypt, this neither fulfilled Britain's security interest of preserving an independent Turkey, nor was it taken very seriously at first.[41] But in combination with these other factors, London soon became alarmed.

Yet, even as late as March 1853, French attempts to ally with Britain were unsuccessful. British policy contended that Turkey should be preserved through the 1841 Straits Convention and that there should be no collaboration with France.[42] By May, Russian troops were ready and the Russian ultimatum to the Porte was issued. Britain informed the Turks that the fleet was available if Constantinople were threatened. Nicholas, meanwhile, informed the British ambassador that he was determined to fight even if the war were long and costly.[43] By this time, London became much more willing to work with France, both because of the worrisome possibility that France could switch support to Russia in exchange for Crete and Egypt[44] and because of the need for French soldiers and coastal ships should it become necessary to defend the Ottoman Empire.

On 13–15 June, first the British and then the French naval squadrons arrived at Besika Bay, and the respective naval officers began planning for their actions and supply in the event of war.[45] On 2 July, Russian troops occupied the Principalities.[46] They ordered the hospodars to pay their tribute to Russia, giving the impression that Russia was preparing either for annexation or war.[47] Nevertheless, Russia declared that the occupation was not an act of war, Britain did not view it as a *casus belli*, and continued diplomatic negotiations – if for no other reason than British policy was still hesitant.[48]

On 4 October, the Porte declared war on Russia[49] and formally requested assistance from the Royal Navy.[50] The Turkish request was initially tabled.[51] While Britain began to collect troops, British policy remained undecided[52] as the British cabinet and public opinion became increasingly polarized. Therefore, Britain made efforts to limit escalation and took a 'half-step', directing the Royal Navy to fight only if Turkish territory were threatened or the Russian fleet left Sevastopol.[53]

On 13 November, the Turks sent a frigate squadron to Sinope despite a British prohibition.[54] This led to the fateful Battle of Sinope of 30 November–2 December, in which the Russians virtually annihilated the Turkish squadron. Sinope was followed by news of a Russian advance on the eastern front – at the same time that the Turkish army on the eastern frontier found itself cut off by the defeat at Sinope.[55] The Russian attempt at a knock-out blow and the seeming ease of Russian victories served only to worsen western fears. Britain (and France) now had to decide whether to give the Porte military support or allow Russia to defeat Turkey with unforeseeable consequences.[56] After Sinope, France and Britain began preparing for war, spending February escorting Turkish warships in the Black Sea. London had already rejected the idea of fighting as Turkish auxiliaries in favor of an Anglo-French alliance as principals.[57]

Once it became clear that Russia would, in all probability, soundly defeat the Turks in the spring, Britain began naval preparations for a two-front war – in the Baltic as well as the Black Sea. The basic British strategy was to attack Sevastopol and destroy the Russian Black Sea fleet in time to switch resources to the Baltic.[58] With the Baltic theater in mind, Britain publicly pressed for Scandinavian neutrality and privately sought Scandinavian assistance.[59] While as late as February[60] France expressed little interest in Baltic operations, France was an integral part of British planning from the beginning.

On 27 February, France and Britain sent an ultimatum to Russia. The ultimatum was set to expire in March – the earliest time the British would be ready to reach Reval in the north and Gallipoli in the south. War at this point was inevitable, 'the timing of war being dependent only on the strategic necessities so apparent to Graham'.[61] On 12 March 1854, France, Britain and the Ottoman Empire executed an alliance treaty. On 28 March, the western powers declared war on Russia.

It is quite clear that Britain entered the ninth Russo-Turkish War to preserve an independent Turkey in order to keep Russia out of the Mediterranean and curtail Russia's southern expansion. Russian actions posed a direct threat to a vital British interest and Britain balanced that threat. The French alliance gave Britain a rare opportunity to move against Russia without having to worry about a French attack. It is not at all surprising, then, that Britain moved to check Russia.

Sardinia

Sardinia is a case of a very small power joining a conflict against a great power. As discussed in Chapter 2, it is not rational for a small power to join a great power conflict for balancing reasons, simply because it is too small to affect the outcome. Sardinia did not have any clear goals in the Black Sea. Sardinia's behavior in the Crimea was predatory, but its ambitions were in Italy. It hoped that by contributing to the western powers' cause it might earn favors that could be cashed in later.

At the close of 1849, there were only two Italian states that Austria did not control either directly or indirectly: the Papal States, which were 'virtually a French protectorate',[62] and Sardinia–Piedmont ('Sardinia'). Sardinia's primary foreign-policy goal, judging by its

behavior in 1848–49, was an independent Italy dominated, if not con-
sumed, by Sardinia. When Sardinia failed to succeed by force of arms,
the new King, Victor Emmanuel, and his minister Cavour, devised a
two-pronged strategy: to create a consensus in favor of unity among
Italian elites, and convince Europe that Sardinia was the guarantor of
a peaceful and orderly transition to a united Italy.[63]

In the spring of 1853, Sardinia discussed the possibility of a defensive alliance with the Ottoman Empire, but the idea was ridiculed by
the Porte: the Ottomans wanted great power support.[64] Nevertheless,
the King and Cavour viewed the crisis and the ensuing war as 'a
chance for their country to play a part on the international scene as a
way of putting the Italian question on the agenda'.[65] By October 1853,
there were rumors of secret treaties between Sardinia and the western
powers, encouraged, no doubt, by France and Britain to pressure
Austria away from Russia. By winter, Britain wanted Sardinia and
Prussia to join the western powers as a means of excluding Austria.[66]

Negotiations between the western powers and Sardinia continued
throughout 1854. Britain wanted Sardinian troops. In late November
1854, Sardinia presented its terms, which included a war loan, pressure on Austria regarding the sequestration issue[67] and a guarantee
that the 'Italian question' would be considered at the peace table.
These terms would have humiliated Austria. Wanting to cooperate
with Austria, at least temporarily, France signed a protocol on 22
December, promising to help preserve the status quo in Italy for the
duration of the conflict. France then cautioned Britain against agreeing to Sardinia's conditions. Facing the prospect of Austro-French
cooperation in Italy, Cavour signed the military alliance without any
of his political conditions being met.[68]

Sardinia concluded an alliance on 26 January 1855, which called
for a 15,000-man combat-ready Sardinian army to be provisioned by
Britain.[69] Sardinia sent these troops to the Crimea where they received
their baptism of fire in the last Battle of Sevastopol. There they paid
the blood price that earned Sardinia a place at the peace table and that
Cavour hoped would be one of the principal elements of a united
Italy.[70]

Cavour's predatory strategy of currying favor with the western
powers nearly fell apart when France signed the convention with
Austria. By that point, however, it was too late to turn back, and an
alliance, even without the guarantees Cavour wanted, was the only
hope of salvaging anything. Amazingly enough, Sardinia did earn a

place at the peace table in 1856. Although Cavour brought back nothing concrete, he did bring the issue of the future of the Italian peninsula to the attention of the major powers.[71]

OR NOT TO JOIN?

There is always a certain difficulty in evaluating a non-event. There are always more states that abstain from a conflict than participate. In this case, selection was based on one of two criteria. First, there are the large German states – Austria and Prussia – whose very absence from the conflict eliminates the Crimean War from the category of 'great' wars in some estimations.[72] Second, there are several small powers, Sweden, Persia, Greece and the USA – whose participation was actively courted and/or deterred by the participants. These six states are discussed in turn.

Austria

Austria never favored another Russo-Turkish war but, as expected, Vienna initially leaned toward Russia. Only after it became clear that Russian aims meant the demise of Turkey and, further, that Russian strategy posed severe difficulties for Austria, did Vienna shift toward a pro-west stance, which culminated in the western alliance and the Austrian ultimatum that forced Russia to the peace table. This was not a case, as a cursory glance might suggest, of hopping aboard the bandwagon. Rather, throughout the war Austria tried to mediate the conflict, keep it within bounds and bring it to a speedy close. Austria tried to minimize the costs – they were high; not maximize gains – there were none.

Austria was the second largest land power in the region and had direct interests in the area of dispute. As a member of the Holy Alliance, Austria had a close relationship with Russia and initial Russian war plans counted on Austrian assistance. If predatory, Austria would be expected to join in and share the spoils with Russia. But, for Austria the costs were too high. From a balancing perspective, Austria seemed a prime candidate for the 'dilemma of the victor's inheritance' – let Russia, France and Britain fight while remaining neutral and thus emerge relatively stronger at the conclusion. Yet Austria provides an interesting exception to the victor's inheritance dilemma. Austria was in too weak a position, both economically and politically, to ride out the conflict. While a significant victory for either side would hurt Austria, neutrality presented costs that were almost as bad. Instead of finding itself in a win/win situation, Vienna was in a lose/lose situation. While the calculations and strategy are similar, the best Austria could do was to minimize the cost.

During the Holy Places Crisis, two principal factors gave the impression that Austria would support Russia against the Ottoman Empire. First, tense relations between Austria and the Porte over disturbances in the Balkans resulted in the Leiningen mission, a heavy-handed Austrian diplomatic effort to force Ottoman troops to withdraw. In late November 1852, the Montenegrins drove the Ottomans from their capital.[73] The Ottomans responded to the revolt while Montenegro appealed to Austria and Russia for assistance. Austria wanted to prevent the revolt from spreading, stop the flow of refugees, and offset Russian influence in the Balkans. Vienna sent a special mission to Constantinople under Leiningen, demanding that the Turks redress grievances or face a joint Austro-Russian invasion. Austrian forces went on alert and Turkey capitulated at the last moment.[74] The success of the Leiningen mission had two important effects. First, 'Buol [Austrian Foreign Minister] and his colleagues had managed to project a bullying, opportunistic image that was dia-metrically counter to their intentions'.[75] Such heavy-handedness suggested that Austria would be more than willing to acquiesce in Ottoman partition for the right share. Moreover, the successful co-operation between the two states led Russia to believe that Russia could direct Austria's foreign policy toward the Ottoman Empire.[76]

Second, to all outward appearances, Russia and Austria had a close relationship and shared interests as members of the Holy Alliance. Austria was indebted to Russia for assistance in quelling the 1848 rev-olutions. As late as May 1853, the Czar still counted on Austrian com-pliance and moral support.[77] Even in July, Nicholas believed that Austria would come around, this despite the fact that Vienna had informed him that Austria would not join a war against Turkey.[78]

Russia was not alone in believing Austria would join forces with it. In the fall of 1852, Czar Nicholas took a trip to Sevastopol, during which he was accompanied by the Austrian Ambassador. This creat-ed the impression of an Austro-Russian alliance against the Turks. This suspicion was seemingly confirmed by the Leiningen mission.

In fact, the Porte believed that Austria was hand-in-glove with Russia either from fear or greed, and Austrian troop concentrations on the Serbian border seemed to confirm the impression.[79]

Britain remained suspicious of Austria throughout the crisis and subsequent war. The personal diplomacy between Czar Nicholas and Emperor Franz Joseph easily gave the impression of collusion. The meeting between the two at Olmütz in September 1853 was perceived in Britain as further proof of an Austro-Russian partition plan.[80]

Despite appearances to the contrary, Austria did not want the Ottoman Empire partitioned. First of all, Austria was much too weak. Vienna suffered from a severe shortage of capital: Austria could not afford even the monetary cost associated with a war. Incipient nationalism threatened its internal stability, a situation which would only be aggravated by attempts to pacify and incorporate new territories.[81] While the Austrian economy was stagnating, Prussia's economic lead continued to grow.[82] Austria was too weak and inefficient to compete economically with Britain and France, even in the neighboring Principalities.[83]

Second, even if Austria were stronger, Franz Joseph did not wish to incorporate more Slavs into the volatile mix of nationalities that comprised the Habsburg Empire. Although some Austrian generals discussed shortening the border to make it more defensible, the costs of occupation, as Vienna discovered when Austria briefly occupied the Principalities with Turkish consent, would surely outweigh the gain. Simply put, Austria was under strain simply trying to hold on to what it had without acquiring more.

Third, in this weakened state, Austria needed the Concert of Europe to preserve the status quo at the least possible cost. Desperately trying to reduce expenditure and worried about internal problems, Austria could not safely rely on its deterrent posture to ward off its enemies. To the extent that the concert stabilized international relations by upholding the status quo and providing for regular diplomatic discourse, it reduced Austria's reliance on military force for its preservation. Anything that weakened the Concert, as a partition of the Ottoman Empire in defiance of the Straits Convention surely would, threatened Austria.

The Menshikov mission was for Austria, as for Britain, the pivotal event in moving Austria from a pro-Russian to an anti-Russian stance. The threat was even more dire for Austria, in that Moldavia and Wallachia already seemed lost to Russia. If the Balkans were lost too, Austria would be hemmed in.[84] Austria's predicament was made even worse by Russian strategy, which threatened to exacerbate Austria's internal problems.

Essentially, Russian strategy promoted Christian uprisings against the Turks as a means to tie down Ottoman manpower and precipitate the Ottoman Empire's collapse. According to Schroeder, 'The Russians brushed aside Francis Joseph's argument that inflammatory appeals from St Petersburg to the Balkan Christians would subvert his own subjects.'[85] This strategy was chosen as the one least likely to provoke the western powers.[86] Yet such a strategy, combined with Russian actions in the Principalities, dealt Austria a serious blow.

Austria did not immediately ally with the western powers; rather Buol tried feverishly, not only during the crisis but even after war began, to mediate a swift end to the war. On 13 October 1853, Vienna declared neutrality, which was accompanied by a large reduction in Austria's standing army. This reduction, which had long been planned, was prompted by financial problems. Austria could not sustain this neutral position unless Russia accepted limits on the conduct and aims of the war.[87] In January, Russia offered Austria joint protectorates in 'liberated' areas and promises of armed assistance to counter French threats in Italy[88] in exchange for continued neutrality, but these offers were rejected. Austria did not want any territorial gains; rather Vienna wanted to eliminate the costs of the war, not only financial, but also the risks posed to its internal stability. By February, Austria and Russia were in conflict over Serbia and it appeared that Russia was going to annex the Principalities. To bolster its position, Austria signed a defensive pact with Prussia in April 1854, and tried to persuade the other German states to join.[89]

Finally, on 3 June, Austria sent Russia an ultimatum demanding evacuation of the Principalities. On 14 June, Austria and Turkey agreed to a convention allowing for Austrian occupation of the Principalities upon Russian evacuation for the duration of the war.[90] Russia evacuated the Principalities – although claiming to do so for strategic reasons – and Austria moved in to maintain order.

With the Russian threat in the Principalities removed (mid-1854) and the campaigning in the Crimea rather than the Danube, Austria saw no reason to intervene in the war.[91] However, as the attack on Sevastopol turned into a siege, France and Britain needed Austrian assistance. Allied demands for an offensive alliance were countered by continued demands for negotiations. By the fall, Buol clearly favored a western alliance because he believed: 'Only a clear treaty relation-ship with the West would keep the sea powers from trying to embar-rass Austria and to force her prematurely into war.'[92] On 2 December 1854, Austria signed a defensive alliance with the western powers.[93]

Late 1854 and early 1855 saw renewed Austrian efforts to negoti-ate a settlement. France and Britain dealt the Vienna peace talks a fatal blow. Austria responded by seeking better relations with Prussia and Germany. The expense of maintaining its mobilization was too great and, in June, Austria demobilized another 62,000 reservists despite western protests.[94]

Following the fall of Sevastopol on 9 September 1855, France began pressuring Austria for another ultimatum, which, if refused, would force Austria to sever relations with Russia. Vienna concurred in an effort to end the war. Austria was still demobilizing and under financial pressure for even more military cuts. Buol was afraid that, if the war did not end at this juncture, it would continue for at least one more campaigning season at a price Austria could not afford.[95] The Austrian ultimatum was delivered on 16 December 1855, and accept-ed by Russia on 15 January, leading to the Paris peace talks that opened on 1 February 1856.

The Crimean War caught Austria between the proverbial rock and a hard place. Unlike the situation envisioned in the 'dilemma of the victor's inheritance', Vienna's susceptibilities placed it in a negative-sum situation where the best option was still one of minimizing losses. If Russia had a major victory, Austria would be hemmed in. Russia fostered revolutionary uprisings in the Balkans as part of its strategy, while the western powers disrupted Austria with uprisings in Italy, either of which threatened Austria's already fragile internal sta-bility. Simply the financial strains of keeping forces on alert were more than Austria could bear. Threatened by the war itself, Vienna first tried other means of balancing, particularly improving relations with Prussia. Austria did whatever it could to end the war as quickly as possible, which ultimately meant allying with the western powers, although Austria did not actually enter the war.

Prussia

Unlike Austria, Prussia indeed profited by the war. Prussia expected no gains in the Crimea, but nonetheless capitalized on neutrality, as two of its three major competitors – France and Russia – squared off against one another. The only danger to Prussia was a major victory by either side.

Prussia sought only territorial gains in northern Germany. However, Berlin did not wish to pursue them at the expense of international embarrassment.[96] Russia had made it clear in the Schleswig–Holstein Crisis of 1848 that it would not allow Prussia to threaten Denmark.[97] Since the allies were courting the Scandinavian countries as part of their Baltic strategy, they were unlikely to support Prussia in such a move. However, weakening Russia's forces in the Baltic might open the path to future Prussian predominance in the area.

There were no gains for Prussia in the Crimea – none were wanted nor offered. Indeed, Berlin was left out of every Russian partition plan. Even had Prussia desired Russian territory in the east, Prussia did not have sufficient manpower to open a new front against Russia without Austria's help. Likewise, Prussia lacked sufficient manpower to open a new front against France in south Germany.

Prussia did not have to balance against either France or Russia; they balanced each other.[98] Meanwhile, neutrality was gradually weakening Austria, Prussia's third competitor. While the disturbances on its frontier threatened renewed domestic unrest, Austria was forced to keep troops on alert at a time when Vienna needed to slash expenditures.

Prussia declared neutrality in the fall of 1853. On 5 December, Berlin signed a protocol with Vienna, followed on 20 April 1854 by an Austro-Prussian defensive alliance.[99] In this way, Prussia could attempt to control Austrian policy while avoiding diplomatic isolation. At the same time, Prussia played off Britain and Russia. As the main conduit for Russian commerce, Prussia grew rich on Russian trade.[100] Nevertheless, Prussia offered Britain support should Austria join with Russia.[101]

Neutrality was the safest and most profitable policy for Prussia. Berlin had no incentive for predation and no reason to balance. In fact, the longer the war continued, the better.

Sweden

Sweden actually allied with the western powers, albeit too late to join in the fighting. Swedish motives were largely predatory – namely, to acquire Finland. Yet, in many respects, Sweden was the 'exception that proved the rule'. Sweden did not want to join an alliance unless it could be assured that the allies' aims and strategy against Russia were sufficiently large to guarantee the acquisition of territory and, moreover, that Russia would be sufficiently weakened to be unable to retake it. Sweden could not afford to stand alone against Russia in the Baltic regardless of temptations offered by the west. It was only with the reduction of the Russian fort at Bomarsund and plans for a vigorous Baltic campaign in 1856, that the conditions were propitious for Swedish gains – largely at allied expense.

A dispute over Finmark, a once common area inhabited by Laplanders on the Russo-Norwegian border, caused a decline in Russo-Swedish relations immediately before the Crimean War.[102] On the surface, this was a petty dispute over Laplanders' fishing and pasturage rights. However, Russian demands for permanent bases on the Norwegian side, coupled with the direct participation of Nesselrode, Russia's Foreign Minister, fed Swedish fears that Russia might invade Norwegian Finmark.[103] Nevertheless, personal relations between Oscar and Nicholas remained cordial.

Despite disagreement over Finmark, there was no serious discussion of using the situation as an opportunity to strike back against Russia as the Holy Places Crisis began to heat up. Rather, Sweden and Denmark, sharing an identical interest in maintaining strict neutrality, reached agreement as early as 14 August 1853 on the definition of that neutrality. They also decided to issue joint declarations in all capitals at the end of October. Russia's initial response was to pressure Sweden for additional concessions, but quickly dropped these demands when the Czar declared war on the western powers.[104]

As soon as the British began making plans for a Baltic campaign to commence in the spring, they realized they needed the Swedish flotilla and pilots.[105] While the allies initially pressed for Scandinavian neutrality, they were already envisioning a Swedish alliance.[106] In April, the allied Admiral Napier met with King Oscar and senior naval officers. The King informed Napier that Sweden did not desire conquests and that a western alliance would not improve his position with Russia. The offer of a subsidy for an 80,000-man army in June did not sway him. Even the offer of the Aland Isles did not tempt Oscar and Sweden refused to occupy the islands following the allied victory there in August.[107]

Meanwhile Nicholas, although confident of Oscar's benign intentions, avoided provoking Sweden.[108] He knew that the maritime powers had more immediate means of inflicting reprisals.[109] Relations between Sweden and Russia continued on a cordial basis through the fall. Yet Swedish neutrality satisfied neither side in the conflict, and Sweden risked diplomatic isolation at the end of the war.

After Czar Nicholas died on 2 March, Oscar began to show more interest in the possible benefits of a western alliance.[110] In April 1855, Oscar's special envoy, Barck, met with Napoleon III first, and later Clarendon, and outlined Sweden's conditions for entering the conflict:

1 France and Britain declare that the object of the war is to render Russia less menacing to Europe and guarantee Finland to Sweden and accompany the declaration with sufficient land and naval forces;
2 Austria subscribes to this convention;
3 Sweden is invited to join the western alliance; and
4 no separate peace.

Britain refused to guarantee Finland and French troops were still tied down in the Crimea. Discussions continued, but Oscar was determined never to enter a war that did not aim to significantly reduce Russia.[111]

After the fall of Sevastopol, Oscar believed a large Baltic campaign would be planned (it was) for 1856, and signed a defensive treaty with the allies on 21 November 1855. When Russia accepted Austria's ultimatum, he was astounded; Napoleon III's success at reconciling England and Russia shocked him further. Sweden joined the allies too late to reap any material benefit.

As his stated conditions made evident, Oscar clearly had predatory intentions in mind. The allied reduction of Bomarsund in the first Baltic campaign removed one of the chief Russian outposts against Sweden. The question of Finmark had been dropped for at least the duration of the war; relations between Sweden and Russia otherwise were fairly good. In consequence, the war improved Sweden's balancing position somewhat.

Nonetheless, the fact that Oscar would not enter into an alliance for two years underscores his estimation of the high political cost of warfare. The demand for virtually unlimited aims against Russia was not to guarantee Sweden's safety; rather, it was to guarantee the safety of Swedish acquisitions. Not only did Oscar want to reap the rewards commensurate with a costly adventure, he also wanted it in such a way that France, Britain and Austria would pay the price by waging an unlimited war against Russia.

Persia

Persia had been the site of Anglo-Russian conflict in the 1830s[112] and neither side was sure which side, if any, Persia would take. Persia would have liked to obtain several Ottoman provinces, and initially cooperated with Russia, mobilizing 75,000 men.[113] However, Britain anticipated the threat and was able to use diplomatic pressure to restrain the Shah.[114] Britain raised the costs of obtaining the provinces to such a degree as to dissuade Persia from allying with Russia.

Greece

Greece was not so easily deterred as Persia. Although independent since 1832, the new state was much smaller than ethnicity would dictate. The war against the Ottoman Empire seemed to provide a prime opportunity for annexing the remaining Ottoman Greek provinces.[115]

King Otto of Greece believed that a Russo-Turkish war would enable him to 'liberate' the remaining Greek provinces.[116] In the spring of 1853, Menshikov ordered Admiral Kornilov to visit King Otto, reinforcing Otto's belief that he could depend on Russian and Austrian support. By early 1854, Greek 'volunteers' were leading insurrections in the Greek provinces. This state of undeclared hostilities brought Turkey to break relations with Greece in late March.[117]

Greece appealed to Russia and Austria for assistance, proposing that they divide the southern Balkans.[118] Austria, however, was under pressure from France and Britain to put down the insurrections and offered no more than token surveillance.[119] The western powers had consistently warned Greece against any action and made it clear that they would fully support the Ottoman Empire. Greek actions not only threatened the Ottoman Empire with internal collapse and greater Russian influence in the Balkans, but Greek risings also threatened the British-held Ionian Islands.[120] King Otto ignored the warnings he received from the sea powers as late as February, believing that their action against Russia would preclude them from bringing an effective force to bear on Greece. He was wrong. By May, the allies sent warships to occupy Piraeus, where they remained until 1857.[121]

Greece was too small to fight the Ottoman Empire under ordinary circumstances and, for that matter, with ordinary means. King Otto seized upon the war as a chance to greatly expand his territory. He disregarded diplomatic warnings and he was only restrained through western armed diplomacy, which greatly increased the costs of his venture.

United States

Although far removed from the action and without any direct interests in the area, there were some concerns that the United States would use the war as an opportunity to expand at the expense of the Western powers. The United States and Britain, and France to a lesser extent, were rivals in the new world. The United States was in the midst of a naval build-up that included six new frigates, authorized in 1854 and launched in 1856.[122] There was concern that Washington would see allied action in the east as an opportunity to snatch allied colonies in the western hemisphere.

The United States had a program for expansion in all directions and President Pierce was ready to set it in motion as early as December 1853,[123] a fact not lost on any of the participants. Russian diplomats approached the United States about a possible alliance.[124] Britain took the American threat seriously enough to plan a reserve fleet in the Channel to demonstrate British strength and ordered two battalions of infantry to Canada as a direct deterrent.[125] The show of force was sufficient to convince the Americans to take the safer and more profitable road, trading with both sides.

Summary

The ninth Russo-Turkish War was widened into the Crimean War through one instance of balancing and two instances of predation. Britain entered the conflict to balance, preserving the Ottoman Empire as a buffer between the British and Russian empires. Both France and Sardinia assisted Britain, although the gains they sought were not in the Crimea, but in Europe. Although there were other states interested in the conflict, most notably Austria, it failed to spread because states were sensitive to the high costs involved.

COMPETING THEORIES

An examination of the events comprising the Crimean War is not only useful for understanding the war widening theory presented in this thesis, but it also helps dispel the two primary counter-arguments: alliances and offense dominance.

Alliances

In its simplest version, the alliance argument predicts that commitments force states to enter wars, either willingly or unwillingly. If states are not pursuing the interests that produced the alliance per se, they are at least acting to preserve their credibility for future alliances. If this argument is true, states should 'line up' on the sides of prewar alliances and support their alliance partners, not switch sides. Obviously, for an alliance to be any kind of direct causal mechanism, it must predate the conflict. The Crimean War disproves this explanation. States did not align according to prewar alliances, nor do any of the wartime alliances predate the conflict. In short, not one instance of war widening was caused by an existing alliance.

Not one of the cases of war widening can be accounted for by the existence of a prewar alliance. The closest thing to an alliance between any of the belligerents would be that some people considered Britain to have an unofficial protectorate over Turkey. This was far from internationally recognized and no real British credibility was involved. In the case of France and Britain, they were naval rivals and their naval arms race actually continued throughout the war. All of the alliances figuring in the Crimean War were made for the specific purpose of fighting that war; they did not contribute to the widening of that war in any way. If anything, as French behavior indicates, the relationship can work the other way – wars cause alliances.

Additionally, alliances can have a dampening impact on war widening and are used by states to constrain each other's behavior. Prussia entered into an alliance with Austria to try to control Vienna; Austria entered into an alliance with the western powers to try to control their behavior and limit their war aims. In this Austria was somewhat successful. Through the Franco-British alliance, France was able to force Britain to the peace table at Paris in 1856. Alliances can have a dampening effect on both war widening and war aims.

Offense Dominance

The offense dominance argument has been used to show why alliances produce war widening. Essentially, it contends that under conditions of offense dominance alliances widen and tighten, so that war by one alliance member triggers action by the remaining alliance members. Although it has already been shown that preexisting alliances did not play a role in widening the Crimean War, it is worth an examination to see if perhaps offense dominance was at work in this instance after all, but manifested differently.

The year 1853 predates all of the technological innovations, such as the tank, which underlie the technological variation of the offense dominance argument. According to one scholar, the first half of the nineteenth century cannot be clearly characterized as either offensive or defensive.[126] And there is no evidence of a belief in offensive dominance ('cult of the offensive'). While it is true that France and Britain were prompted to insert ground forces in the Crimea for fear that Russia would crush the Turkish army, this fear was prompted by the existing force inequality, not by any belief in the superiority of the offense over the defense. At best, the offense dominance argument does not apply to the Crimean War because it cannot be categorically described as either defense or offense dominant. At worst, the Crimean War weakens the argument by presenting a case it cannot explain.

CONCLUSION

The Crimean War occurred in the post-1815 time period, which was a period of high political cost to warfare. Therefore, one should expect little or no predatory behavior and the amount of war widening should be limited to the extent that the Crimean War (or rather the ninth Russo-Turkish War) threatened to upset the balance of power. On the surface, the relatively small amount of widening that occurred (as compared with the Napoleonic Wars, World War I, etc.) would seem to support this thesis, but the closer examination provided in this case paints a somewhat more complex picture.

Of the three states that joined the conflict – France, Britain and Sardinia – only Britain was clearly balancing. Sardinia, on the other hand, was clearly predatory. Sardinia's small size meant balancing behavior in a great power conflict would have made little sense. Sardinia chose a predatory policy, which was potentially suicidal, especially given the losses it suffered in 1848–49. However, once it determined on such a policy, the means it chose – tying its policy to the actions of great powers (bandwagoning) – made sense.

French policy was predatory when viewed as a long-term plan for breaking the constraints imposed on it by the Concert of Europe and thus paving the way for expanded influence in Germany and Italy. It could be argued, although less convincingly, that Paris' attempt to upset the Concert was really balancing against the threat of an anti-French coalition. Regardless, France was very conscious of the costs of warfare, and it was France that was unwilling to engage in an unlimited war against Russia.

That the six states considered most likely to join in the conflict were deterred from doing so substantiates the theory more than the examination of the states that did join. Austria made it very clear that the cost of war more than outweighed any potential gain and Prussia profited handsomely from its neutrality. The United States and Persia were fairly easily deterred from their predatory ambitions; Greece needed to be dissuaded with a bit more force. Even Sweden, while eventually joining the alliance in the hope of acquiring Finmark, was deterred by the cost and was only willing to join with the assurance that the costs would be borne by France and Britain.

The Crimean War also provides some insight into the relationship between strategy and war widening. Russia's attempt at a knock-out blow against the Ottoman Empire is what sufficiently alarmed the western powers to bring in ground forces. While such a strategy may have made sense if one were concerned about preventing war widening for predatory reasons – that is, preempting it – it is especially dangerous if war widening is likely to occur for balancing reasons because it increases the threat.

It would be an overstatement to assert that the Crimean War fully endorses the theory of war widening presented in this thesis. Sardinia and France are anomalous, if explainable. But, when all of the widening possibilities which did *not* occur are taken into account, the Crimean War reasonably supports the thesis. Moreover, the Crimean War clearly undermines the alternative arguments.

NOTES

1. L. Thouvenel, *Nicholas I et Napoléon III: Les Préliminaires de la Guerre de Crimée 1852–1854 d'après les Papiers Inédits de M. Thouvenel* (Paris: Ancienne Maison Michel Lévy Frères, 1891), p. 215.
2. Sweden joined the coalition too late to enter the fighting and is not considered a combatant in the war.
3. See Paul M. Kennedy, *The Rise and Fall of British Naval Mastery* (London: The Ashfield Press, 1983), pp. 171–2.
4. Members of the Russian Orthodox Church. Orthodoxy was the official religion of Russia and was even a state department.
5. The Convention of Balta Liman was signed in 1838; under it Britain won extensive tariff concessions and opened up the Ottoman Empire to British trade. See Ann Pottinger Saab, *The Origins of the Crimean Alliance* (Charlottesville, VA: University Press of Virginia, 1977), p. 3. Turkey was Britain's best trading partner in the region. See Andrew D. Lambert, *The Crimean War: British Grand Strategy, 1853–56* (Manchester: Manchester University Press, 1990), p. 3; David Wetzel, *The Crimean War: A Diplomatic History* (Boulder, CO: East European Monographs, distributed by Columbia University Press, New York, 1985), p. 15.
6. A customs union of north German states. See Paul W. Schroeder, *Austria, Great Britain, and the Crimean War: The Destruction of the European Concert* (Ithaca, NY: Cornell University Press, 1972), p. 4.
7. See ibid., p. 23.
8. For all of the details, especially regarding Austrian mediation attempts, see ibid. For the Ottoman perspective, see Saab, *The Origins of the Crimean Alliance.*
9. Saab, *The Origins of the Crimean Alliance*, p. 96.
10. The treaty ending the Napoleonic Wars also specified that, should Napoleon or a member of his family again rule France, the coalition against France was reactivated.
11. David M. Goldfrank, *The Origin of the Crimean War* (London: Longman, 1994), p. 28.
12. L.Thouvenel, *Nicholas I et Napoléon III*, pp. 35–7, 86.
13. Goldfrank, *The Origin of the Crimean War*, p. 76; Saab, *The Origins of the Crimean Alliance*, p. 156.
14. Schroeder, *Austria, Great Britain, and the Crimean War*, p. 23.
15. There is more about Napoleon III's Italian policy in the discussions on Austria and Sardinia.
16. Saab, *The Origins of the Crimean Alliance*, p. 36.
17. Goldfrank, *The Origin of the Crimean War*, p. 37.
18. Thouvenel wrote to Castelbajac on 30 April 1853 that it was clear no one at St Petersburg would help France retreat honorably. Thouvenel, *Nicholas I et Napoléon III*, p. 126.
19. Lambert, *The Crimean War*, p. 17.
20. Goldfrank, *The Origin of the Crimean War*, p. 137.
21. Norman Rich, *Why the Crimean War? A Cautionary Tale* (Hanover, NH: University Press of New England, 1985), p. 99.
22. Goldfrank, *The Origin of the Crimean War*, p. 167.
23. Saab, *The Origins of the Crimean Alliance*, p. 54.
24. Ibid., p. 98.
25. Ibid., p. 126. More on the effect of Sinope on Britain later.
26. Saab, quoting Napoleon III, ibid., p. 126.

27. Lambert, *The Crimean War*, p. 83.
28. Saab, *The Origins of the Crimean Alliance*, p. 133; Schroeder, *Austria, Great Britain, and the Crimean War*, p. 132.
29. Thouvenel, *Nicholas I et Napoléon III*, p. 232.
30. See Goldfrank, *The Origin of the Crimean War*, pp. 174–5.
31. Castelbajac to Thouvenel, 23 September 1853, in Thouvenel, *Nicholas I et Napoléon III*, p. 227.
32. For details, see Saab, *The Origins of the Crimean Alliance*, pp. 2–9.
33. Ibid., p. 9.
34. Ibid., p. 7. Essentially the millet system defined individuals' relationship to the state according to religious/ethnic group, rather than a direct and presumably equal status as citizen or subject.
35. Goldfrank, *The Origin of the Crimean War*, p. 49.
36. Andrew D. Lambert, *The Crimean War*, pp. xx–xxi.
37. Goldfrank, *The Origin of the Crimean War*, p. 128.
38. There is considerable disagreement among scholars as to what Nicholas's intentions in the Crimea actually were – whether his intentions were benign, only to be masked by the manner in which he conducted his diplomacy, on whether the Holy Places Crisis was an excuse for Russia to extend its influence in the Balkans and Black Sea at the expense of the Ottoman Empire, or even whether Nicholas had become eccentric with age. From the standpoint of the other powers, this sort of subtlety is meaningless; Russian actions were a direct threat to the Ottoman Empire and, by extension, to British (and Austrian) security interests. See Albert Seaton, *The Crimean War: A Russian Chronicle* (London: B. T. Batsford, 1977), pp. 40–1; Goldfrank, *The Origin of the Crimean War*, p. 117; David Saunders, *Russia in the Age of Reaction and Reform: 1801––1881*, Longman History of Russia (London: Longman, 1992), p. 191; Thouvenel, *Nicholas I et Napoléon III*, p. 215.
39. Goldfrank, *The Origin of the Crimean War*, p. 97.
40. Ibid., pp. 109–10.
41. Saab, *The Origins of the Crimean Alliance*, pp. 15–16.
42. Lambert, *The Crimean War*, p. 17.
43. Goldfrank, *The Origin of the Crimean War*, p. 171.
44. Lambert, *The Crimean War*, p. 20.
45. Ibid., pp. 39–40.
46. Ibid., p. 22.
47. Goldfrank, *The Origin of the Crimean War*, p. 190.
48. Saab, *The Origins of the Crimean Alliance*, pp. 54, 92.
49. Ibid., p. 95.
50. Lambert, *The Crimean War*, p. 50.
51. Saab, *The Origins of the Crimean Alliance*, p. 96.
52. Lambert, *The Crimean War*, pp. 50–1.
53. Saab, *The Origins of the Crimean Alliance*, pp. 98–9.
54. Lambert, *The Crimean War*, p. 60.
55. Saab, *The Origins of the Crimean Alliance*, pp. 117, 119.
56. Ibid., p. 117.
57. Goldfrank, *The Origin of the Crimean War*, p. 227.
58. Ibid., p. 243; Lambert, *The Crimean War*, pp. 64–5.
59. Ibid., p. 73. There is more on this subject when Sweden's role is discussed.
60. Ibid., p. 74.
61. Ibid., p. 77.

62. Roger Absalom, *Italy since 1800: A Nation in the Balance?* (London: Longman, 1995), p. 33.
63. Absalom, *Italy since 1800*, p. 31.
64. Saab, *The Origins of the Crimean Alliance*, pp. 46–7.
65. Absalom, *Italy since 1800*, p. 37.
66. Schroeder, *Austria, Great Britain, and the Crimean War*, p. 136.
67. A problem resulting from Austrian repression and punitive measures against revolutionaries – generally exile and property seizure.
68. Schroeder, *Austria, Great Britain, and the Crimean War*, pp. 237–9.
69. Lambert, *The Crimean War*, p. 196.
70. Albin Cullberg, *La Politique du Roi Oscar I pendant la Guerre de Crimée: Etudes Diplomatiques sur les Négociations Secrètes entre les Cabinets de Stockholm, Paris, St Petersbourg et Londres les Années 1853–1856* (Stockholm: Författarens Förlag, 1912), p. 1:13.
71. Absalom, *Italy since 1800*, p. 37.
72. According to Goldfrank, 'Since the seventeenth century all major wars in Europe have been at least partially German wars. The Crimean War was not a "great" war because the Germans themselves did not wish it to be one.' Goldfrank, *The Origin of the Crimean War*, p. 282. It seems to me that the statement is only partially true. 'Great' wars seem to be so judged, in part, by their results. By refusing to cater to British war aims, which included reducing Russia, Napoleon III is in large measure responsible for limiting the war.
73. Goldfrank, *The Origin of the Crimean War*, p. 101.
74. Schroeder, *Austria, Great Britain, and the Crimean War*, pp. 24–6.
75. Saab, *The Origins of the Crimean Alliance*, p. 22.
76. Schroeder, *Austria, Great Britain, and the Crimean War*, p. 28.
77. Goldfrank, *The Origin of the Crimean War*, p. 170; Saab, *The Origins of the Crimean Alliance*, p. 52.
78. Schroeder, *Austria, Great Britain, and the Crimean War*, pp. 44–5.
79. Saab, *The Origins of the Crimean Alliance*, pp. 60, 67–8.
80. Schroeder, *Austria, Great Britain, and the Crimean War*, p. 70.
81. Goldfrank, *The Origin of the Crimean War*, pp. 14, 19; Schroeder, *Austria, Great Britain, and the Crimean War*, pp. 15–17; Saunders, *Russia in the Age of Reaction and Reform*, p. 198.
82. Schroeder, *Austria, Great Britain, and the Crimean War*, p. 4.
83. Ibid., p. 212.
84. Ibid., p. 14.
85. Ibid., p. 42. See also Saab, *The Origins of the Crimean Alliance*, p. 134.
86. Goldfrank, *The Origin of the Crimean War*, p. 220.
87. Schroeder, *Austria, Great Britain, and the Crimean War*, pp. 84–6.
88. Ibid., pp. 138–41.
89. Ibid., pp. 166, 178.
90. Ibid., pp. 180–2.
91. Ibid., p. 201.
92. Ibid., p. 215.
93. Ibid., p. 232.
94. Ibid., pp. 278, 295, 302.
95. Ibid., pp. 314, 326.
96. Goldfrank, *The Origin of the Crimean War*, p. 19.
97. Lambert, *The Crimean War*, p. 6.
98. Goldfrank argues that Prussia did not join with Russia because it could not provision the 200,000 Russian troops that would be needed against France. Goldfrank, *The Origin of the Crimean War*, p. 256.

99. Schroeder, *Austria, Great Britain, and the Crimean War*, pp. 114, 166.
100. Lambert, *The Crimean War*, pp. 78, 182.
101. Goldfrank, *The Origin of the Crimean War*, p. 238.
102. At this time Russia had annexed Finland, and Sweden and Norway were a dual monarchy.
103. Cullberg, *La Politique du Roi Oscar I pendant la Guerre de Crimée*, pp. 1:7–20. It is not certain whether Russia pursued the issue because of domestic politics (to show the Finns the benefit of union with Russia) or whether the issue was seized upon as a pretext for further expansion in the Baltic. However, there is a certain similarity between Russian policy in the Baltic and the Balkans. In both cases, Russia was acting under the guise of advancing the rights and privileges of peoples on the fringe of its empire as a pretext for further expansion of the empire.
104. Cullberg, *La Politique du Roi Oscar I pendant la Guerre de Crimée*, pp. 1:31–41. See also Goldfrank, *The Origin of the Crimean War*, p. 235, and Lambert, *The Crimean War*, p. 73.
105. Goldfrank, *The Origin of the Crimean War*, p. 236. Denmark was assumed to be too close to Russia.
106. Lambert, *The Crimean War*, pp. 73, 75.
107. Cullberg, *La Politique du Roi Oscar I pendant la Guerre de Crimée*, pp. 1:69, 75–6. The offer of the Aland Isles included the now reduced Russian fort at Bomarsund. While Bomarsund was obviously not sufficiently fortified to stand against allied naval forces, it was useful against Sweden and had, in fact, been fortified by Russia in violation of a Russo-Swedish treaty.
108. Cullberg, *La Politique du Roi Oscar I pendant la Guerre de Crimée*, p. 1:81.
109. Goldfrank, *The Origin of the Crimean War*, p. 235.
110. Cullberg attributes this to a personal relationship and moral obligation between Oscar and Nicholas, but it could also be that Alexander II was seen as less threatening because he had been a vocal opponent of the war.
111. Cullberg, *La Politique du Roi Oscar I pendant la Guerre de Crimée*, pp. 2:42–4, 56.
112. Goldfrank, *The Origin of the Crimean War*, p. 50.
113. Saab, *The Origins of the Crimean Alliance*, pp. 121–2.
114. Lambert, *The Crimean War*, p. 64.
115. For example, Epirus, Thessaly, Macedonia, Chalcedice.
116. Saab, *The Origins of the Crimean Alliance*, p. 104.
117. Schroeder, *Austria, Great Britain, and the Crimean War*, p. 173; Saab, *The Origins of the Crimean Alliance*, p. 146.
118. Ibid., p. 145.
119. Schroeder, *Austria, Great Britain, and the Crimean War*, p. 173.
120. Saab, *The Origins of the Crimean Alliance*, p. 142.
121. Ibid., p. 147.
122. Kenneth J. Hagan, *This People's Navy: The Making of American Sea Power* (New York: The Free Press, 1991), pp. 139–40. See also Russell F. Weigley, *The American Way of War: A History of United States Military Strategy and Policy* (Bloomington, IN: Indiana University Press, 1977), p. 63.
123. Goldfrank, *The Origin of the Crimean War*, p. 256.
124. Schroeder, *Austria, Great Britain, and the Crimean War*, p. 204; Goldfrank, *The Origin of the Crimean War*, p. 256.
125. Lambert, *The Crimean War*, pp. 269, 291.
126. Jack Levy, 'The Offensive/Defensive Balance of Military Technology: A Theoretical and Historical Analysis', *International Studies Quarterly*, 28 (1984), p. 232.

— 6 —

World War I

All nations want peace, but they want a peace that suits them.
Jacky Fisher[1]

World War I was selected as a case study for three principal reasons. First, it is the cornerstone case for the offense dominance argument, particularly the 'cult of the offensive' variant that was developed to explain the outbreak of this war.[2] Second, World War I is also a strong case for the alliance argument, given the attention paid by both historians and contemporaries to the roles of the alliance blocs in spreading the conflict. Third, while World War I provides a good case for these two opposing arguments, it is problematic for the war widening argument presented in this thesis, because it occurred at a time when the theory predicts that one of the principal causes for war widening, predation, should not be present and that war widening in general, therefore, should have been less likely.

Examination of the case shows, as the theory predicts, that the great powers entered the conflict for balancing reasons. Despite the resemblance in scope to eighteenth-century conflicts, the motivation behind World War I differed dramatically, in that the great powers did not widen the conflict for predatory reasons. Small states, however, remained predatory, unable to affect the general balance of power, but willing to ride on great power coat-tails to enhance their regional position. The alliance argument explains the initial outbreak well, but suffers, if anything, a negative correlation for smaller states. Furthermore, the alliances were responsible more for the diplomatic environment prompting the outbreak of war and the duration of the conflict than for the widening of the war. Offense dominance fails to explain why this war widened, even if one were to accept its argument for the war's outbreak. By contrast, the war widening theory explains why World War I widened.

This chapter begins with a brief review of what the war widening theory predicts about World War I. A discussion of the war as a case study follows. The case presentation includes state-by-state reviews of the reasons each participant entered the conflict followed by a brief discussion of the more notable abstainers. Upon conclusion of the case presentation, two competing arguments are assessed. The first is the role of alliances, not only how much of the widening resulted from preexisting alliances, but also whether the alliances had any independent impact on the situation. The second argument assesses offense dominance in both its variants, technological and ideological. The conclusion weighs the explanatory power of the war widening argument tested in this thesis against its principal opponents on their strongest case.

THEORETICAL PREDICTIONS

Predation

World War I broke out in an era when warfare had a high political cost. France lost Alsace and Lorraine in the Franco-Prussian War and, more recently, Russia suffered revolutionary turmoil following its loss to Japan. World leaders were acutely aware that any European conflict would be costly in both blood and treasure.[3] Therefore, great powers had virtually no incentive to engage in predatory war widening.

According to the war widening theory, small powers, on the other hand, are not bound by the same restrictions. While small powers suffered horrendous costs in warfare, such as Bulgaria's losses in the Second Balkan War, the opportunity afforded by great power war is seemingly irresistible. Often restrained from aggression by their regional balance of power or threats from the great powers, small powers can use great power conflicts as a shield behind which to attack their neighbors and improve their position. Moreover, if the great powers themselves are not in the conflict to increase their own territory, they are more willing to offer their adversaries' possessions as incentives to smaller states. Unable to affect the global balance of power, and thus not bound by it, small powers are free to shift their allegiance to whichever coalition offers the greatest prospects, also mitigating the costs. Thus any great power war, regardless of the era, offers small states an incentive for predation. When great powers are balancing, the opportunities can be even greater.

Balancing

Balancing predicts that, when the political cost of warfare is high, as was true in the post-Napoleonic period, great powers should enter ongoing conflicts only for balancing reasons. War widening usually lessens, because balancing logic dictates that states enter an ongoing conflict only when that conflict: (1) threatens their interests; or (2) threatens to shift the balance of power adversely; and (3) all other balancing options are exhausted. But the theory does not predict when balancing is necessary. The power distribution in a particular situation determines that need.

Europe in 1914 meets all three requirements. It was dominated by two roughly equal alliance blocs, France–Russia and Germany–Austria. Russia was growing stronger, while Austria was in decline. In the crises that occurred over the previous decade, Great Britain repeatedly backed France and Russia, seemingly foreclosing other balancing options for Germany and Austria. Thus, a central European war fulfills the balancing requirements. And so, great powers were under tremendous pressure to balance. Small states, however, had no incentive to balance because they could not affect the balance of power either way.

WORLD WAR I: HISTORIOGRAPHY

Historians have not yet reached consensus on the cause(s) of World War I.[4] Because the discussion of the cause of the war was so highly politicized from the start, as evidenced by the 'war guilt' clause in the Treaty of Versailles, this bloody and costly conflict has been attributed to such varying causes as a German bid for hegemony,[5] 'secret alliances', and bungling diplomats. Perhaps Paul Kennedy puts it best:

> As with most complex happenings, the First World War offers so much data that conclusions can be drawn from it to suit any *a priori*

hypothesis which contemporary strategists and politicians wish to advance.[6]

The discussion of causes is further complicated because, as Corelli Barnett puts it, 'The First World War had causes but no objectives.'[7] That is, it differed from previous wars in that most of the participants were not at war in an effort to seize or defend pieces of territory per se.

The most important issue for war widening is determining which states are initial combatants and which states are neutrals. In other words, is World War I the widening of an Austro-Serbian conflict or did it begin as a general war? While an interesting story can be told of World War I as yet another Balkan war, this chapter will proceed on the somewhat more conventional basis of a war initiated between Germany, Belgium, Russia and France, as well as Austria and Serbia.

There are several reasons for including so many states as initial combatants in World War I, although it does make the case rather exceptional. The first reason is temporal: these states all entered the conflict at virtually the same time. As Jack Levy writes, 'World War I comes close to simultaneous entry by all great powers, in that the Austrian and Serbian decisions for a local war cannot be separated, either chronologically or analytically, from German, Russian and French decisions for a general European war.'[8]

The second and most important reason for treating World War I as a war that was initiated as a general war, is that it conforms to the way it is commonly treated by international relations scholars.[9] Applying the war widening thesis to the same story facilitates comparison with other international relations research. For most international relations theorists, as well as analytic historians, Germany is at the heart of the origins of World War I. For theories of inadvertent or accidental war, World War I is the best, and perhaps only, historical example.[10] These historians and theorists place Germany at the center of events, assuming that Germany could have prevented the Austro-Serbian war.

Likewise, scholars interested in power transition arguments and preventive war theories hone in on the relationship between Germany and Russia.[11] Scholars interested in deterrence examine the relationship between Great Britain and Germany. Could a more explicit British commitment to France have deterred Germany?[12] And lastly, one of the counter-arguments to this war widening argument: did a

belief in the superiority of the offense, manifested in the war plans of
the great powers, cause the outbreak of World War I? This argument
places Germany in the central explanatory position as well.[13]

Britain is not included as an initial participant for two reasons.
First, as will be discussed in a later section, Britain entered the war
several days after the Continental powers. Second, it was not initially
clear to the other combatants, or within the British Cabinet itself,
whether Britain would, in fact, enter the war.[14] Even France did not
count on the arrival of the British Expeditionary Force (BEF). When
General Joffre drafted Plan 17, he left a 110-mile stretch of his left
flank exposed, to be covered by the BEF if it arrived. But Joffre
believed that the German army would be coming through the
Ardennes so that the fighting would be on the right.[15] Therefore,
Britain is treated as the first neutral to widen the conflict.

The drawback to treating World War I as a conflict with such an
explosive start is that it hampers a direct comparison with one of the
primary counter-arguments: offense dominance. By conceding that so
many states were initiators, it leaves uncontested the claim that a false
belief in offense dominance led to the outbreak of the war. This chapter can at best only show that offense dominance did not contribute
to the further widening of the conflict – a claim Van Evera does not
make.

The outbreak of World War I is a familiar one. On 28 June 1914,
Austrian Archduke Franz Ferdinand was assassinated. At the end of
a five-week crisis, Germany launched the infamous Schlieffen plan,[16]
attacking Belgium en route to France. Austria was left to hold Russia
and Serbia until Germany could swing forces back to the east. Austria,
Serbia, Russia, Germany, Belgium and France were at war.

TO JOIN? THE GREAT POWERS

Britain

Much of the historical discussion of Britain's entry into World War I
has focused on whether a clearer declaration by Britain prior to the
war would have deterred Germany and why such a declaration was
not made. Such speculation is moot, because German military
planners had already factored British military participation into the

equation and discounted it.[17] Furthermore, a blockade had limited effectiveness against Germany, particularly in a war that almost all believed would be short.[18] The question to ask of the British case, therefore, is not whether Britain could have prevented German entry; rather, why did Britain itself enter the conflict? Britain did not fight World War I out of an obligation to France or Belgium, but rather to prevent German hegemony on the Continent, and the threat such domination would pose to itself.[19]

Prior to World War I, Germany and the United States overtook Britain in industrial output. However, as an imperial and naval power, in addition to its role as a commercial and financial center, Britain remained the top power, although this position was under pressure from all sides. Thus, London tried to preserve the status quo, although doing so increasingly resembled a juggling act.[20] The Franco-Russian alliance precluded Britain's old Crimean policy. British overtures to Germany to provide manpower for the Near East failed, but those to Japan succeeded in 1902. Russia's defeat in the Russo-Japanese War, particularly the destruction of its navy, gave Britain some respite in the east. Britain also signed an agreement with Russia on the Middle East in 1907. The Russo-Japanese War gave further impetus to the Anglo-French Entente Cordiale, because both France and Britain wanted to limit the spread of their respective allies' conflicts.[21] Initial British relationships with France and Russia began primarily as attempts to resolve colonial differences and consolidate Britain's position.

These agreements coincided with and were furthered by the development of the German navy and allowed Britain to concentrate force against it in the North Sea.[22] Britain considered the German North Sea Fleet a direct threat to British security, and in fact Admiral Fisher saw Germany as 'the only probable enemy' as early as 1903,[23] five years before the dreadnought race. The British army followed suit in 1905.[24] Germany initiated a series of Anglo-German naval negotiations in 1909 in which Berlin offered to slow down naval development in exchange for colonial concessions. These talks culminated in 1912 with the Haldane mission. However, Britain was unwilling to promise neutrality in a European war, and Germany was unwilling to make any significant naval reductions.[25] Nevertheless, Anglo-German relations were good otherwise, and agreements on colonial issues were ready for signature when the war broke out.[26]

As Germany grew and became a greater threat, British relations with France strengthened. There was no formal alliance between France and Britain, and joint staff talks remained unofficial, although they were approved by Grey, the British Prime Minister.[27] The first joint war plans were made in July 1911 and called for a seven-division (six infantry and one cavalry) British Expeditionary Force – however, the navy did not make arrangements for their transport until early 1912.[28] The British situation was difficult. It only made sense to help France if, unaided, France would be crushed. And yet, to avoid merely joining France's defeat, British assistance must be powerful enough to prevent it, a difficult proposition for a country short of manpower and long on obligations.[29] Therefore Grey and Churchill refused any sort of binding agreement with France that might restrict British freedom of action.[30] By the spring of 1914, all of the Anglo-French staff work was complete, but it was secret.[31] Parliament was ignorant of the turn Anglo-French relations had taken, and France remained unsure of British support when war broke out.

Was the German violation of Belgium a colossal blunder that ensured British belligerence? No. Britain was a guarantor of Belgian neutrality by two 1839 treaties,[32] yet when the danger of a Franco-German war arose in 1887 the British government informed Belgium not to expect assistance.[33] As late as 29 July 1914, the British Cabinet assumed both France and Germany would violate Belgian neutrality, leaving British action a matter of policy, not legal obligation.[34] While Britain did not go to war to rescue Belgium, it did provide a useful issue around which various centers of opinion in Britain could coalesce, ensuring an earlier and more united response than would otherwise have been possible.[35]

As the crisis broke in July 1914, Britain had no alliances on the Continent, only an entente with France and three years of joint war-planning. However, a German defeat of France would not only make Germany a European hegemon (a long-term threat to British security), but also could provide Germany with Atlantic naval bases, which would be a real and immediate threat to the British Isles. After it became clear that British mediation proposals had failed, on 30 July Britain requested a pledge from both Germany and France to respect Belgian neutrality; Germany refused. British policy was still unresolved and on 1 August the Cabinet refused to call up the naval reserves.[36] Lloyd George believed that the sides were fairly well-matched and that initially neither side would win decisively. Therefore, he believed, British interests would be best served by waiting for the stalemate to maximize British bargaining leverage – essentially following the strategy prescribed for neutrals by the 'dilemma of the victor's inheritance'.[37] In a complete about-face, the next day London worried France might be crushed.[38] Britain learned of the German ultimatum to Belgium on 3 August.[39] Grey used the Belgian ultimatum to garner support in Parliament, which he followed with an ultimatum to Germany on 4 August. With no satisfactory answer, Britain and Germany were at war at midnight.[40]

Despite the British declaration of war against Germany, the Anglo-French war plans did not automatically take effect, although the British war book system had all necessary orders ready for signature.[41] The proper role of the BEF – whether to fight as is or to provide the nucleus for an expanded force, to have a unified or separate command, and where and how best to fight for British interests – remained to be debated by the Cabinet. The BEF did not begin embarkation until 9 August, and only on 12 August did Britain decide to go ahead with the original deployment plan at Maubeuge, but with only four infantry divisions.[42] An alliance between Britain, France and Russia was not formed until 4 September, when the parties signed the Pact of London pledging not to conclude a separate peace.[43]

Britain was forced to consolidate its position in the years preceding World War I as its preeminence was challenged by the growing power of the United States, Germany and Russia. London was able to reach an accommodation with the United States and Russia because their conflicts were limited to specific colonial matters, and neither Russia nor the USA had the naval power to challenge Britain's world position. Germany was a different matter. Germany and Britain were able to reach agreement on many colonial differences, but that did little to ease Germany's more general threat to Britain's world dominance. With Germany already having a strong navy and industrial output outpacing its own, Britain could not allow Germany to defeat France and become a European hegemon with access to Atlantic naval ports. Britain had to balance that threat directly with military force.

Japan

Japan, admitted to great power status following its victory over Russia in 1905, continued to gain strength in the early twentieth century, largely through territorial aggrandizement to offset its own relatively resource-poor territory. Japanese participation in World War I was no different. While the other powers waged total war in Europe, Japan seized the opportunity to expand its holdings in China.

Japan entered into an alliance with Britain in 1902.[44] While only the most liberal interpretation would confirm that Japan acted in accordance with this agreement, it did serve to provide a thin veil of diplomatic cover for its actions. Like the other great powers, Japan had a stake in China that gradually eroded not only Chinese territory, but Chinese sovereignty as well. Japan expanded its stake by a 1907 treaty with Russia that had secret provisions for dividing Manchuria.[45] When the war began, the Anglo-Japanese treaty gave Japan cover to attack German possessions in China and elsewhere in the Pacific.[46] Japan coveted Kiao-Chow, which gave access to northern China and which, most importantly, was rich with the raw materials Japan needed.[47]

Japan wasted little time. On 2 August 1914, Japan informed Germany that, while desiring neutrality, treaty obligations bound it to defend Britain's Asian empire – despite the fact that London did not issue an ultimatum to Germany until 4 August. The states interested in Asia, including the Allies, were not fooled, but with their energies needed in Europe they were powerless to prevent it. On 11 August, the United States attempted to mediate a German-Japanese neutralization of Asia, to which Washington received a favorable reply from Germany on 13 August. This only hastened Japanese actions. Fearing its hands would be tied diplomatically, Japan issued an ultimatum to Germany on 15 August, demanding that Germany hand over Kiao-Chow. When Germany made no reply, Japan declared war on 25 August, two days *after* besieging the German base, Tsingtao.[48] Japan continued to make profitable inroads into China as the European war dragged on and the other powers were unable to interfere.[49]

Alone among the great powers during World War I, Japanese action was clearly predatory; it seized the opportunity the war provided to expand its territory and greatly improve its position. Japan was not balancing; the balance of power at issue was in Europe. Nor was Japan protecting Britain's interests in Asia because Germany was willing to keep the war out of China. Japan saw that with the European great powers tied down, it could expand virtually unopposed. This it did with great success.

The United States

The United States was not part of the European alliance system in the early twentieth century; indeed, American concerns were predominantly based in the western hemisphere. This isolationism suited the belligerents who, foreseeing a short war, saw no need for US assistance. The British, who later would become desperate for American materiel and manpower, initially disdained any US meddling. Without direct interest in the conflict and unprepared for a war of that magnitude, the United States not surprisingly declared neutrality when the conflict began. The interesting story is why and how the United States became increasingly involved as the war dragged on, finally entering in time to tip the scales in favor of the Allies and winning a significant seat at the peace table.

At the beginning of the twentieth century, the United States was a great power without being part of the great power system.[50] The United States had most of the hallmarks of a great power: industrial output, population, land mass. As to military force, the US army was smaller than that of Portugal,[51] but the US navy 'was first-class by any standard'.[52] The United States had taken some tentative steps toward joining the great power system, participating in Algeciras (1906), but ignoring the Second Moroccan Crisis. Likewise, after many failed attempts, the United States passed a number of arbitration treaties in 1913 and 1914, but these committed it to very little.[53] American interests were largely outside Europe, and military planning, such as it was, focused on Japan and Mexico.[54]

The US response to the opening of hostilities was to ask the belligerents to abide by the 1909 Declaration of London, which delineated neutral shipping rights but which the parties had not, however, formally ratified. The Central Powers agreed, contingent on the Allies, but the British, fearing loss of their naval superiority, essentially rejected the request. Washington protested at the British response.[55] Meanwhile, the United States was also having problems with Britain's ally, Japan. Japan and Germany both violated Chinese neutrality, but China and the USA feared Japan had wider aspirations in China. These fears were confirmed in January 1915 when Japan presented China with its infamous 'Twenty-one Demands'. Unwilling to fight Japan, the United States only refused to recognize the agreement that China had been forced to sign.[56]

After the beginning of the war which saw friction between the

USA and the Allies, things improved. Although Britain cut off the considerable American trade with the Central Powers and neutrals, the Allies bought up the difference, creating a modest war boom in a previously depressed US economy.[57] As this economic relationship strengthened, 'the United States became the larder, arsenal, and bank of the Allies and acquired a direct interest in Allied victory that was to bemuse the postwar apostles of economic determinism for a long time.'[58] Nevertheless, it was not the close Anglo-American economic relationship that prompted US entry into the war. Rather, it was the desire for a seat at the peace table and a growing fear of German hegemony.

President Wilson hoped to keep the USA out of the war by ending it. He tried repeatedly during the conflict to negotiate a settlement between the belligerents. However, as the war progressed and more blood and treasure were expended, whichever side held the advantage wanted victor's terms to which the other, with hopes bolstered by the presence of allies, would not accede.[59] Wilson's attempts at mediation failed and hopes of influencing the shape and character of the postwar world as a neutral died with them.[60]

Berlin declared that Germany would resume unrestricted submarine warfare on 1 February 1917, prompting Wilson to break relations with Germany. By refusing President Wilson's mediation efforts, and by resuming unrestricted warfare, Germany threatened American national interests.[61] Submarine warfare raised the specter of a German victory by cutting off the Allies from the US supplies on which they increasingly relied. Germany wanted to take advantage of the Allies' dependence on the United States. Although submarine warfare itself was the pretext for US entry, it was really the prospect of German hegemony that prompted the American move.[62] US strategists had decided that the fighting itself posed no real threat to the United States or to the Monroe Doctrine as long as the war was being waged in Europe. US military planning during the war, including the 1916 Naval Act, was geared toward dealing with the victor.[63] Now it appeared that Germany could emerge victorious, with dominance over Europe, shattering hopes for a favorable postwar balance. If Great Britain were defeated, the Royal Navy could no longer serve as a shield protecting the western hemisphere from other European powers, as it had been doing for years.[64] Wilson asked Congress for a Declaration of War on 2 April 1917.

At first the United States declared war only on Germany – not only because Germany was the only belligerent to wage unrestricted submarine warfare, but also in hopes of drawing off its allies. When that failed, Washington declared war on Austria in December. The USA did not, however, become one of the Allies. Instead, it was an 'associated power'.[65]

The United States entered World War I to prevent a German victory and gain some leverage at the peace table in order to help implement a stable postwar balance of power. The United States did not enter the war because of any alliance commitments; it maintained none, either before or after it entered. As long as there was a stalemate in Europe, it was not immediately threatened, and indeed prospered. But, facing the prospect of German hegemony over Europe, combined with such industrial and naval power, the United States chose to defend its interests immediately rather than await the potential long-term threat.

TO JOIN? SMALLER POWERS

Turkey

Turkey did not enter the war until November 1914, after its German ally committed an act of war in its name. Whether Turkey would have finally taken up arms otherwise is a matter for speculation. Turkey did have strong motives for throwing in its lot with the Central Powers. An alliance with Germany and Austria would balance against Russia and its Balkan allies and, if victorious, allow Turkey to recover some of its lost European territory.

Turkey's obvious internal weakness, manifested by the Young Turk Revolution of 1908, made it a tempting target for its traditional adversaries, especially Russia, with ambitions in the Balkans, as well as dubious Italian claims to Turkey's African provinces. The threat of the First Balkan War forced Turkey to accept Italian gains in Africa in 1912;[66] and Turkey suffered considerably at the hands of the Balkan League.

Although Turkey managed to recapture a small amount of territory in the Second Balkan War, it still had lost almost all of its wealthier European territory. As a result of warfare from 1911 to 1913, Turkey was left with its poorer Asiatic provinces and had been bled white.[67] Turkey's traditional ally, Britain, had turned down its request for a permanent alliance in 1911,[68] having given up hope on it, and was cooperating closely with Turkey's most dangerous foe, Russia. Weak and friendless, Turkey turned toward Germany which, alone of the great powers, had no interest in Turkish territory.[69]

Prospects for more solid relations with Germany seemed good. Whereas other states saw the Young Turk Revolution as a sign that Turkey's demise was drawing near, Germany saw potential for Turkish rejuvenation and an opportunity to be a patron, expanding Germany's already considerable economic penetration. Fearful of Russian intrigues, in 1913 Turkey requested that its British and German military missions be strengthened. The German military instructor, Liman von Sanders, precipitated an international crisis because of his dual status as commander of the corps defending Constantinople. Although Germany resolved the crisis, it is worth noting that Turkey refused to give in to Russian demands.[70]

Turco-German relations hit a snag over Greece. Germany wanted Turkey to form an alliance with Greece. Turkey, however, did not want an alliance with Greece, which had designs on Constantinople and might well antagonize Bulgaria. In October 1913, Turkey and Bulgaria secretly negotiated an offensive alliance against Greece. But fear of Russia and Romania caused Bulgaria to pull out. By early July 1914, a Turco-Greek conflict seemed imminent.[71] This conflict was put on hold as war between Austria and Serbia appeared more likely, with its potential to create more favorable conditions. On 13 July, Turkey quietly let Austria know that the time was 'favorable for a final settlement of accounts with Serbia' and that Turkey would not stand in the way.[72]

Early in 1914, Turkey had offered an alliance to Germany, hoping for an alliance with Bulgaria and the Central Powers to protect its rear.[73] Germany initially turned it down but, as the crisis became acute in late July, Berlin was suddenly interested. When Turkey made a formal request for an offensive and defensive alliance against Russia on 28 July, Germany immediately accepted. Turkey had some last-minute reservations about such an unequivocal move – that is, until Britain seized two Turkish battleships being built in British shipyards.[74]

The alliance with Germany was signed on 3 August. To limit its exposure, the only steps Turkey took in response to the crisis were to mobilize and declare armed neutrality.[75] As an incentive for more active Turkish participation, Germany sold Turkey two battleships, the *Goeben* and the *Breslau*, which Germany had moved into the Black Sea with Turkish permission on 10 August.[76] Turkey also signed a secret treaty with Bulgaria on 6 August.[77] However, none of this was sufficient to impel Turkey to declare war. Italy and Romania, instead of joining the Central Powers, declared neutrality; England intervened swiftly; Bulgaria did nothing – all of which significantly decreased the prospects of swift victory for the Central Powers. Thereafter Turkey took a wait-and-see approach, negotiating the price of its neutrality with the Allies.[78]

In October, Germany forced Turkey's hand. The former *Goeben* and *Breslau* were still commanded by a German admiral. Under his orders, they shelled Sevastopol, Odessa and Feodosia on 28 October. Prompted by this act, Russia declared war on Turkey on 4 November; Britain and France declared war on 5 November.[79]

Turkey was engaged in World War I for reasons of both balancing and predation. The outbreak of the war spurred German interest in a Turkish alliance, providing Turkey's only option for balancing against Russia. At the same time, the conflict in the Balkans afforded Turkey the opportunity to settle old scores and regain lost territory. It is not clear which motive was stronger; since each dictated the same policy, Turkey was not forced to choose between them.

Italy

Italy's initial response to the July Crisis was to declare neutrality. Not only did Italy not feel bound by the Triple Alliance to join the Central Powers, but also, after negotiations with the Allies, Italy switched sides and declared war on Austria the following year. There is no conceivable argument to be made that Italy entered the war due to alliance commitments, mobilization schedules, or an overriding belief in the efficacy of offensive action as is frequently argued for the August 1914 belligerents. Nor did Italy enter the conflict for balancing reasons – at the time of its entry it was perfectly situated to allow others to pay the blood price for it. Rather, Italy joined the Allies because it believed they would win and saw an opportunity to seize Trieste and Trentino[80] – Austrian territory that Rome had long coveted.

Italian foreign policy in the years preceding World War I is not as inconsistent as it first seems. Rather, Italian policy reflects Italy's weakness and the fact that its own strategic interests did not coincide neatly with either alliance system. Italy's common frontier with Austria, irredentist politics and Balkan interests meant perennial conflict with Austria. By the same token, Italy's lengthy coastline implied a strategic and economic threat from the French navy.[81] Italy could not handle either threat alone – let alone both – because it was far too weak. The Italian economy was largely agricultural with low productivity; industrial growth was shaky; Italy was unable to provide its own energy needs; and the transportation system was also inadequate.[82] In short, all of the factors that not only constitute economic power, but translate it into military power, conspired to place Italy in a position markedly inferior to its neighbors. The obvious solution would be an alliance with Germany and Britain against Austria and France, but this was, of course, precluded by the Austro-German alliance and Franco-British entente. Much of Italy's 'fickleness' in international relations must be viewed in terms of this dilemma; it was too weak to power its own course while its preferred allies were in turn allied with its enemies.

Italy tried to solve its strategic dilemma with a German alliance. However, Germany would not reach an agreement with Italy separate from Austria.[83] Italy joined the Triple Alliance in 1882, which stipulated mutual defense against France 'and benevolent neutrality if a signatory, having been threatened, was driven to make war itself'.[84] Italy began to lose faith in the value of the Triple Alliance when Rome discovered that it was of little or no use in furthering its colonial ambitions, a fact made abundantly clear by its 1896 humiliation at Adowa and reinforced by its war in Libya.[85] Nevertheless, Italy continued to renew the Triple Alliance, signing the final renewal on 5 December 1912 and a naval convention the following year. Furthermore, the Italian military was encouraged to work closely with these allies, who were informed in February 1914 that Italy would indeed be able to send an army to the Rhine in event of war, as their agreement stipulated.[86]

As Rome became disillusioned with its ability to use the Triple Alliance to further Italian expansionist aims, and battered by a trade war with France, Italy decided to switch tactics. Between 1897 and 1899, Italy ended its trade war and in 1900 exchanged notes with France respecting each other's interests in Libya and Morocco. This was followed by a secret agreement in 1902 whereby Italy promised neutrality in any conflict in which France was 'provoked'.[87] Italy's disillusionment with the Triple Alliance deepened after the Bosnian

Crisis (1909) in no small measure because Austria did not live up to the Balkan compensation stipulations agreed to in 1887.[88] Therefore, Italy and Russia signed a secret agreement at Racconigi in October 1909 recognizing each other's interests in Tripoli and the Straits respectively, and aiming at diplomatic cooperation against Austria in the Near East.[89] After the French were guaranteed Morocco following the Agadir Crisis, Italy moved against Libya to fulfill the Racconigi agreement. Despite the diplomatic resolution with Turkey in 1912, this turned out to be a strategic blunder that drained Italian manpower into 1915.[90] Friction arose between Italy and both alliance groups, but soon faded into insignificance in the shadow of the Balkan Wars.

As the July Crisis broke, Italy had a long-standing alliance with Germany and Austria, and a conflicting set of agreements with France and Russia, although the latter were secret and did not have quite the standing of the Triple Alliance. It is interesting to note that France and Russia made no attempt to break Italy away from Germany and Austria; to the contrary, they found Italy a useful dead weight in the Triple Alliance.[91] Italy's allies, in fact, treated it as a silent partner; it was not consulted as the crisis developed, despite Germany's urgings to Austria.[92] Nevertheless, the Italian Chief of Staff assumed Italy would fulfill its obligations and asked the War Minister to declare a state of readiness. The Italian military was surprised when, on 2 August, the government declared neutrality.[93] Italy did not declare neutrality on principle. To the contrary, Italy believed entry was necessary to ensure great power status. But, however willing the Italian military was, it was nevertheless unprepared.[94] The decision hinged on timing – determining which side would be victorious and ensuring maximum compensation.[95] The Battle of the Marne (5–10 September 1914), tactically a stalemate but a strategic victory for the entente, decided the issue of which side to join, although Italy continued to hear German offers in a bid to raise its price.[96] Despite Italy's membership in the Triple Alliance, the entente had a better history of furthering Italian expansionist aims; this time was no exception, because the entente could offer more than the Triple Alliance.[97] Italy wanted Anglo-French naval pressure against Austria to assist with the seizure of Trieste. After months of haggling, the Treaty of London was signed on 26 April 1915. Italy pledged to denounce the Triple Alliance and to enter the war shortly in exchange for Trentino, Trieste, Istria, much of Dalmatia and other 'dangerously vaguely worded compensations in Asia Minor and Africa'.[98] Nevertheless, when Italy declared war on 23 May 1915, it was only against Austria, not against Germany. Italy attempted to maintain only a partial involvement in the war in pursuit of its aims. A surprise Austrian attack in May 1916 changed everything, and Italy declared war on Germany on 28 August – in exchange for more compensations, of course.[99]

Italy joined World War I to gain additional territory. Rome did not need to join for balancing purposes; its best-case scenario was for both France and Austria to sustain heavy losses. Italy did not join to fulfill alliance obligations; in fact, it disregarded them. Instead, when it appeared clear which side would win, Italy hopped on the bandwagon for the biggest compensation package.

Bulgaria

Bulgaria did not join the conflict until October 1915. Bulgaria was too weak to figure significantly in the war plans of either alliance bloc, and Bulgaria itself was more interested in its regional balance of power, which at that point was tilted heavily against it. When events turned more favorable, Bulgaria joined in to reap some of the spoils at Serbia's expense.

Bulgaria's position in the international system was not unlike that of Italy, except that Bulgaria was even weaker and more vulnerable. Bulgaria was crushed by Serbia, Greece, Romania and Turkey during the Second Balkan War (1913), which, largely of its own making, also cost it Russian support.[100] While Bulgaria's conflict with Serbia had cost it Russian support, it made an alliance with Austria natural, and both parties were interested in coming to an arrangement.[101] However, Germany initially vetoed an Austro-Bulgarian alliance because of Berlin's long-standing alliances with Bulgaria's enemies, Greece and Romania.

During the crisis Russia, Germany and Austria advised Bulgaria to remain neutral. Greece and Romania further warned Bulgaria that an attack against Serbia would also result in war with them. At any rate, from a purely balancing perspective, it was clear that Bulgaria's interests would be best served by allowing Austria to defeat Serbia and absorb the costs. Thus, on 28 July, Bulgaria pledged to maintain strict neutrality.[102]

After Turkey allied with Germany, the great powers decided that

Bulgaria might be useful. On 11 August, Russia tried to persuade Bulgaria to adopt a policy of benevolent neutrality and resistance to any Turkish offensive. But all Russia was able to offer in return, because of its ties to Serbia, were Istip and Radovic. These were insufficient, and Bulgaria declined the Russian offer the next day. Meanwhile, Germany had taken a sudden interest in Bulgaria, going so far as to secure Romanian permission for a Bulgarian attack on Serbia. However, Austria abruptly lost interest in a Bulgarian alliance, perhaps because the concessions necessary would have precluded a negotiated settlement.[103] At any rate, the declarations of neutrality by Italy and Romania made a Central Powers' victory less promising and reinforced Bulgaria's own decision for neutrality.

As the war progressed, both sides persisted in their attempts to win Bulgaria's favor. The entente was hampered, however, by its relationship with Serbia, which possessed the territory Bulgaria wanted. Pressure from the Central Powers increased when Romania closed its borders to German supply shipments in June 1915. However, the major factor in Bulgaria's decision was the prospect for local success, which increased dramatically when the Central Powers repulsed the Allied Gallipoli invasion in August 1915. Bulgaria made an alliance with the Central Powers on 6 September and took the field with them against Serbia in October.[104]

Bulgaria did not join World War I to balance. It could not affect the great power balance, and Austria was handling its regional balancing needs. Nor was Bulgaria responding to alliance ties. When the momentum of the war in the Balkans shifted in favor of the Central Powers, Bulgaria joined their cause to reclaim territory from Serbia.

Romania

Romania, like Bulgaria, was primarily concerned with the situation in the Balkans. Unlike its neighbor, Romania was not friendless; rather, the Austro-Serbian conflict caught it between conflicting alliance commitments in a seemingly unwinnable situation. Romania initially declared neutrality but, when it saw an opportunity to realize a gain with seemingly little risk, it seized it.

At the time of the July Crisis, Romania was part of the Triple Alliance, which had been renewed in February 1913. This fact was kept secret from the Romanian public, which was very anti-Austrian due to the treatment of ethnic Romanians in Transylvania. Romania was also bound to Serbia by the Treaty of Bucharest (1913). With an Austro-Serbian war in the offing, there was no way Romania could satisfy both obligations. On 30 July, Russia offered Romania Transylvania; on 1 August, Germany offered Bessarabia. These were only of value to Romania should Austria or Russia respectively be rendered too weak to recover the territory later. With the outcome of the war uncertain, and fearful of incurring the vengeance of the victors, Romania tried to steer a path between them. On 3 August, the Romanian Crown Council voted for neutrality. Publicly, Romania pledged respect for the Treaty of Bucharest if violated by Bulgaria, but secretly agreed, as a sop to Austria, to remain neutral if Bulgaria attacked Serbia.[105]

By definition, Romanian neutrality was pro-Russian, in that it freed more Russian troops to invade Galicia.[106] On 2 October, Romania reached an agreement with Russia for benevolent neutrality in exchange for 'recognizing her [Romania's] rights to annex the Rumane regions of the Austro-Hungarian Monarchy excepting the Bukovina'.[107] This was as far as Romania was willing to go despite repeated Allied attempts to induce more active participation in the war.[108] These Allied attempts were hindered by the poor performance at Gallipoli in 1915, so much so that Romania initially refused the posting of a French general for fear of compromising its neutrality.[109]

That changed in 1916. The initial success of the Russian Brusilov offensive (June to September 1916) promised to knock Austria out of the war. Eager to grasp its promised prizes – possession is a better arbiter than promises – Romania declared war on Germany and Austria on 27 August, and marched virtually unopposed into Transylvania, until attacked from behind by Bulgaria.[110]

Romania entered the war solely to seize Transylvania, at a time when doing so appeared virtually cost-free. Romania honored none of its prewar alliance commitments; it neither entered with the Central Powers nor came to Serbia's aid when it was attacked by Bulgaria. Unconcerned with balancing, Romania aimed solely to seize Transylvania at little or no cost to itself.

Greece

Greece did not immediately enter World War I, despite an alliance commitment and despite diplomatic pressure from both sides. Greek ambitions and balancing considerations dictated that it join the Allies against Turkey. But the Allies were unable to give it the support it required to make the strategy pay off.

Greece had allied with Serbia against Bulgaria and a 'third power' – Austria – on 1 June 1913. The Austrian declaration of war on Serbia clearly met the treaty requirements. Nevertheless, Greece remained neutral. Greek fear of being left open to attack by Turkey and Bulgaria deterred it from assisting Serbia, which could not help it anyway because of complete involvement with Austria. In short, Greece could not fulfill its treaty obligations without putting itself at mortal risk.[111]

Greece's primary concern was Turkey. The months immediately preceding the July Crisis had threatened a Turco-Greek war over the Aegean islands and the Turkish expulsion of Greeks from Asia Minor. Although this conflict was mediated by Germany, which along with France had backed Greece at the 1913 Treaty of Bucharest, relations were still threatening.[112]

Germany tried to coerce Greece into siding with Austria by threatening to break relations. The Allies tried to form an alliance with Greece, which failed because of inadequate concessions, conflicting interests with Russia over Constantinople, and an inability to provide Greece with concrete support. Nevertheless, in October 1915 it appeared that Greece would join with the Allies. But the pro-German King Constantine dismissed Prime Minister Venizélos, and declared that Greece would remain neutral.[113] In another turnabout, Constantine abdicated on 12 June 1917. In the intervening period, the Allies had been using Greek territory as a staging ground for operations in support of Serbia. The new king, Alexander, reappointed Venizélos and, on 27 June 1917, Greece joined the Allies.

Greece entered the war both to balance against Turkey and to seize Turkish territory. It was unable and unwilling to do so, however, until the Allies had built up sufficient force in the area to support it and Turkey had begun to weaken.

OR NOT TO JOIN?

The previous discussion of warring states makes it clear that few states with an interest in the outcome of World War I refrained from participating in the conflict. There were, however, a few notable exceptions.

Scandinavia

The Scandinavian states – Sweden, Denmark and Norway – remained
neutral in the war, although their leanings differed. Sweden was pro-
German and anti-Russian; Norway was pro-English; Denmark was
anti-German. Despite these differing outlooks, all three, in consulta-
tion with each other, declared neutrality between 4 and 5 August.
Denmark was too vulnerable to a German invasion to risk any
attempt at liberating the Schleswig Danes. Sweden could not be sure
of a Central Powers victory sufficient to assure it of satisfactory gains
in Finland against Russia. Norway feared coming out for England
with a potentially hostile Sweden combining forces with Germany
against it. In this way, much like a three-legged stool, they deterred
each other and combined to keep Scandinavia neutral.[114]

Summary

World War I occurred in a period where there was a high political cost
to warfare, yet there was still a considerable amount of war widening.
This thesis predicts that when the political cost of warfare is high, as
in the post-Napoleonic period, great powers should join ongoing conflicts only for balancing reasons, not for predation. Because the incentives for balancing are fewer than for predation, the overall amount of
war widening should be smaller. That did not hold true in World War
I. Why?

Of the three great powers that widened the conflict, Great Britain
and the United States were balancing, as the theory predicts. Japan,
the other great power, was clearly predatory. The overall level of
widening was fueled by the entry of small powers. These behaved pre-
dictably. None jumped in immediately. Each sought to use the war to
enhance its position, but only when it appeared to have the inside
edge, with the great powers bearing the brunt of the cost.

COMPETING THEORIES

Two competing theories have been used to explain war widening:
alliances and offense dominance. These are important arguments
because of what they imply about crisis stability and the ways in
which states can be inadvertently drawn into other states' wars. The

implications have been used to form the basis of present and future nuclear policy. Chapter 2 discusses theoretical problems with these arguments. As both rely heavily on World War I, it is reasonable at this point to reexamine them in light of the evidence to determine whether they really fit the case on which they are based.

Alliances

The alliance argument holds that alliances cause wars to widen, in that two-party wars are more likely to spread the wider and tighter the prewar alliance systems are. Did alliances widen World War I?

First of all, the only states involved in the war honoring a prewar alliance commitment were Germany (to support Austria) and France and Russia (to support Serbia). To the extent that these states are initial combatants, it appears that there is evidence supporting the proposition that the alliances caused the outbreak of a general conflict as opposed to a two-party war. But the explanatory power of the alliance argument ends there; it fails to explain why the war widened. Britain did not have a prewar alliance with either France or Russia; Britain deliberately limited itself to the Entente Cordiale to keep its hands free. Furthermore, Britain had shown in the past that it did not consider itself bound by the treaties on Belgian neutrality. And, once Britain entered, it would be a gross overstatement to say that, in attacking German possessions in China, Japan was fulfilling the terms of the Anglo-Japanese treaty. Of the remaining states that entered the conflict, Italy and Romania fought *against* their prewar alliance partners; Turkey and Bulgaria fought under alliances agreed to *after* the outbreak of hostilities; and the USA fought *without* an alliance at all.

The alliances, including those formed during this war, had their greatest effect not on the outbreak of the conflict, but on the conduct and duration of the war. Alliances ensured that even a state that was decisively beaten in any campaign was encouraged to remain in the conflict by the hope and promise of aid from allies, a situation apparently unrecognized by contemporaries.[115] This situation was exacerbated by the promises of compensations made to induce the smaller states to join the conflict – promises that could be kept only by extracting territory from an utterly defeated adversary. As these intrawar alliances grew, the prospects for a negotiated settlement diminished.[116]

Alliances do not account for any of the widening in World War I beyond the initial outbreak. Great Britain entered without an alliance. Japan entered against Britain's wishes, ostensibly fulfilling a treaty that did not need to be fulfilled. As the war dragged on, the great powers made new alliances with small powers specifically to prosecute the war, even reversing prewar arrangements. In these instances, the causal relationship is clearly reversed; war widening caused the alliances. Alliances also prolonged the war by increasing hopes of aid from allies and promising concessions that could only be delivered with absolute victory.

Offense Dominance

Offense dominance occurs when a state decides that 'it is easier to destroy the other's army and take its territory than it is to defend one's own'.[117] Ostensibly, offense dominance exacerbates the security dilemma producing more frequent wars with more participants.[118] The offense dominance argument has two variants. The straightforward technological version argues that certain weaponry and other technology can favor either defensive or offensive action. The ideological version argues that whether or not technology favors offense or defense is immaterial; what matters is what decision-makers believe a future war will look like.

No current writers argue that the technological innovations in warfare in the decades prior to World War I, such as the machine gun and barbed wire, produced genuine offense dominance. To the contrary, the ideological variant argues that decision-makers mistakenly *believed* that technology favored the offense when, in fact, it favored the defense. However, characterizing 1914 Europe as defense dominant is just as wrong as labeling it offense dominant. After the Battle of the Marne, the Western Front did become relatively static, characterized by trench warfare favoring the defender, but we should not forget how very close Germany came to succeeding. Moreover, the Eastern Front remained a war of maneuver,[119] and the failure of various eastern offensives stemmed from typical causes such as poor generalship and lack of support from neighboring units, among others, and not from domination of defense.

Cult of the Offensive

The ideological variant of the offense dominance argument skirts the issue of technology by arguing that the state of military technology in and of itself is irrelevant; what matters is what decision-makers believe about their world. In his influential article, 'The Cult of the Offensive and the Origins of the First World War',[120] Stephen Van Evera argues: 'The cult of the offensive was a principal cause of the First World War, creating or magnifying many of the dangers which historians blame for causing the July crisis and rendering it uncontrollable.'[121] Van Evera uses the cult of the offensive to explain the origin of World War I, not why it subsequently widened. Including Germany, France and Russia as initial combatants has eliminated the ability to tackle Van Evera's argument head on.

There is considerable evidence that the great powers that widened the conflict, Great Britain and Japan, believed that the war would be short. Was this due to a belief in offense dominance, or something else?

The British case is interesting, because Prime Minister Lloyd George changed his opinion literally overnight.[122] Nevertheless, the change came after days (31 July–3 August) of very difficult Cabinet wrangling.[123] Niall Ferguson charges that the decision was at least in part fueled by domestic political considerations.[124] Moreover, the initial reports from France indicated that the BEF was not needed so long as the Royal Navy protected the French coast.[125] So it does not appear that the British decision was determined by a cult of the offensive.

The Japanese case is driven more by the fear of US intervention than by fear of the European war ending too soon. The same European conflict that opened the opportunity against China also removed the Royal Navy as a buffer between the United States and Japan. While the United States was unable to do more than protest Japan's actions against China in August 1914, the opening of the Panama Canal that same month meant that the United States would soon be able, if Washington chose, to put more forces in the Pacific.[126]

Moreover, the belief that a future war will be short does not mean that there was any belief in offense dominance. Before 1914, the vast majority of European decision-makers believed that any future war would have to be short. This belief did not stem from any belief in offensive or defensive dominance. Instead, the short-war myth derived from the interaction of modern mass armies and modern economies. How could economies possibly continue to function when such a large proportion of their manpower had been siphoned off to fight? They reasoned they could not, and therefore, if the victory of one of the combatants did not cut the war short, world economic collapse surely would.[127] Two important strategic implications arise from this proposition. First, there is not enough time to adopt a strategy of remaining on the defensive and counterattacking when the adversary is spent. Even if a shot is never fired, the cost associated with keeping that much manpower mobilized and out of the economy for too great a time may mean defeat in and of itself. Second, should the war bog down and its end emerge not through armed victory, but by economic paroxysm, it is best to be fighting on the enemy's territory. That way one is in a better negotiating position, because the enemy will have to make concessions to have its territory restored. Furthermore, the destruction inherent in any sort of warfare has been inflicted on the adversary and not on one's own territory. The short-war myth did not arise from a belief in the superiority of the offense. Rather, the belief that the war must be short helped drive the development of an offensive strategy.

The offense dominance argument is not used to explain why any of the other states entered World War I. Most of these states entered after the stalemate was reached in the west, which, had decision-makers been afflicted by a cult of the offensive, would have cured them. It is interesting to note that no such belief in offense dominance seems to have affected naval strategy. To the contrary, according to one writer, both the British and German admiralties spent the crisis 'in the grip of the cult of the defensive'.[128]

CONCLUSION

The theory of war widening presented here makes several predictions based on the level of perceived political cost to warfare. Because World War I occurred after the Napoleonic Wars, the political cost of warfare was high. Therefore, under this theory, great powers would enter the conflict only to balance. Moreover, the theory predicts that because predation is removed as a cause of great power widening in the post-Napoleonic era, the overall level of widening in such wars should be lower. In contrast, small powers should join only existing wars, particularly great power wars, for predatory reasons. This tendency should increase with the length of the conflict, as great powers are willing to offer more for assistance.

The case examination reveals that balancing was the dominant force behind great power widening in World War I. Britain entered the war early, acting to preserve vital interests and maintain a favorable balance of power. The United States was satisfied to profit from the conflict as long as it was a stalemate. Once it appeared that Germany could break the deadlock, the United States intervened to prevent the establishment of German hegemony in Europe. The only exception to this balancing trend was Japan. Japanese actions in China were clearly predatory. The involvement of the great powers half a world away dramatically lowered the cost of warfare in Asia, providing Japan with a golden opportunity to expand its empire. Overall, the theory performs well in explaining why great powers joined the conflict.

The case examination also corroborated the expectations about small power participation. All of the small powers that entered the conflict did so because they saw an opportunity to improve their position. A few cases, such as Turkey, were over-determined because a predatory policy coincided neatly with a balancing policy. The small states did not join at the outbreak of the conflict, waiting instead for an opportune time when the fortunes of war appeared to be in their favor. Greece did not enter until June 1917. Ironically, because the great powers were balancing and not attempting to seize territory for themselves, they were more willing to bargain away their adversaries' assets, creating greater opportunities for small power predation.

The prediction that does not hold is the overall level of widening. Despite the fact that the political cost of warfare was high, the war widened on a vast scale. This was not due to any misconceptions by world leaders; decision-makers knew the war would entail very high costs – in blood, treasure and, most important, the political future of their state. But this high degree of great power balancing opened the door for predation by the small states.

The case history finds little evidence to substantiate the offense dominance argument in either the technological or the ideological variant. Almost all of the widening that occurred, with the exception of Britain and Japan, came after the Battle of the Marne, which dashed whatever belief did or did not exist in the superiority of the offense. The best case which can be made would apply to Britain, which only waited several days before reinforcing France. However, the evidence for London's decision is mixed, and a strong argument can be made that, given the relative strength of Germany, the British decision made sense without any belief in the superiority of the offense but solely on examination of the force ratios.

The alliance argument does not fare much better than offense dominance. Few states entered the war to fulfill their prewar alliance commitments, just as many or more states entered the war in opposition to such prewar commitments. States pursued their strategic interests regardless of alliances. Alliances were useful for explaining other aspects of World War I, but fail to explain why it widened.

The war widening theory developed here fares reasonably well in explaining World War I, which is a difficult case for this theory. On examination, the exceptionally high degree of widening, which contradicts general expectations, was due to an exceptionally high degree of balancing by great powers. These, in turn, provided inducements for predation by small powers, such as Turkey, Romania, Bulgaria and Italy. The two counter-arguments – offense dominance and alliances – explain very little of the case.

NOTES

1. Quoted in Robert K. Massie, *Dreadnought: Britain, Germany and the Coming of the Great War* (New York: Random House, 1991), p. 406.
2. See Stephen Van Evera, 'The Cult of the Offensive and the Outbreak of the First World War', *International Security*, 9, 1 (Summer 1984), pp. 58–107.
3. See Michael Howard, 'Men against Fire: Expectations of War in 1914', *International Security*, 9, 1 (Summer 1984), reprinted in Steven E. Miller, ed., *Military Strategy and the Origins of the First World War: An International Security Reader* (Princeton, NJ: Princeton University Press, 1985), pp. 41–57.
4. For a concise description of the historiography of this war, see James Joll, *The Origins of the First World War* (London: Longman, 1984), pp. 1–7.
5. Fritz Fischer's thesis has not gone away, but has been passed on to a new generation of scholars. For example, see Hartmut Pogge von Strandmann, 'Germany and the Coming of War', in R. J. W. Evans and Hartmut Pogge von Strandmann, eds, *The Coming of the First World War* (Oxford: Clarendon Press, 1988), pp. 87–123 at 97, in which he writes: 'In the present state of research, the evidence that Germany and Austria started the war and dragged the rest of the powers into it is even stronger than in the early 1960s when Fritz Fischer published his analysis of German war aims and policies.'
6. Paul M. Kennedy, 'The First World War and the International Power System', *International Security*, 9, 1 (Summer 1984), reprinted in Steven E. Miller, ed., *Military Strategy and the Origins of the First World War: An International Security Reader* (Princeton, NJ: Princeton University Press, 1985), pp. 7–40, see 37.

7. Corelli Barnett, *The Swordbearers: Supreme Command in the First World War* (Bloomington, IN: Indiana University Press, 1963), p. 18.
8. Jack Levy, 'Big Wars, Little Wars and Theory Construction', *International Interactions*, 16, 3 (1990), pp. 215–24, see 222, n. 18.
9. The most significant exception to this is Geoffrey Blainey, who treats World War I as the escalation of an initial Austro-Serbian war. See Geoffrey Blainey, *The Causes of War*, 3rd edn (New York: The Free Press, 1988), pp. 236–7.
10. For example, see Luigi Albertini, *The Origins of the War of 1914*, trans. Isabella M. Massey, 3 vols (Oxford: Oxford University Press, 1952); Richard Ned Lebow, *Nuclear Crisis Management: A Dangerous Illusion* (Ithaca, NY: Cornell University Press, 1987); Barbara Tuchman, *The Guns of August* (New York: Macmillan, 1962); L. C. F. Turner, *Origins of the First World War* (New York: W. W. Norton, 1970).
11. That Germany wanted war is, of course, the central tenet of the Fischer thesis. See Fritz Fischer, 'German War Aims 1914–1918 and German Policy before the War', in Barry Hunt and Adrian Preston, eds, *War Aims and Strategic Policy in the Great War 1914–1918* (London: Croom Helm, 1977), pp. 105–23. Recently, an even stronger version of the argument has been propounded by Dale Copeland, *The Origins of Major War* (Ithaca, NY: Cornell University Press, 2000).
12. For example, Jack Levy concludes: 'No war would have occurred in the absence of the German assumption that Britain would stay neutral in a continental conflict.' Jack S. Levy, 'Preferences, Constraints and Choices in July 1914', *International Security*, 15, 3 (Winter 1990/91), pp. 151–86, see 185.
13. Van Evera, 'The Cult of the Offensive and the Origins of the First World War', pp. 58–107.
14. Niall Ferguson, *The Pity of War: Explaining World War I* (New York: Basic Books, 1999), p. 81.
15. S. R. Williamson, 'Joffre Reshapes French Strategy, 1911–1913', in Paul M. Kennedy, ed., *The War Plans of the Great Powers, 1880–1914* (London: George Allen & Unwin, 1979), pp. 133–54, see 148.
16. For an excellent discussion of the Schlieffen Plan, see Gerhard Ritter, *The Schlieffen Plan: Critique of a Myth*, trans. Andrew and Eva Wilson (Westport, CT: Greenwood Press, 1979).
17. John H. Maurer, *The Outbreak of the First World War: Strategic Planning, Crisis Decision Making and Deterrence Failure*, Praeger Studies in Diplomacy and Strategic Thought Series, B. J. C. McKercher, ed. (Westport, CT: Praeger, 1995), p. 36. See also Marc Trachtenberg, 'The Meaning of Mobilization in 1914', *International Security*, 15, 3 (Winter 1990/91), pp. 120–50, see 135.
18. Paul Kennedy, *Strategy and Diplomacy 1870–1945: Eight Studies* (London: George Allen & Unwin, 1983), p. 61.
19. Michael Brock, 'Britain Enters the War', in R. J. W. Evans and Hartmut Pogge von Strandmann, eds, *The Coming of the First World War* (Oxford: Clarendon Press, 1988), pp. 145–78, see 160–1. Niall Ferguson argues that Britain did not need to balance against Germany and that the German threat was manufactured by Grey and other Germanophobes. See Ferguson, *The Pity of War*, esp. ch. 2.
20. Paul Kennedy, *The Rise and Fall of the Great Powers: Economic Change and Military Conflict from 1500 to 2000* (New York: Random House, 1987), pp. 231–2.
21. Sidney Bradshaw Fay, *The Origins of the World War*, 2 vols, 2nd revd edn (New York: The Free Press, 1966) pp. 1:153–4, 219.
22. Fay, *The Origins of the World War*, p. 1:235.
23. Kennedy, *Strategy and Diplomacy 1870–1945*, p. 142.

24. J. McDermott, 'The Revolution in British Military Thinking from the Boer War to the Moroccan Crisis', in Paul M. Kennedy, ed., *The War Plans of the Great Powers, 1880–1914* (London: George Allen & Unwin, 1979) pp. 99–117, see 107–8. McDermott argues, however, that bureaucratic politics played a significant role in this shift, as the army officers in England wanted to do more than supply reinforcements for India's defense and Germany was a more 'practical' adversary than Russia (pp. 106–8).

25. Fay, *The Origins of the World War*, pp. 1:299–311.

26. Ibid., p. 1:312; Kennedy, *Strategy and Diplomacy 1870–1945*, p. 24.

27. McDermott, 'The Revolution in British Military Thinking from the Boer War to the Moroccan Crisis', pp. 111–12.

28. David G. Herrmann, *The Arming of Europe and the Making of the First World War* (Princeton, NJ: Princeton University Press, 1996), pp. 154–6.

29. Brock, 'Britain Enters the War', p. 147.

30. Fay, *The Origins of the World War*, pp. 1:320–3.

31. Tuchman, *The Guns of August*, p. 55.

32. Brock, 'Britain Enters the War', p. 147.

33. Barnett, *The Swordbearers*, p. 19.

34. Brock, 'Britain Enters the War', p. 154.

35. Ibid., p. 175.

36. Tuchman, *The Guns of August*, p. 96.

37. Maurer, *The Outbreak of the First World War*, p. 105.

38. Brock, 'Britain Enters the War', p. 155.

39. Fay, *The Origins of the World War*, p. 2:542; Brock, 'Britain Enters the War', p. 159.

40. Tuchman, *The Guns of August*, p. 129; Fay, *The Origins of the World War*, pp. 2:542–6.

41. Tuchman, *The Guns of August*, pp. 113, 131.

42. Ibid., pp. 202–5.

43. Ibid., p. 322; John Gooch, 'Soldiers, Strategy and War Aims in Britain 1914–1918', in Barry Hunt and Adrian Preston, eds, *War Aims and Strategic Policy in the Great War 1914–1918* (London: Croom Helm, 1977), pp. 21–40, see 27.

44. Fay, *The Origins of the World War*, p. 1:141.

45. Ibid., p. 1:218.

46. Kennedy, *The Rise and Fall of the Great Powers*, p. 256.

47. Albertini, *The Origins of the War of 1914*, p. 3:695.

48. Ibid., pp. 694–8; R. Ernest Dupuy and Trevor N. Dupuy, *The Encyclopedia of Military History: From 3500 BC to the Present*, 2nd revd edn (New York: Harper & Row, 1986), p. 944.

49. Tuchman, *The Guns of August*, p. 271.

50. According to Kennedy, 'The United States had definitely become a Great Power. But it was not part of the Great Power system.' Kennedy, *The Rise and Fall of the Great Powers*, p. 248.

51. Robert H. Ferrell, *Woodrow Wilson and World War I: 1917–1921* (New York: Harper & Row, 1985), p. 11.

52. Kenneth J. Hagan, *This People's Navy: The Making of American Sea Power* (New York: The Free Press, 1991), p. 247.

53. Alexander DeConde, *A History of American Foreign Policy: Vol. 2, Global Power (1900 to the Present)*, 3rd edn (New York: Charles Scribner's Sons, 1978), pp. 3–6.

54. J. A. S. Grenville, 'Diplomacy and War Plans in the United States, 1890–1917',

in Paul M. Kennedy, ed., *The War Plans of the Great Powers, 1880–1914* (London: George Allen & Unwin, 1979), pp. 23–38, see 34, 36–7; DeConde, *A History of American Foreign Policy*, pp. 20, 37–9; Edward M. Coffman, 'The American Military and Strategic Policy in World War I', in Barry Hunt and Adrian Preston, eds, *War Aims and Strategic Policy in the Great War 1914–1918* (London: Croom Helm, 1977), pp. 67–84, see 71.

55. DeConde, *A History of American Foreign Policy*, p. 42; Tuchman, *The Guns of August*, pp. 334–5.

56. DeConde, *A History of American Foreign Policy*, pp. 20–1; Grenville, 'Diplomacy and War Plans in the United States, 1890–1917', p. 34.

57. DeConde, *A History of American Foreign Policy*, pp. 43–4.

58. Tuchman, *The Guns of August*, p. 337.

59. John Milton Cooper, Jr, *The Warrior and the Priest: Woodrow Wilson and Theodore Roosevelt* (Cambridge, MA: Belknap Press of Harvard University Press, 1983), pp. 290–5, 310; DeConde, *A History of American Foreign Policy*, pp. 52–4.

60. Ferrell, *Woodrow Wilson and World War I*, p. 2.

61. Bernadotte E. Schmitt and Harold C. Vedeler, *The World in the Crucible: 1914–1919* (New York: Harper & Row, 1984), p. 252.

62. DeConde, *A History of American Foreign Policy*, p. 56.

63. Grenville, 'Diplomacy and War Plans in the United States, 1890–1917', pp. 35–7; Coffman, 'The American Military and Strategic Policy in World War I', pp. 69–73; Ferrell, *Woodrow Wilson and World War I*, pp. 15, 33.

64. Hagan, *This People's Navy*, p. 242.

65. DeConde, *A History of American Foreign Policy*, p. 57.

66. Joll, *The Origins of the First World War*, p. 163.

67. Albertini, *The Origins of the War of 1914*, p. 605.

68. Tuchman, *The Guns of August*, p. 139.

69. Albertini, *The Origins of the War of 1914*, p. 607.

70. Fay, *The Origins of the World War*, p. 1:513.

71. Albertini, *The Origins of the War of 1914*, pp. 608–9.

72. Ibid., p. 610.

73. Ibid., p. 611.

74. Tuchman, *The Guns of August*, p. 140.

75. Albertini, *The Origins of the War of 1914*, p. 615; Tuchman, *The Guns of August*, p. 141.

76. Tuchman, *The Guns of August*, pp. 159–60.

77. Albertini, *The Origins of the War of 1914*, p. 616.

78. Ibid., p. 617; Tuchman, *The Guns of August*, p. 160.

79. Ibid., p. 161.

80. Richard Bosworth, *Italy and the Approach of the First World War* (New York: St Martin's Press, 1983), pp. 50, 57.

81. Kennedy, *The Rise and Fall of the Great Powers*, p. 206. For example, a trade war with France in 1896 battered an Italian economy already weakened by bad harvests. See Bosworth, *Italy and the Approach of the First World War*, p. 52.

82. Bosworth, *Italy and the Approach of the First World War*, pp. 6–19; Kennedy, *The Rise and Fall of the Great Powers*, p. 205.

83. John Whittam, 'War Aims and Strategy: The Italian Government and High Command 1914–1919', in Barry Hunt and Adrian Preston, eds, *War Aims and Strategic Policy in the Great War 1914–1918* (London: Croom Helm, 1977), pp. 85–104, see 86.

84. Bosworth, *Italy and the Approach of the First World War*, p. 54.

85. Ibid., pp. 52, 99–105; Fay, *The Origins of the World War*, pp. 1:143–4.

86. Whittam, 'War Aims and Strategy', p. 88; Bosworth, *Italy and the Approach of the First World War*, p. 118.
87. Bosworth, *Italy and the Approach of the First World War*, pp. 59–61; Fay, *The Origins of the World War*, pp. 1:143–7.
88. Bosworth, *Italy and the Approach of the First World War*, p. 58.
89. Fay, *The Origins of the World War*, pp. 1:396, 406–8.
90. Bosworth, *Italy and the Approach of the First World War*, p 125.
91. Fay, *The Origins of the World War*, p. 1:345.
92. Bosworth, *Italy and the Approach of the First World War*, p. 121.
93. Whittam, 'War Aims and Strategy', p. 89.
94. Bosworth, *Italy and the Approach of the First World War*, p. 125.
95. Ibid., pp. 122–3.
96. Whittam, 'War Aims and Strategy', p. 90; Bosworth, *Italy and the Approach of the First World War*, pp. 123, 131.
97. Whittam, 'War Aims and Strategy', p. 91.
98. Bosworth, *Italy and the Approach of the First World War*, p. 134.
99. V. H. Rothwell, *British War Aims and Peace Diplomacy 1914–1918* (Oxford: Clarendon Press, 1971), p. 57; Whittam, 'War Aims and Strategy', p. 94.
100. Albertini, *The Origins of the War of 1914*, p. 583; Fay, *The Origins of the World War*, p. 1:444.
101. Albertini, *The Origins of the War of 1914*, p. 596.
102. Ibid., p. 588.
103. Ibid., pp. 589–91, 596.
104. Ibid., p. 591.
105. Ibid., pp. 558–77.
106. Maurer, *The Outbreak of the First World War*, p. 57.
107. Albertini, *The Origins of the War of 1914*, p. 580; Gooch, 'Soldiers, Strategy and War Aims in Britain 1914–1918', p. 27.
108. Rothwell, *British War Aims and Peace Diplomacy 1914-1918*, pp. 25, 78.
109. Glenn E. Torrey, 'Biographical Introduction: Henri-Mathias Berthelot (1861–1931)', in Glenn E. Torrey, ed., *General Henri Berthelot and Romania: Mémoires et Correspondance 1916–1919* (Boulder, CO: East European Monographs, 1987), pp. ix–xxxix, see xiv.
110. Albertini, *The Origins of the War of 1914*, p. 583; Fay, *The Origins of the World War*, p. 1:444.
111. Albertini, *The Origins of the War of 1914*, pp. 625, 628, 630.
112. Ibid., pp. 626–7.
113. Ibid., pp. 634–7, 642–4; Dupuy and Dupuy, *The Encyclopedia of Military History*, p. 952.
114. Albertini, *The Origins of the War of 1914*, pp. 662–76.
115. Kennedy, 'The First World War and the International Power System', p. 11; idem, *The Rise and Fall of the Great Powers*, pp. 254–6.
116. Gooch, 'Soldiers, Strategy and War Aims in Britain 1914–1918', p. 27.
117. Robert Jervis, 'Cooperation under the Security Dilemma', *World Politics*, 30, 2 (January 1978), pp. 167–214, see 187.
118. Robert Jervis, 'Offense, Defense, and the Security Dilemma', in *International Politics: Enduring Concepts and Contemporary Issues*, 3rd edn (New York: HarperCollins, 1992), pp. 146–69, see 148.
119. Michael Howard, 'Men against Fire: The Doctrine of the Offensive in 1914', in *Makers of Modern Strategy: From Machiavelli to the Nuclear Age*, Peter Paret, ed. (Princeton, NJ: Princeton University Press, 1986), pp. 510–26, see 522.
120. Van Evera, 'The Cult of the Offensive and the Origins of the First World War'.

121. Ibid., p. 58.
122. Brock, 'Britain Enters the War', p. 155.
123. Turner, *Origins of the First World War*, p. 111.
124. Ferguson, *The Pity of War*, pp. 162–6.
125. Ibid., p. 167.
126. Hagan, *This People's Navy*, p. 247.
127. Michael Howard, *War in European History* (Oxford: Oxford University Press, 1976), p. 112; Michael Howard, 'Europe on the Eve of the First World War', in R. J. W. Evans and Hartmut Pogge von Strandmann, eds, *The Coming of the First World War* (Oxford: Clarendon Press, 1988), pp. 1–17, see 5; Maurer, *The Outbreak of the First World War*, pp. 3–8; Brock, 'Britain Enters the War', p. 169.
128. Maurer, *The Outbreak of the First World War*, p. 103.

— 7 —

Conclusion

Why do wars widen? We cannot contain conflicts without first determining why they spread. This study tested three theoretical explanations of war widening: alliances, offense dominance, and the predation and balancing explanation. Alliances and offense dominance both failed to explain why conflicts spread. In addition to theoretical problems, neither the alliance nor the offense dominance argument fits the facts of the four cases examined in this study. The war-widening theory developed in this study far surpassed the other two in explanatory power. Most importantly, it can also be used to predict future trends better than alternative explanations.

I argued that war widening depends on the political cost of warfare, which in turn causes predation and balancing. When the political cost of warfare is low – that is, when states are in little danger of being destroyed – they are more likely to join other states' conflicts as predatory opportunities present themselves. Conversely, when the political cost of warfare is high – that is, when war entails the risk of annihilation – states are less likely to join wars for predatory reasons, but will join them for balancing reasons. However, not all wars carry with them the possibility to significantly shift the balance of power. Additionally, states have means to balance short of intervention, such as alliances or economic development. Since the incentives for balancing are fewer than the incentives for predation, war widening in general is more likely in periods when the political cost of warfare is low (indecisive) than in periods when it is high (decisive).

The study identified two periods of political cost for the time period under examination. The political cost associated with warfare was low for the period 1700–1803 and high thereafter. Based on the level of political cost, the argument predicts that the period

1700–1803 should be characterized by a high level of war widening. Moreover, such widening should be driven by predation. Conversely, during the period after 1803, wars should widen less frequently. When great powers do enter ongoing conflicts, they should be balancing.

More specifically, the theory predicted that during the Seven Years' War there should be a large amount of war widening because of predation, since the war occurred when the political cost of warfare was low. This was substantiated both by the large number of participants, and an examination which revealed that their motives were, in fact, predatory. Austria, Russia and Sweden entered the Anglo-French war in order to partition Prussia. Saxony would also have attacked Prussia, had not Frederick the Great invaded Saxony first. Only Spain, which entered late, was balancing. Neither of the alternative explanations – alliances nor offense dominance – were able to explain this case. The alliances that figured prominently in the conflict were formed *after* the conflict began. Austria used the Anglo-French war to engineer the Diplomatic Revolution necessary to create the predatory coalition against Prussia. Clearly, offense dominance fails because this was a period in history of limited war, a period characterized as 'defense dominant'.

The French Revolutionary War and War of Liberation illustrate the transition from an era of low political cost to one of high political cost. That is, together they encompassed the shift to decisive warfare, as Napoleon Bonaparte combined the developments of the preceding generation with the energy released by the French Revolution to make the move to total war. By focusing on the first and final coalitions of the Napoleonic Wars, I highlighted the change from predation to balancing. Again, most of the alliances were formed (and often changed) after the war began. The First Coalition was a predatory coalition formed precisely to take advantage of the French Revolution. There was a large amount of widening in the First Coalition, when leaders still believed warfare carried little risk of significant loss. The War of Liberation illustrates how difficult it was to form a balancing coalition against Napoleon, and how only the threat of French hegemony enabled a balancing coalition to form and become strong enough to defeat Imperial France. Again, most of the alliances were formed *during* the conflict, not before, so that alliances cannot be a significant factor in the widening of the war. Prussia and Austria changed over to the Russian side only after Napoleon's invasion failed. Offense dominance could account for the widening of the

War of Liberation but not of the French Revolution, and even that assertion is dubious.

The Crimean War showed how a war that had a tremendous potential to widen, in terms both of the location of the conflict and the number of states interested in its outcome, in fact widened very little. That so little widening did occur is attributable to the fact that states were aware of the high political cost of warfare. This was an especially striking feature of Austrian behavior, driving both Vienna's decision to stay out of the conflict, as well as attempts to negotiate a settlement. There were no incentives for predatory behavior, and the endemic factors which inhibit balancing were operative. Therefore, the Crimean War was largely contained. Yet again, the alliances were formed *during* the conflict and offense dominance provided little explanation.

World War I was the final case study. The Great War is the most difficult for the war widening theory to explain, while it is the strongest case for both the alliance argument and the offense dominance argument. Indeed, it is the seminal case for that progeny of offense dominance, the cult of the offensive. Nevertheless, even if the role of alliances is accepted for the outbreak of the war, alliances had no bearing on the widening of the war. Again, alliances were formed after the conflict began and states even changed sides. Italy was the most notable state to change sides, but smaller states, such as Romania and Greece, were caught between conflicting alliance commitments. The United States did not just enter the war without a pre-war alliance, Washington did not even form one during the conflict. Offense dominance cannot explain why World War I widened beyond its outbreak. Any overriding belief in offence dominance died at the Battle of the Marne.

The cases also substantiated the assertion that balancing by great powers provides predatory opportunities for small states. Sweden in the War of Liberation, Sardinia in the Crimean War, Romania, Bulgaria, Greece and Italy in World War I – all were lured in by generous compensations offered by great powers not interested in the spoils for themselves. These small states based their decisions on a combination of the prospects for success and the particular prizes available.

The war widening theory developed in this study, explained the four cases in the study very well. The two counter-arguments developed from the theoretical literature, alliances and offense dominance, did not. The main criticism of the war widening theory advanced in this study is that it is not *one* explanation, but *two*, albeit linked by the same independent variable. Seemingly in defense of the theory, Clausewitz wrote: 'Critical research is faced with a serious intrinsic one [problem]: effects in war seldom result from a single cause; there are usually several concurrent causes.'[1] In the same vein, I believe that what this argument gives up in parsimony, it gains in explanatory richness.

Further Research

This study made no attempt to test the war widening theory against civil wars. The closest comparison to a civil war would be the case of the French Revolutionary War. In that case, the revolution was seen to weaken France, making it more vulnerable to predation by other states. The logical question to arise is whether or not civil wars are more likely to widen than interstate conflicts, because the former invite predation. Or if, to the contrary, the zero-sum nature of civil wars raises the level of political cost, dampening the predatory behavior that drives most war widening.

Another avenue of research suggested by this book involves alliances. Some cases saw states use warfare as a means to create new alliances, cement existing alliances or strengthen their position within alliances. For example, Austria used the outbreak of the Anglo-French colonial phase of the Seven Years' War to engineer the Diplomatic Revolution against Prussia. Likewise, France allied with Britain to fight in the Crimea to break out of its diplomatic isolation. Conversely, France used its new relationship with Britain to restrain its war aims, perhaps dampening the possibility of further spread. How prevalent is this behavior and, from a policy standpoint, is it effective? While the conventional wisdom holds that alliances widen wars, this study indicates that, if there is a causal relationship at all, it is reversed: war widening causes alliances.

The Future of War Widening

The theory proposed in this study indicated one primary variable that influences the likelihood of war widening: the political cost of warfare. We are currently in an era characterized by a high political cost to warfare; losing a war may entail the destruction of a state as a political (and perhaps even physical) entity. Even the costs of winning a war may exceed the benefits. Therefore, great powers are unlikely to enter other states' conflicts unless all three of the following conditions are met:

1   The war threatens to adversely shift the balance of power.
2   No other state appears likely to redress the balance of power.
3   All other balancing options are exhausted.

What foreseeable developments might reverse this trend? War widening may be made more likely in one of two ways. Either the international political situation can make it more likely that the above three conditions are simultaneously fulfilled, or the political cost of warfare can drop.

Even if the political cost of warfare remains high, developments in international politics may affect the likelihood that great powers feel compelled to widen wars in order to balance. And, if that occurs, the widening can be explosive because of the predatory opportunities afforded to small states.

Whether or not a war threatens to shift the balance of power is something that can only be determined on a case-by-case basis. But this tendency can generally be related to the polarity of the international system. Currently, the United States is so far ahead of the other great powers that a war between any other two great powers would not cause a significant shift in the balance of power. This could change over the long term, most simply by a decline in US power or the rise of one or more other powers, such as the fullest expression of the European Union as a sovereign, political unit.

American dominance has partially solved the collective good problem associated with maintaining the balance of power. This has been reinforced by United Nations (UN) activism. Should there be a political shift in American politics back to isolationism, the collective good problem would reemerge. Increased war widening would not necessarily result because of buck-passing tendencies. But it would be more likely once the international community accepted that it could no longer depend on US action.

Rapid economic growth has given states more tools to balance internally. Although dominated by the USA, a looser international system gives states other balancing options. Just as in the decades preceding World War I, it would take a series of crises or small wars to exhaust all of these balancing options. Therefore, war widening for balancing purposes is not likely for the foreseeable future. What about predatory war widening? Will the political cost of warfare fall to the point where predatory war widening by great powers resurfaces?

Nuclear proliferation is one of the most pressing issues of the day and it could have a profound impact on war widening. Generally, nuclear weapons are considered beneficial in that they raise the cost of warfare, make it more dangerous and less productive, and thus greatly enhance deterrence. Will nuclear proliferation affect the political cost of warfare, and thereby the likelihood of future wars to widen?

In making his optimistic assessment of the effects of nuclear proliferation, Ken Waltz argues: 'Nuclear weapons deter adversaries from attacking one's vital, and not one's minor, interests.'[2] Thus, during the Cold War, the United States and the Soviet Union fought a significant number of what are termed 'proxy wars'. These were limited engagements from the perspective of the superpowers, which were reasonably secure in the knowledge these conflicts would remain limited, precisely because of their nuclear deterrent posture. Martin van Creveld echoes the point when he asserts: 'A strong case could be made that wherever nuclear weapons have appeared or their presence is even strongly suspected, major interstate warfare on any scale is slowly abolishing itself.'[3] He then contends that, in the case of India and Pakistan, 'military operations have invariably been confined to border incidents'.[4] But, has nuclear deterrence been *too* successful? If, as Waltz contends, 'the unconditional surrender of a nuclear nation cannot be demanded',[5] then does that not also mean that nuclear states can engage in wars against non-nuclear states or on the periphery, with little or no risk to their survival?[6] Or, as Barry Posen asks, will nuclear weapons 'come to be viewed as a shield that protects conventional conquests from *any* [emphasis in original] challenger, including a great power heavily armed with its own nuclear weapons?'.[7] While Posen points out that nuclear weapons have yet to be used in such a manner, it is a possibility that needs to be considered seriously. It could be that the ultimate high cost weaponry has, counterintuitively, lowered the political cost of warfare for those that possess it. And, according to the war widening explanation presented here, that will raise the likelihood of war widening.

In a countervailing trend, changes in the structure of the international system may raise the political cost of warfare, making predation less attractive and wars less likely to widen. During the Cold War, the United States and the Soviet Union managed conflicts between their respective allies in the Middle East, in effect limiting the political cost for those states by removing the threat of annihilation.[8] The end of the Cold War and the collapse of bipolarity lifted these restraints, as the USSR stood to the side while the United States and its allies expelled Iraq from Kuwait in 1991. Although Saddam Hussein's regime was not forced to pay the ultimate price, that was arguably more due to American self-restraint than inability. If the end of the Cold War and bipolarity has the effect of removing artificial limits on the cost of war, returning warfare to its 'natural' state, then the end of the Cold War may make war widening less likely by raising political cost. The future may depend on the role of the United Nations.

With the end of the Cold War, the United Nations has taken on a more active role in international affairs, including armed intervention by 'peace keepers'. Ostensibly these activities have been motivated by humanitarian concerns. But, they have an unintended consequence: they can lower the political cost of warfare. The UN lowers the political cost of warfare for its members by providing an umbrella under which they can spread the costs of action among each other. To the extent that this process is or can be influenced by interested states, this UN activism can lower the political costs of warfare, creating incentives for predatory war widening.

There are additional factors that seem to point toward a future decrease in the incidence of war widening. While this study has focused primarily on the costs of warfare, there are, of course, the gains to be considered. For states with modern economies, the primary goal of most predatory warfare – territory – is less important. Much of what propels modern economies, and thus state power, is only indirectly linked to the territory states encompass. Nationalism has made conquered peoples more difficult to incorporate into another political unit. And population, measured as pure numbers, has become less a measure of state power than it used to be. However, the same nationalism that has made foreign territory difficult to annex, and thus less desirable, has created a new problem: refugees. Wars impose a cost on neighboring states by creating a flood of refugees. It is entirely conceivable that states may intervene in wars simply to minimize the costs to their own political, economic and social infrastructure posed by this refugee 'collateral' damage.

These four trends – nuclear proliferation, the end of the Cold War,

UN activism and the declining value of predation – must be balanced against each other to determine if political cost will fall. To a great extent, the end of the Cold War and UN activism cancel each other out. In other words, the limits on warfare imposed by the Soviet–American rivalry have been replaced by others imposed by the UN. The most important issue is whether the potential for nuclear proliferation to lower the cost of warfare is counterbalanced by the declining value of the gains usually conferred by predation. But, as French behavior in the Crimean War illustrated, the gains sought through predation can be non-territorial, and would not be affected by nationalism and economic factors that lessen the value of territorial conquest. This largely leaves the issue of nuclear proliferation. If the argument about nuclear proliferation is correct, that it will lower the political cost of warfare for nuclear states, then the political cost of warfare will decrease, and future wars will be more and more likely to widen.

There is nothing in the international political system that indicates war widening for balancing reasons should reemerge in the near future. It is inevitable, however, that American dominance will fade, but even then it should be many years before states exhaust their available balancing options. Whether or not the political cost of warfare falls to the point where the incentives for predatory war widening return for the great powers hinges on the effects and scope of nuclear proliferation.

Policy Implications

At present, the political cost of warfare remains high. The driving force behind war widening is the need of great powers to balance against adverse shifts in the balance of power. If balancing war widening occurs, predatory opportunities will be created for small powers, with the potential for explosive escalation. But, such a situation can be prevented. States will not enter an interstate conflict unless it threatens to shift the balance of power, and other balancing options have been exhausted. Here is where policy can make a difference.

One way states balance is by generating power internally through economic growth and improving efficiency. While there will always be concerns about relative growth, efforts that promote the world economy will generally assist most states in their attempt to balance internally. Many states have untapped reserves of power that can be realized through modernization of, not just their economies, but their political structures as well.

The other way states balance is through alliances. While alliances do not cause wars to widen, they can, under certain conditions, prevent war widening. As the transition from a bipolar to a multipolar international system progresses, and US dominance fades, the opportunities for various alliance combinations should increase. This will assist states in their balancing efforts, but only so long as the alliances remain responsive to changes in the international power structure across issue areas. The rigid alliance blocs that dominated the diplomatic landscape during the Cold War, such as NATO, can be detrimental in a multipolar world. More flexibility is retained by building separate coalitions for different issues. And flexibility is the key to preserving balancing options for all states.

Lastly, policy should seek to prevent a return to an era of low political cost warfare. Of the foreseeable trends, nuclear proliferation appears most likely to create that effect. Of course, nuclear weapons have not been used in warfare for close to 60 years, which lends a sort of surreal aspect to any discussion of how their spread will lower the political cost of warfare. Nevertheless, the ability of nuclear weapons to safeguard vital interests does seem to lower the political cost of warfare by, perversely, removing the risk of annihilation introduced by Napoleon. For this reason, nuclear proliferation should be actively prevented, if possible, and managed, if not. It would be the ultimate irony if the doomsday weapon of the modern world returned us to the limited war of the eighteenth century.

NOTES

1. Carl von Clausewitz, *On War*, trans. Michael Howard and Peter Paret, eds (Princeton, NJ: Princeton University Press, 1976), p. 157.
2. Scott D. Sagan and Kenneth N. Waltz, *The Spread of Nuclear Weapons: A Debate* (New York: W. W. Norton, 1995), p. 16.
3. Martin Van Creveld, 'Through a Glass, Darkly: Some Reflections on the Future of War', *Naval War College Review*, 53, 4 (Autumn 2000), pp. 25–44, see 32.
4. Van Creveld, 'Through a Glass, Darkly', p. 35.
5. Sagan and Waltz, *The Spread of Nuclear Weapons*, p. 29.
6. Van Creveld reaches a different conclusion as to the ultimate effect of nuclear proliferation. He sees nuclear proliferation marginalizing interstate conflict, with future conflict being conducted largely by terrorist organizations. See Martin Van Creveld, *Nuclear Proliferation and the Future of Conflict* (New York: The Free Press, 1993), pp. 124–5. In yet a different conclusion, upon examining wars between nuclear and non-nuclear states, T. V. Paul contends that percep-

tions of a 'nuclear taboo' lead non-nuclear states to believe that nuclear states are self-deterred. See T. V. Paul, 'Nuclear Taboo and War Initiation in Regional Conflicts', *Journal of Conflict Resolution*, 39, 4 (December 1995), pp. 696–717, see 699. However, these are peripheral conflicts and, according to Waltz, excluded from the nuclear deterrent. See Sagan and Waltz, *The Spread of Nuclear Weapons*, p. 25. While President Eisenhower suggested that an American nuclear threat helped end the fighting in the Korean War, recent historical research sheds some doubt on that issue. See John Lewis Gaddis, *We Now Know: Rethinking Cold War History* (Oxford: Clarendon Press, 1997), pp. 107–8.

7. Barry R. Posen, 'US Security Policy in a Nuclear-armed World or: What if Iraq had had Nuclear Weapons?' *Security Studies*, 6, 3 (Spring 1997), pp. 1–31, see 5.

8. Norman Cigar, 'Iraq's Strategic Mindset and the Gulf War: Blueprint for Defeat', *Journal of Strategic Studies*, 15, 1 (March 1992), pp. 1–29, see 9.

Appendices

APPENDIX A
WAR WIDENING, 1700–1973

No.	War	Duration (years)	Total widen- ing	Preda- tors	Great power predators	Balancers	Great power balancers
1	Great Northern War (1700–21)	21	6	6	2	0	0
2	War of Spanish Succession (1701–13)	12	7	5	1	2	2
3	War of the Quadruple Alliance (1716–20)	4	6	3	1	3	3
4	British-Spanish War (1727–29)	2	0	0	0	0	0
5	War of Polish Succession (1733–39)	6	7	7	3	0	0
6	War of Austrian Succession (1739–48)	9	9	6	2	3	2
7	Seven Years' War (1754–63)	9	6	5	2	1	1
8	Russo-Turkish-Polish War (1768–74)	6	1	0	0	1	0
9	War of American Revolution (1775–83)	8	2	2	2	0	0
10	War of Bavarian Succession (1778–79)	1	0	0	0	0	0
11	Ottoman War (1787–92)	3	3	3	1	0	0

APPENDIX A (CONTINUED)

No.	War	Duration (years)	Total widen-ing	Preda-tors	Great power predators	Balancers	Great power balancers
12	French Revolutionary Wars (1792–1802)	10	10	8	2	2	1
13	Napoleonic Wars (1803–14)	11	12	2	0	10	4
14	Hundred Days (1815)	1	0	0	0	0	0
15	Neapolitan War (1815)	1	0	0	0	0	0
16	Franco-Spanish War (1823)	1	0	0	0	0	0
17	Russo-Turkish War (1828–29)	1	0	0	0	0	0
18	Austro-Sardinian War (1848–49)	1	1	1	1	0	0
19	First Schleswig-Holstein War (1848)	1	1	0	0	1	0
20	Crimean War (1853–56)	3	3	2	1	1	1
21	War of Italian Unification (1859)	1	1	1	1	0	0
22	Franco-Mexican War (1862–67)	5	0	0	0	0	0
23	Second Schleswig-Holstein War (1864)	1	0	0	0	0	0
24	Austro-Prussian War (1866)	1	1	1	1	0	0
25	Franco-Prussian War (1870–71)	1	0	0	0	0	0
26	Russo-Turkish War (1877–78)	1	1	1	0	0	0
27	Sino-French War (1884–85)	1	0	0	0	0	0
28	Russo-Japanese War (1904–5)	1	0	0	0	0	0
29	Italo-Turkish War (1911–12)	1	0	0	0	0	0

APPENDIX A (CONTINUED)

No.	War	Duration (years)	Total widen-ing	Preda-tors	Great power predators	Balancers	Great power balancers
30	World War I (1914–18)	4	8	4	2	3	1
31	Manchurian War (1931–33)	2	0	0	0	0	0
32	Italo-Ethiopian War (1935–36)	1	0	0	0	0	0
33	Sino-Japanese War (1937–41)	4	1	0	0	1	1
34	Russo-Japanese War (1939)	1	0	0	0	0	0
35	World War II (1939–45)	6	8	4	2	4	3
36	Korean War (1950–53)	3	2	0	0	2	2
37	Russo-Hungarian War (1956)	1	0	0	0	0	0
38	Sinai War (1956)	1	0	0	0	0	0
39	Sino-Indian War (1962)	1	0	0	0	0	0
40	Vietnam War (1965–73)	8	1	0	0	1	1

APPENDIX B

The following is the list of wars used to develop Appendix A and Table 1.1 presented in Chapter 1. This list is based on the list of wars used by Jack Levy.[1] It is, however, shorter than Levy's list. This is because several of the wars he identifies as separate conflicts are, according to the war widening thesis, part of the same war. Military historians treat wars as separate conflicts if they have little effect on each other, in terms of either strategy or operations. Diplomatic historians separate wars based on political objectives. The contention of the war widening argument is, however, that states may enter ongoing conflicts for reasons entirely distinct from, and sometimes in opposition to, the objectives of the initial combatants. According to this proposition, two wars are treated as one if the decision-making in the second war was contingent on the existence of the first. For example, the Great Northern War (1700–21) includes two Russo-Turkish wars because the Ottoman Empire's decision for war against Russia was affected by Russia's preoccupation with its war against Sweden. In another instance, I have included the Russo-Turkish War in the Napoleonic Wars because, despite Levy's assertion to the contrary, it is intimately linked to the person of Napoleon himself, who drew the Turks into war against Russia.[2]

I have also relied on Levy's definition of great powers.[3] This includes both Italy and Japan. As Levy concedes, the inclusion of Italy among the great powers is 'a difficult one'.[4] And Italy most certainly does not behave the way the argument suggests a great power should behave. Japan, too, is counted as a great power although, in the Japanese case, distance may be keeping it out of the great power system.

The war widening theory presented in this study concerns itself only with neutrals who joined ongoing conflicts. Neutrals who were unarguably attacked by one of the initial combatants have been removed from the study, and are listed below in the wars where this occurred. This results in lowering the amount of widening in several cases, with the largest effect being on World War II, where seven neutrals were removed from the widening count.

The number of states in Europe has changed dramatically since 1700. Had every state been counted, it would have greatly inflated the amount of widening that occurred in the eighteenth century, leading to an extreme bias in favor of the war widening arguments put forth. To remove this bias, only one Italian state was counted, and of the German states, only Prussia, Saxony and Bavaria were included.

Lastly, only states that were independent political units when a conflict began were counted. So, while Wright lists Czechoslovakia as a participant in World War I because it was involved territorially,[5] I count only Austria-Hungary because Czechoslovakia did not have an independent foreign policy in 1914.

LIST OF WARS, 1700–1973 (AS SHOWN IN APPENDIX A)

1   *Great Northern War (1700–21)*

- Includes Russo-Turkish War (1710–12)
- Includes Ottoman War (1716–18)
- Initiated between: Russia, Denmark and Sweden
- Widened by addition of: Great Britain, Netherlands, Prussia, Saxony, Poland, Turkey
- Great powers: Great Britain, Netherlands, Sweden, Austria
- Predators: Great Britain, Poland, Prussia, Netherlands, Saxony, Turkey
- Great power predators: Great Britain, Netherlands

- End of the war marks the end of Sweden as a great power and the beginning of Russia as a great power
- Great Britain and the Netherlands joined on Russian side after Russian victories in the Baltic
- TOTAL STATES: 9
- TOTAL WIDENING: 6
- TOTAL PREDATORS: 6
- GREAT POWER PREDATORS: 2
- TOTAL BALANCERS: 0
- GREAT POWER BALANCERS: 0

2   *War of Spanish Succession (1701–13)*

- Initiated between: France, Spain
- Widened by addition of: Great Britain, Netherlands, Portugal, Austria, German Empire, Prussia, Savoy
- Great powers: France, Great Britain, Netherlands, Spain, Austria
- Predators: Portugal, Austria, German Empire, Prussia, Savoy
- Balancers: Great Britain, Netherlands
- Great power predators: Austria
- Great power balancers: Great Britain, Netherlands
- TOTAL STATES: 9
- TOTAL WIDENING: 7
- TOTAL PREDATORS: 5
- GREAT POWER PREDATORS: 1
- TOTAL BALANCERS: 2
- GREAT POWER BALANCERS: 2

3   *War of the Quadruple Alliance (1716–20)*

- Outgrowth of Ottoman War (1716–18): Spain used Ottoman War as cover to attack Austria by seizing Sardinia
- Initiated between: Turkey, Venice
- Widened by addition of: Austria, Spain, France, Great Britain, Netherlands, Savoy
- Great powers: France, Great Britain, Spain, Austria
- Predators: Netherlands, Spain, Savoy
- Great power predators: Spain
- Balancers: France, Great Britain, Austria
- Great power balancers: France, Great Britain
- TOTAL STATES: 8
- TOTAL WIDENING: 6
- TOTAL PREDATORS: 3
- GREAT POWER PREDATORS: 1
- TOTAL BALANCERS: 3
- GREAT POWER BALANCERS: 3

4   *British-Spanish War (1727–29)*

- Initiated between: Great Britain, Spain
- No widening
- TOTAL STATES: 2
- TOTAL WIDENING: 0

5   *War of Polish Succession (1733–39)*

- Includes Russo-Austrian War
- Initiated between: Russia, Poland
- Widened by addition of: France, Spain, Austria, Prussia, Savoy, Saxony, Turkey
- Great powers: France, Spain, Austria, Russia
- Predators: France, Spain, Austria, Prussia, Savoy, Saxony, Turkey
- Great power predators: France, Spain, Austria
- Great power balancers: none
- TOTAL STATES: 9
- TOTAL WIDENING: 7
- TOTAL PREDATORS: 7
- GREAT POWER PREDATORS: 3
- TOTAL BALANCERS: 0

6   *War of the Austrian Succession (1739–48)*

- Includes Russo-Swedish War
- Initiated between: Austria, Prussia
- Widened by addition of: France, Great Britain, Netherlands, Spain, Bavaria, Savoy, Saxony, Russia, Sweden
- Great powers: France, Great Britain, Spain, Austria, Prussia, Russia
- Predators: France, Spain, Bavaria, Savoy, Saxony, Sweden
- Balancers: Great Britain, Netherlands, Russia
- Great power predators: France, Spain
- Great power balancers: Great Britain, Russia
- TOTAL STATES: 11
- TOTAL WIDENING: 9
- TOTAL PREDATORS: 6
- GREAT POWER PREDATORS: 2
- TOTAL BALANCERS: 3
- GREAT POWER BALANCERS: 2

7   *Seven Years' War (1754–63)*

- Initiated as Anglo-French colonial war
- Widened by addition of: Spain, Austria, German Empire, Saxony, Russia, Sweden
- Great powers: France, Great Britain, Spain, Prussia, Russia
- Predators: Austria, German Empire, Saxony, Russia, Sweden
- Balancers: Spain, Prussia
- Great power predators: Austria, Russia
- Great power balancers: Spain
- TOTAL STATES: 8
- TOTAL WIDENING: 6
- TOTAL PREDATORS: 5
- GREAT POWER PREDATORS: 2
- TOTAL BALANCERS: 1
- GREAT POWER BALANCERS: 1

8   *Russo-Turkish-Polish War (1768–74)*

- Outgrowth of Confederation of Bar; Turkey joins when Russia chases Poles into Turkish territory

- Leads to first partition of Poland
- Initiated between: Russia, Poland
- Widened by addition of: Turkey
- Great powers: Russia
- Predators: none
- Balancers: Turkey
- TOTAL STATES: 3
- WIDENING: 1
- TOTAL PREDATORS: 0
- TOTAL BALANCERS: 1
- GREAT POWER BALANCERS: 0

9 *War of American Revolution (1775–83)*

- Initiated between: Great Britain, USA
- Widened by addition of: France, Spain, Netherlands
- Great powers: France, Great Britain, Spain
- Predators: France, Spain
- Great power predators: France, Spain
- Balancers: none
- NEUTRALS ATTACKED BY INITIAL COMBATANTS: 1
- TOTAL STATES: 5
- TOTAL WIDENING: 2
- TOTAL PREDATORS: 2
- GREAT POWER PREDATORS: 2
- TOTAL BALANCERS: 0

10 *War of Bavarian Succession (1778–79)*

- Initiated between: Austria, Prussia
- No widening
- TOTAL STATES: 2
- TOTAL WIDENING: 0

11 *Ottoman War (1787–92)*

- Combined with Russo-Swedish War
- Initiated between: Russia, Turkey
- Widened by addition of: Austria, Denmark, Sweden
- Great powers: Austria, Russia
- Predators: Austria, Denmark, Sweden
- Great power predators: Austria
- Great power balancers: none
- TOTAL STATES: 5
- TOTAL WIDENING: 3
- TOTAL PREDATORS: 3
- GREAT POWER PREDATORS: 1
- TOTAL BALANCERS: 0

12 *French Revolutionary Wars (1792–1802)*

- Combines First and Second Coalitions
- Initiated between: France, Austria, Prussia
- Widened by addition of: Great Britain, Netherlands, Portugal, Spain, German

Empire, Sardinia, Saxony, Denmark, Russia, Sweden, Turkey
- Great powers: France, Great Britain, Spain, Austria, Prussia, Russia
- Predators: Spain, German Empire, Sardinia, Saxony, Denmark, Russia, Sweden, Portugal
- Balancers: Great Britain, Netherlands
- Great power predators: Spain, Russia
- Great power balancers: Great Britain
- TOTAL STATES: 14
- NEUTRALS ATTACKED BY INITIAL COMBATANTS: 1
- TOTAL WIDENING: 10
- TOTAL PREDATORS: 8
- GREAT POWER PREDATORS: 2
- TOTAL BALANCERS: 2
- GREAT POWER BALANCERS: 1

13 Napoleonic Wars (1803–14)

- Initiated between: France, Great Britain
- Widened by addition of: Austria, Russia, Prussia, Saxony, Spain, Portugal, Denmark, Bavaria, Naples, USA, Sweden, Turkey
- Great powers: France, Great Britain, Prussia, Russia, Austria, Spain
- Predators: Sweden, Turkey
- Balancers: Prussia, Russia, Austria, Spain, Portugal, Denmark, Saxony, Bavaria, USA, Naples
- Great power predators: none
- Great power balancers: Spain, Austria, Russia, Prussia
- TOTAL STATES: 14
- TOTAL WIDENING: 12
- TOTAL PREDATORS: 2
- GREAT POWER PREDATORS: 0
- TOTAL BALANCERS: 10
- GREAT POWER BALANCERS: 4

14 Hundred Days (1815)

- Initiated between: France, Great Britain, Netherlands, Spain, Austria, Naples, North Germany, Prussia, Russia, Sweden
- No widening
- TOTAL STATES: 10
- TOTAL WIDENING: 0

15 Neapolitan War (1815)

- Initiated between: Austria, Naples
- No widening
- TOTAL STATES: 2
- TOTAL WIDENING: 0

16 Franco-Spanish War (1823)

- Initiated between: France, Spain
- No widening
- TOTAL STATES: 2
- TOTAL WIDENING: 0

17 *Russo-Turkish War (1828–29)*

- Initiated between: Russia, Turkey
- No widening
- TOTAL STATES: 2
- TOTAL WIDENING: 0

18 *Austro-Sardinian War (1848–49)*

- Initiated between: Austria, Sardinia
- Widened by addition of: France
- Great powers: France, Austria
- Predators: France
- Great power predators: France
- TOTAL STATES: 3
- TOTAL WIDENING: 1
- TOTAL PREDATORS: 1
- TOTAL GREAT POWER PREDATORS: 1
- TOTAL BALANCERS: 0

19 *First Schleswig-Holstein War (1848)*

- Initiated between: Prussia, Denmark
- Widened by addition of: Sweden
- Great powers: Prussia
- Predators: none
- Balancers: Sweden
- TOTAL STATES: 3
- TOTAL WIDENING: 1
- TOTAL PREDATORS: 0
- TOTAL BALANCERS: 1
- TOTAL GREAT POWER BALANCERS: 0

20 *Crimean War (1853–56)*

- Initiated between: Russia, Turkey
- Widened by addition of: Great Britain, Sardinia, France
- Great powers: France, Great Britain, Russia
- Predators: France, Sardinia
- Balancers: Great Britain
- Great power predators: France
- Great power balancers: Great Britain
- TOTAL STATES: 5
- TOTAL WIDENING: 3
- TOTAL PREDATORS: 2
- GREAT POWER PREDATORS: 1
- TOTAL BALANCERS: 1
- GREAT POWER BALANCERS: 1

21 *War of Italian Unification (1859)*

- Initiated between: Austria, Sardinia
- Widened by addition of: France
- TOTAL STATES: 3

- TOTAL WIDENING: 1
- TOTAL PREDATORS: 1
- GREAT POWER PREDATORS: 1
- TOTAL BALANCERS: 0

22 *Franco-Mexican War (1862–67)*

- Initiated between: France, Great Britain, Spain, Mexico
- Widening: none
- Veracruz occupied because of Mexican debt crisis; France decided to conquer Mexico, taking advantage of US Civil War; could alternatively be coded as widening of US Civil War with France as only widener
- TOTAL STATES: 4
- TOTAL WIDENING: 0

23 *Second Schleswig-Holstein War (1864)*

- Initiated between: Austria, Prussia, Denmark
- Widening: none
- TOTAL STATES: 3
- TOTAL WIDENING: 0

24 *Austro-Prussian War (1866)*

- Initiated between: Prussia, Austria, Saxony
- Widened by addition of: Italy
- Great powers: Prussia, Austria, Italy
- Predators: Italy
- Great power predators: Italy
- TOTAL STATES: 4
- TOTAL WIDENING: 1
- TOTAL PREDATORS: 1
- GREAT POWER PREDATORS: 1
- TOTAL BALANCERS: 0

25 *Franco-Prussian War (1870–71)*

- Initiated between: France, Prussia
- No widening
- TOTAL STATES: 2
- TOTAL WIDENING: 0

26 *Russo-Turkish War (1877–78)*

- Initiated between: Russia, Turkey
- Widened by addition of: Serbia
- Predators: Serbia
- Great power predators: none
- TOTAL STATES: 3
- TOTAL WIDENING: 1
- TOTAL PREDATORS: 1
- GREAT POWER PREDATORS: 0
- TOTAL BALANCERS: 0

27 *Sino-French War (1884–85)*

- Initiated between: France, China
- No widening
- TOTAL STATES: 2
- TOTAL WIDENING: 0

28 *Russo-Japanese War (1904–5)*

- Initiated between: Russia, Japan
- No widening
- TOTAL STATES: 2
- TOTAL WIDENING: 0

29 *Italo-Turkish War (1911–12)*

- Initiated between: Italy, Turkey
- No widening
- TOTAL STATES: 2
- TOTAL WIDENING: 0

30 *World War I (1914–18)*

- Initiated between: Germany, Austria, France, Belgium, Russia, Serbia
- Widened by: Great Britain, Bulgaria, Greece, Romania, China, Japan, Turkey, USA
- Great powers: France, Great Britain, Austria, Germany, Italy, Russia, Japan, USA
- Predators: Italy, Bulgaria, Greece, Japan, Romania
- Balancers: Great Britain, China, USA
- Great power predators: Italy, Japan
- Great power balancers: Great Britain, USA
- TOTAL STATES: 14
- TOTAL WIDENING: 8
- TOTAL PREDATORS: 4
- GREAT POWER PREDATORS: 2
- TOTAL BALANCERS: 3
- GREAT POWER BALANCERS: 1

31 *Manchurian War (1931–33)*

- Initiated between China, Japan
- No widening
- TOTAL STATES: 2
- TOTAL WIDENING: 0

32 *Italo-Ethiopian War (1935–36)*

- Initiated between: Italy, Ethiopia
- No widening
- TOTAL STATES: 2
- TOTAL WIDENING: 0

33 *Sino-Japanese War (1937–41)*

- Initiated between: China, Japan

- Widened by addition of: Great Britain
- Great powers: Japan, Great Britain
- Balancers: Great Britain
- TOTAL STATES: 3
- TOTAL WIDENING: 1
- TOTAL PREDATORS: 0
- TOTAL BALANCERS: 1
- GREAT POWER BALANCERS: 1

34   *Russo-Japanese War (1939)*

- Initiated between: USSR, Japan
- No widening
- TOTAL STATES: 2
- TOTAL WIDENING: 0

35   *World War II (1939–45)*

- Initiated between: Germany, Poland, USSR
- Widened by addition of: Belgium, France, Great Britain, Netherlands, Hungary, Bulgaria, Greece, Romania, Yugoslavia, China, Japan, USA, Italy, Norway, Denmark
- Great Powers: France, Great Britain, Germany, USSR, Japan, Italy, USA
- Predators: Japan, Italy, Hungary, Bulgaria
- Balancers: France, Great Britain, USA, China
- Great power balancers: France, Great Britain, USA
- TOTAL STATES: 18
- NEUTRALS ATTACKED BY INITIAL COMBATANTS: 7
- TOTAL WIDENING: 8
- TOTAL PREDATORS: 4
- GREAT POWER PREDATORS: 2
- TOTAL BALANCERS: 4
- GREAT POWER BALANCERS: 3

36   *Korean War (1950–53)*

- Initiated between: North Korea, South Korea
- Widened by addition of: USA, China
- Great powers: China, USA
- Balancers: China, USA
- Great power balancers: China, USA
- TOTAL STATES: 4
- TOTAL WIDENING: 2
- TOTAL BALANCERS: 2
- GREAT POWER BALANCERS: 2

37   *Russo-Hungarian War (1956)*

- Initiated between: USSR, Hungary
- No widening
- TOTAL STATES: 2
- TOTAL WIDENING: 0

38 *Sinai War (1956)*

- Initiated between: Great Britain, France, Israel, Egypt
- No widening
- TOTAL STATES: 4
- TOTAL WIDENING: 0

39 *Sino-Indian War (1962)*

- Initiated between: India, China
- No widening
- TOTAL STATES: 2
- TOTAL WIDENING: 0

40 *Vietnam War (1965–73)*

- Initiated between: North Vietnam, South Vietnam
- Widened by addition of: USA
- TOTAL STATES: 3
- TOTAL WIDENING: 1
- TOTAL BALANCERS: 1
- GREAT POWER BALANCERS: 1

NOTES

1. Jack Levy, *War in the Modern Great Power System, 1495–1975* (Lexington, KY: University Press of Kentucky, 1983), pp. 70–3.
2. Ibid., p. 67. For the Franco-Turkish alliance, see Vernon J. Puryear, *Napoleon and the Dardanelles* (Berkeley, CA: University of California Press, 1951), p. 99.
3. Levy, *War in the Modern Great Power System*, p. 47.
4. Ibid., p. 41.
5. Quincy Wright, *A Study of War*, 2nd edn (Chicago, IL: University of Chicago Press, 1965), p. 646.

Select Bibliography

Absalom, Roger, *Italy since 1800: A Nation in the Balance?* (London: Longman, 1995).

Albertini, Luigi, *The Origins of the War of 1914*, trans. Isabella M. Massey (Oxford: Oxford University Press, 1952).

Alexander, Don W., 'French Replacement Methods during the Peninsular War, 1808–1814', *Military Affairs*, 44, 4 (1980), pp. 192–7.

Altfeld, Michael F. and Bruce Bueno de Mesquita, 'Choosing Sides in Wars', *International Studies Quarterly*, 23, 11 (March 1979) pp. 87–112.

Art, Robert J. and Robert Jervis, eds, *International Politics: Enduring Concepts and Contemporary Issues*, 3rd edn (New York: HarperCollins, 1992).

Art, Robert J. and Kenneth N. Waltz, eds, *The Use of Force: Military Power and International Politics* (Lanham, MD: University Press of America, 1988).

Asprey, Robert B., *The German High Command at War: Hindenburg and Ludendorff Conduct World War I* (New York: William Morrow, 1991).

Bain, R. Nisbet, *Gustavus III and his Contemporaries, 1746–1792: An Overlooked Chapter of Eighteenth Century History* (London: Kegan Paul, Trench, Trübner, 1894).

Barnett, Corelli, *The Swordbearers: Supreme Command in the First World War* (Bloomington, IN: Indiana University Press, 1963).

Barton, H. Arnold, *Scandinavia in the Revolutionary Era, 1760–1815* (Minneapolis, MN: University of Minnesota Press, 1986).

Baugh, Daniel A., 'Great Britain's "Blue Water" Policy, 1689–1815', *International History Review*, 10 (1988), pp. 33–58.

Bayly, C.A., *Imperial Meridian: The British Empire and the World 1780–1830* (London: Longman, 1989).

Berghahn, Volker R. and Martin Kitchen, eds, *Germany in the Age of Total War* (Totowa, NJ: Barnes & Noble, 1981).

Bernhardi, Friedrich von, *Germany and the Next War*, trans. Allen H. Powles (New York: Longmans, Green, 1914).

Bertrand, Louis and Charles Petrie, *The History of Spain*, 2nd edn (New York: Macmillan, 1952).

Black, Jeremy, *European Warfare 1660–1815* (New Haven, CT: Yale University Press, 1994).

Blainey, Geoffrey, *The Causes of War*, 3rd edn (New York: The Free Press, 1988).

Blanning, T. C. W., *The Origins of the French Revolutionary War* (London: Longman, 1986).

Bloch, Camille, *The Causes of the World War: An Historical Summary*, trans. Jame Soames (New York: Howard Fertig, 1968 [first English pub. 1935]).

Bloem, Walter, *The Advance from Mons 1914*, trans. G. C. Wynne (London: Peter Davies, 1930).

Blumenthal, Henry, *France and the United States: Their Diplomatic Relations, 1789–1914* (Chapel Hill, NC: University of North Carolina Press, 1970).

Bosworth, Richard, *Italy and the Approach of the First World War* (New York: St Martin's Press, 1983).

Brock, Michael, 'Britain Enters the War', in R. J. W. Evans and Hartmut Pogge von Strandmann, eds, *The Coming of the First World War* (Oxford: Clarendon Press, 1988), pp. 145–78.

Broglie, Le Duc de, *The King's Secret: Being the Secret Correspondence of Louis XV with his Diplomatic Agents from 1752 to 1774* (London: Cassell, Peter & Galpin, 1879).

Broglie, Le Duc de, *L'Alliance Autrichienne* (Paris: Calmann Levy, 1897).

Bueno de Mesquita, Bruce and Randolph M. Siverson, 'War and the Survival of Political Leaders: A Comparative Study of Regime Types and Political Accountability', *American Political Science Review*, 89, 4 (December 1995), pp. 841–55.

Carter, Alice Clare, *The Dutch Republic in Europe and the Seven Years' War* (London: Macmillan, 1971).

Cate, Curtis, *The War of the Two Emperors: The Duel between Napoleon and Alexander, Russia 1812* (New York: Random House, 1985).

Chapman, Charles E., *A History of Spain: Founded on the Historia de España y de la Civilización Española of Rafael Altamira* (New York: The Free Press, 1918).

Charteris, Evan, *William Augustus Duke of Cumberland and the Seven Years' War* (London: Hutchinson, 1925).

Childs, John, *Armies and Warfare in Europe: 1648–1789* (New York: Holmes and Meier, 1982).

Cigar, Norman, 'Iraq's Strategic Mindset and the Gulf War: Blueprint for Defeat', *Journal of Strategic Studies*, 15, 1 (March 1992), pp. 1–29.

Clausewitz, Carl von, *On War*, trans. Michael Howard and Peter Paret, eds (Princeton, NJ: Princeton University Press, 1976).

Coffman, Edward M., 'The American Military and Strategic Policy in World War I', in Barry Hunt and Adrian Preston, eds, *War Aims and Strategic Policy in the Great War 1914–1918* (London: Croom Helm, 1977), pp. 67–84.

Cooper, Duff, *Talleyrand* (New York: Fromm International Publishing, 1986 [orig. pub. 1932]).

Cooper, John Milton, Jr, *The Warrior and the Priest: Woodrow Wilson and Theodore Roosevelt* (Cambridge, MA: Belknap Press of Harvard University Press, 1983).

Copeland, Dale C., *The Origins of Major War* (Ithaca, NY: Cornell University Press, 2000).

Cosmas, Graham A., *An Army for Empire: The United States Army in the Spanish American War* (Columbia, MI: University of Missouri Press, 1971).

Craig, Gordon A., *War, Politics, and Diplomacy* (New York: Frederick A. Praeger, 1966).

Crosby, Alfred W., Jr, *America, Russia, Hemp and Napoleon: American Trade with Russia and the Baltic, 1783–1812* (Columbus, OH: Ohio State University Press, 1965).

Cullberg, Albin, *La Politique du Roi Oscar I pendant la Guerre de Crimée: Etudes Diplomatiques sur les Négociations Secrètes entre les Cabinets de Stockholm, Paris, St Petersbourg et Londres les Années 1853–1856* (Stockholm: Författerens Förlag, 1912).

Dard, Emile, *Napoleon and Talleyrand*, trans. Christopher R. Turner (London: D. Appleton-Century, 1937).

DeConde, Alexander, *The Quasi-War: The Politics and Diplomacy of the Undeclared War with France 1797–1801* (New York: Charles Scribner's Sons, 1966).

DeConde, Alexander, *A History of American Foreign Policy: Vol. 2, Global Power (1900 to the Present)*, 3rd edn (New York: Charles Scribner's Sons, 1978).

Delbrück, Hans, *History of the Art of War within the Framework of Political History: Vol. 4, The Modern Era*, trans. Walter J. Renfroe, Jr, Contributions in Military History, 39 (Westport, CT: Greenwood Press, 1985 [orig. published Berlin, 1920]).

Duffy, Christopher, 'The Seven Years' War as a Limited War', in Gunther E. Rothenberg, Béla K. Kiràly and Peter F. Sugar, eds, *East Central European Society and War in the Pre-Revolutionary Eighteenth Century*, East European Monographs, 122 (Boulder, CO: Social Science Monographs, 1982).

Duffy, Christopher, *The Military Life of Frederick the Great* (New York: Atheneum, 1986).

Dupuy, R. Ernest and Trevor N. Dupuy, *The Encyclopedia of Military History: from 3500 BC to the Present*, 2nd revd edn (New York: Harper & Row, 1986).

Egan, Clifford, *Neither Peace Nor War: Franco-American Relations, 1803–1812* (Baton Rouge, LA: Louisiana State University Press, 1983).

Eldon, Carl William, 'England's Subsidy Policy towards the Continent during the Seven Years' War', unpub. dissert., University of Pennsylvania, 1938.

Entick, John, *The General History of the Late War* (London: Edward Dilly & John Millan, 1763).

Evans, R. J. W., 'The Habsburg Monarchy and the Coming of War', in *The Coming of the First World War*, R. J. W. Evans and Harmut Pogge von Strandmann, eds (Oxford: Clarendon Press, 1988), pp. 33–55.

Evans, R. J. W. and Harmut Pogge von Strandmann, eds, *The Coming of the First World War* (Oxford: Clarendon Press, 1988).

Fay, Sidney Bradshaw, *The Origins of the World War*, 2 vols, 2nd revd edn (New York: The Free Press, 1966).

Ferguson, Niall, *The Pity of War: Explaining World War I* (New York: Basic Books, 1999).

Ferrell, Robert H., *Woodrow Wilson and World War I: 1917–1921* (New York: Harper & Row, 1985).

Fischer, Fritz, 'German War Aims 1914–1918 and German Policy before the War', in Barry Hunt and Adrian Preston, eds, *War Aims and Strategic Policy in the Great War 1914–1918* (London: Croom Helm, 1977), pp. 105–23.

Fisher, Alan W., *The Russian Annexation of the Crimea: 1771–1783* (Cambridge: Cambridge University Press, 1970).

Foote, Shelby, *The Civil War: A Narrative: Vol. 2, Fredericksburg to Meridian* (New York: Random House, 1963).

Gaddis, John Lewis, *We Now Know: Rethinking Cold War History* (Oxford: Clarendon Press, 1997).

Glaser, Charles, 'Political Consequences of Military Strategy: Expanding and Refining the Spiral and Deterrence Models', *World Politics*, 44, 4 (July 1992), pp. 497–538.

Godechot, Jacques, Beatrice F. Hyslop and David L. Dowd, *The Napoleonic Era in Europe* (New York: Holt, Rinehart & Winston, 1971).

Goldfrank, David M., *The Origins of the Crimean War* (London: Longman, 1994).

Gooch, G. P., *The Second Empire* (London: Longmans, Green, 1960).

Gooch, John, 'Soldiers, Strategy and War Aims in Britain 1914–1918', in Barry Hunt and Adrian Preston, eds, *War Aims and Strategic Policy in the Great War 1914–1918* (London: Croom Helm, 1977), pp. 21–40.

Grenville, J. A. S., 'Diplomacy and War Plans in the United States, 1890–1917', in
    Paul M. Kennedy, ed., *The War Plans of the Great Powers, 1880–1914* (London:
    George Allen & Unwin, 1979), pp. 23–38.
Haeussler, Helmut, *General William Groener and the Imperial German Army* (Madison,
    WI: State Historical Society of Wisconsin for the Department of History,
    University of Wisconsin, 1962).
Hagan, Kenneth J., *This People's Navy: The Making of American Sea Power* (New York:
    The Free Press, 1991).
Haldi, Stacy Bergstrom, 'War Widening', unpub. dissert., University of Chicago,
    2000.
Haldi, Stacy Bergstrom, 'The Influence of Logistics on War Widening', *Defense and
    Security Analysis*, 18, 1 (March 2002), pp. 3–14.
Hassall, Arthur, *The Balance of Power: 1715–1789*, Vol. 6, in *Periods of European
    History*, Arthur Hassall, ed. (New York, Macmillan, 1907).
Herrmann, David G., *The Arming of Europe and the Making of the First World War*
    (Princeton, NJ: Princeton University Press, 1996).
Holcroft, Thomas, Jr, *Posthumous Works of Frederick II, King of Prussia: Vol. 2, The
    History of the Seven Years' War, Part 1* (London: G. G. J. and J. Robinson, 1789).
Holt, Lucius Hudson and Alexander Wheeler Chilton, *A Brief History of Europe from
    1789 to 1815* (New York: Macmillan, 1920).
Horsman, Reginald, *The Causes of the War of 1812* (New York: A. S. Barnes, 1962).
Howard, Michael, *War in European History* (Oxford: Oxford University Press, 1976).
Howard, Michael, 'Men against Fire: Expectations of War in 1914', *International
    Security*, 9, 1 (Summer 1984), reprinted in Steven E. Miller, *Military Strategy and
    the Origins of the First World War: An International Security Reader* (Princeton, NJ:
    Princeton University Press, 1985), pp. 41–57.
Howard, Michael, 'Men against Fire: The Doctrine of the Offensive in 1914', in Peter
    Paret, ed., *Makers of Modern Strategy: From Machiavelli to the Nuclear Age*
    (Princeton, NJ: Princeton University Press, 1986), pp. 510–26.
Howard, Michael, 'Europe on the Eve of the First World War', in R. J. W. Evans and
    Hartmut Pogge von Strandmann, eds, *The Coming of the First World War* (Oxford:
    Clarendon Press, 1988).
Hunt, Barry D., 'Introduction', in Barry Hunt and Adrian Preston, eds, *War Aims and
    Strategic Policy in the Great War 1914–1918* (London: Croom Helm, 1977), pp.
    9–20.
Hunt, Barry and Adrian Preston, eds, *War Aims and Strategic Policy in the Great War
    1914–1918* (London: Croom Helm, 1977).
Huntington, Samuel P., *The Soldier and the State: The Theory and Politics of Civil–
    Military Relations* (Cambridge: Belknap Press of Harvard University Press, 1957,
    1985).
Ingrao, Charles W., 'Habsburg Strategy and Geopolitics during the Eighteenth
    Century', in Gunther E. Rothenberg, Béla K. Kiràly and Peter F. Sugar, eds, *East
    Central European Society and War in the Pre-revolutionary Eighteenth Century*, East
    European Monographs, 122 (Boulder, CO: Social Science Monographs, 1982).
Jervis, Robert, 'Cooperation under the Security Dilemma', *World Politics*, 30, 2
    (January 1978), pp. 167–214.
Jervis, Robert, 'Domino Beliefs and Strategic Behavior', in Robert Jervis and Jack
    Snyder, eds, *Dominoes and Bandwagons: Strategic Beliefs and Great Power
    Competition in the Eurasian Rimland* (New York: Oxford University Press, 1991).
Jervis, Robert, 'Offense, Defense and the Security Dilemma', in *International Politics:
    Enduring Concepts and Contemporary Issues*, 3rd edn (New York: HarperCollins,
    1992), pp. 146–69.

Johnson, Douglas, 'French War Aims and the Crisis of the Third Republic', in Barry Hunt and Adrian Preston, eds, *War Aims and Strategic Policy in the Great War 1914–1918* (London: Croom Helm, 1977), pp. 41–54.

Joll, James, *The Origins of the First World War* (London: Longman, 1984).

Keegan, John, *A History of Warfare* (New York: Alfred A. Knopf, 1993).

Kennedy, Paul, *The War Plans of the Great Powers, 1880–1914* (London: George Allen & Unwin, 1979).

Kennedy, Paul M., *The Rise and Fall of British Naval Mastery* (London: The Ashfield Press, 1983).

Kennedy, Paul, ed., *Strategy and Diplomacy 1870–1945: Eight Studies* (London: George Allen & Unwin, 1983).

Kennedy, Paul M., 'The First World War and the International Power System', *International Security*, 9, 1 (Summer 1984), reprinted in Steven E. Miller, *Military Strategy and the Origins of the First World War: An International Security Reader* (Princeton, NJ: Princeton University Press, 1985), pp. 7–40.

Kennedy, Paul, *The Rise and Fall of the Great Powers: Economic Change and Military Conflict from 1500 to 2000* (New York: Random House, 1987).

Kraehe, Enno E., *Metternich's German Policy: Vol. 1, The Contest with Napoleon, 1799–1814* (Princeton, NJ: Princeton University Press, 1963).

Lambert, Andrew D., *The Crimean War: British Grand Strategy, 1853–56* (Manchester: Manchester University Press, 1990).

Lebow, Richard Ned, *Nuclear Crisis Management: A Dangerous Illusion* (Ithaca, NY: Cornell University Press, 1987).

Levy, Jack, *War in the Modern Great Power System, 1495–1975* (Lexington, KY: University Press of Kentucky, 1983).

Levy, Jack S., 'The Offensive/Defensive Balance of Military Technology: A Theoretical and Historical Analysis', *International Studies Quarterly*, 28 (1984), pp. 219–38.

Levy, Jack S., 'Big Wars, Little Wars, and Theory Construction', *International Interactions*, 16, 3 (1990), pp. 215–24.

Levy, Jack S., 'Preferences, Constraints, and Choices in July 1914', *International Security*, 15, 3 (Winter 1990/91), pp. 151–86.

Licklider, Roy, 'The Consequences of Negotiated Settlements in Civil Wars, 1945–1993', *American Political Science Review*, 89, 3 (September 1995), pp. 681–90.

Lieber, Kier, 'Grasping the Technological Peace: The Offense–Defense Balance and International Security', *International Security*, 25, 1 (Summer 2000), pp. 71–104.

Lieven, D. C. B., *Russia and the Origins of the First World War* (New York: St Martin's Press, 1983).

Livermore, H. V., *A New History of Portugal*, 2nd edn (London: Cambridge University Press, 1976).

Ludwig, Emil, *Napoleon*, trans. Eden and Cedar Paul (New York: Boni & Liveright, 1926).

Maistre, Joseph Marie, Comte de, *Memoires Politiques et Correspondance Diplomatique de Joseph de Maistre*, Albert Blanc, ed., 3rd edn (Paris: M. Levy, 1864).

Martin, Albert, *1812: The War Nobody Won* (New York: Atheneum, 1985).

Massie, Robert K., *Dreadnought: Britain, Germany and the Coming of the Great War* (New York: Random House, 1991).

Maurer, John H., *The Outbreak of the First World War: Strategic Planning, Crisis Decision Making, and Deterrence Failure*, Praeger Studies in Diplomacy and Strategic Thought Series, B. J. C. McKercher, ed. (Westport, CT: Praeger, 1995).

McDermott, J., 'The Revolution in British Military Thinking from the Boer War to the Moroccan Crisis', in Paul M. Kennedy, ed., *The War Plans of the Great Powers*,

1880–1914 (London: George Allen & Unwin, 1979), pp. 99–117.

McNeill, William H., *The Pursuit of Power: Technology, Armed Force and Society since AD 1000* (Chicago, IL: University of Chicago Press, 1982).

Mearsheimer, John, 'Back to the Future', in Sean M. Lynn-Jones, ed., *The Cold War and After: Prospects for Peace* (Cambridge, MA: MIT Press, 1991), pp. 141–92.

Mearsheimer, John, *The Tragedy of Great Power Politics* (New York: W. W. Norton, 2001).

Menning, Bruce W., *Bayonets before Bullets: The Imperial Russian Army, 1861–1914* (Bloomington, IN: Indiana University Press, 1992).

Miller, Steven E., ed., *Military Strategy and the Origins of the First World War: An International Security Reader* (Princeton, NJ: Princeton University Press, 1985).

Mommsen, Wolfgang J., 'The Topos of Inevitable War in Germany in the Decade before 1914', in Volker R. Berghahn and Martin Kitchen, eds, *Germany in the Age of Total War* (Totowa, NJ: Barnes & Noble, 1981), pp. 23–45.

Mourot, B., ed., *La Diplomatie et La Guerre 1814: Le Traité de Chaumont-en-Bassigny* (Colombey-Les-Deux-Eglises: St Martin, 1988).

Mowat, R. B., *The Diplomacy of Napoleon* (London: Edward Arnold, 1924).

Mowat, R. B., *Europe 1715–1815* (New York: Longmans, Green, 1929).

Müffling, Baron Carl von, *The Memoirs of Baron von Müffling: A Prussian Officer in the Napoleonic Wars* (London: Greenhill Books, 1997 [orig. pub. 1853]).

Muir, Rory, *Britain and the Defeat of Napoleon 1807–1815* (New Haven, CT: Yale University Press, 1996).

New York Times, 25 March 1999.

Oliva, L. Jay, *Misalliance: A Study of French Policy in Russia during the Seven Years' War* (New York: New York University Press, 1964).

Oren, Ido, 'The War Proneness of Alliances', *JCR*, 34, 2 (1990), pp. 208–23.

Organski, A. F. K. and Jacek Kugler, *The War Ledger* (Chicago, IL: University of Chicago Press, 1980).

Paret, Peter, 'Napoleon and the Revolution in War', in Peter Paret, ed., *Makers of Modern Strategy from Machiavelli to the Nuclear Age* (Princeton, NJ: Princeton University Press, 1986), pp. 123–42.

Paret, Peter, ed., *Makers of Modern Strategy from Machiavelli to the Nuclear Age* (Princeton, NJ: Princeton University Press, 1986).

Paul, T. V., 'Nuclear Taboo and War Initiation in Regional Conflicts', *Journal of Conflict Resolution*, 39, 4 (December 1995), pp. 696–717.

Perkins, Bradford, *Prologue to War: England and the United States 1805–1812* (Berkeley, CA: University of California Press, 1963).

Petre, F. Loraine, *Napoleon and the Archduke Charles: A History of the Franco-Austrian Campaign in the Valley of the Danube in 1809* (London: Greenhill Books, 1991).

Posen, Barry R., *The Sources of Military Doctrine: France, Britain and Germany between the World Wars* (Ithaca, NY: Cornell University Press, 1984).

Posen, Barry R., 'US Security Policy in a Nuclear-armed World or: What if Iraq had had Nuclear Weapons?' *Security Studies*, 6, 3 (Spring 1997), pp. 1–31.

Puryear, Vernon J., *Napoleon and the Dardanelles* (Berkeley, CA: University of California Press, 1951).

Quester, George H., *Offense and Defense in the International System* (New Brunswick, NJ: Transaction Books, 1988).

Rich, Norman, *Why the Crimean War? A Cautionary Tale* (Hanover, NH: University Press of New England, 1985).

Riley, J. P., *Napoleon and the World War of 1813: Lessons in Coalition Warfighting* (London: Frank Cass, 2000).

Ritter, Gerhard, *The Schlieffen Plan: Critique of a Myth*, trans. Andrew and Eva Wilson, (Westport, CT: Greenwood Press, Publishers, 1979).

Roberts, Michael, *The Age of Liberty: Sweden 1719–1772* (Cambridge: Cambridge University Press, 1986).

Ropp, Theodore, *War in the Modern World* (New York: Collier Books, 1962).

Ross, Steven T., *European Diplomatic History 1789–1815: France against Europe* (Garden City, NY: Anchor Books, 1969).

Rothenberg, Gunther E., *The Art of Warfare in the Age of Napoleon* (Bloomington, IN: Indiana University Press, 1978).

Rothenberg, Gunther E., Béla K. Kiràly and Peter E. Sugar, eds, *East European Society and War in the Pre-Revolutionary Eighteenth Century*, East European Monographs, 122 (Boulder, CO: Social Science Monographs, 1982).

Rothwell, V. H., *British War Aims and Peace Diplomacy 1914–1918* (Oxford: Clarendon Press, 1971).

Saab, Ann Pottinger, *The Origins of the Crimean Alliance* (Charlottesville, VA: University Press of Virginia, 1977).

Sagan, Scott D. and Kenneth N. Waltz, *The Spread of Nuclear Weapons: A Debate* (New York: W. W. Norton, 1995).

Saunders, David, *Russia in the Age of Reaction and Reform: 1801–1881*, Longman History of Russia (London: Longman, 1992).

Schama, Simon, *Citizens: A Chronicle of the French Revolution* (New York: Alfred A. Knopf, 1989).

Schlieffen, General Fieldmarshal Count Alfred von, *Cannae* (Leavenworth, KS: Command and General Staff School Press, 1931).

Schmitt, Bernadotte E. and Harold C. Vedeler, *The World in the Crucible: 1914–1919* (New York: Harper & Row, 1984).

Schroeder, Paul W., *Austria, Great Britain, and the Crimean War: The Destruction of the European Concert* (Ithaca, NY: Cornell University Press, 1972).

Schroeder, Paul W., *The Transformation of European Politics 1763–1848* (Oxford: Clarendon Press, 1994).

Schweizer, Karl W., *Frederick the Great, William Pitt, and Lord Bute: The Anglo-Prussian Alliance, 1756–1763* (New York: Garland Publishing, 1991).

Schweller, Randall, 'Bandwagoning for Profit: Bringing the Revisionist State Back In', *International Security*, 10, 1 (Summer, 1994), pp. 72–107.

Schweller, Randall, *Deadly Imbalances: Tripolarity and Hitler's Strategy of World Conquest* (New York: Columbia University Press, 1998).

Seaton, Albert, *The Crimean War: A Russian Chronicle* (London: B. T. Batsford, 1977).

Sherrard, O. A., *Lord Chatham: Pitt and the Seven Years' War* (London: The Bodley Head, 1955).

Shimshoni, Jonathan, 'Technology, Military Advantage and World War I: A Case for Military Entrepreneurship', *International Security*, 15, 3 (Winter 1990/91), pp. 187–215.

Siverson, Randolph M. and Harvey Starr, *The Diffusion of War: A Study of Opportunity and Willingness* (Ann Arbor, MI: University of Michigan Press, 1991).

Smoke, Richard, *War: Controlling Escalation* (Cambridge, MA: Harvard University Press, 1977).

Snyder, Jack, *The Ideology of the Offensive: Military Decision Making and the Disasters of 1914* (Ithaca, NY: Cornell University Press, 1984).

Spring, D. W., 'Russia and the Coming of War', in R. J. W. Evans and Hartmut Pogge von Strandmann, eds, *The Coming of the First World War* (Oxford: Clarendon Press, 1988), pp. 57–86.

Stagg, J. C. A., *Mr Madison's War: Politics, Diplomacy and Warfare in the Early American Republic, 1783–1830* (Princeton, NJ: Princeton University Press, 1983).

Strachan, Hew, *European Armies and the Conduct of War* (London: Unwin Hyman, 1983).

Strandmann, Hartmut Pogge von, 'Germany and the Coming of War', in R. J. W. Evans and Hartmut Pogge von Strandmann, eds, *The Coming of the First World War* (Oxford: Clarendon Press, 1988), pp. 87–123.

Szabo, Franz A. J., *Kaunitz and Enlightened Absolutism 1753–1780* (Cambridge: Cambridge University Press, 1994).

Tapié, Victor-L., *The Rise and Fall of the Habsburg Monarchy*, trans. Stephen Hardman (New York: Praeger Publishers, 1971).

Tellis, Ashley, 'The Drive to Domination: Toward a Pure Theory of Realist Politics', unpub. dissert., University of Chicago, 1994.

Thouvenel, L., *Nicholas I et Napoléon III: Les Préliminaires de la Guerre de Crimée 1852–1854 D'Apres les Papiers Inédits de M. Thouvenel* (Paris: Ancienne Maison Michel Lévy Frères, 1891).

Torrey, Glenn E., 'Biographical Introduction: Henri-Mathias Berthelot (1861–1931)', in Glenn E. Torrey, ed., *General Henri Berthelot and Romania: Mémoires et Correspondance 1916–1919* (Boulder, CO: East European Monographs, 1987), pp. ix–xxxix.

Trachtenberg, Marc, 'The Meaning of Mobilization in 1914', *International Security*, 15, 3 (Winter 1990/91), pp. 120–50.

Tuchman, Barbara W., *The Guns of August* (New York: Macmillan, 1962).

Turner, L. C. F., *Origins of the First World War* (New York: W. W. Norton, 1970).

Turner, L. C. F., 'The Significance of the Schlieffen Plan', in Paul M. Kennedy, ed., *The War Plans of the Great Powers, 1880–1914* (London: George Allen & Unwin, 1979), pp. 199–221.

Van Creveld, Martin, *Supplying War: Logistics from Wallenstein to Patton* (Cambridge: Cambridge University Press, 1977).

Van Creveld, Martin, *Nuclear Proliferation and the Future of Conflict* (New York: The Free Press, 1993).

Van Creveld, Martin, 'Through a Glass, Darkly: Some Reflections on the Future of War', *Naval War College Review*, 53, 4 (Autumn 2000), pp. 25–44.

Van Evera, Stephen, 'The Cult of the Offensive and the Origins of the First World War', *International Security*, 9, 1 (Summer 1984), pp. 58–107.

Van Evera, Stephen, 'Offense, Defense and the Causes of War', *International Security*, 22, 4 (Spring 1998), pp. 5–43.

Veale, F. J. P., *Frederick the Great: His Life and Place in History* (London: Hamish Hamilton, 1912).

Walker, Geoffrey J., *Spanish Politics and Imperial Trade, 1700–1789* (Bloomington, IN: Indiana University Press, 1979).

Walt, Stephen M., *The Origins of Alliances* (Ithaca, NY: Cornell University Press, 1987).

Walter, Barbara, 'The Critical Barrier to Civil War Settlement', *International Organization*, 51, 3 (Summer 1997), pp. 335–64.

Walter, Jakob, *The Diary of a Napoleonic Foot Soldier*, Marc Raeff, ed. (New York: Doubleday, 1991).

Warner, Charles Dudley, ed., Hamilton Wright Mabia, Lucia Gilbert Runkle and George Henry Warner, assoc. eds, *A Library of the World's Best Literature* (New York: J. A. Hill, 1896–1902).

Weigley, Russell F., *The American Way of War: A History of United States Military Strategy and Policy* (Bloomington, IN: Indiana University Press, 1977).

Weigley, Russell F., *The Age of Battles: The Quest for Decisive Warfare from Breitenfeld to Waterloo* (Bloomington, IN: Indiana University Press, 1991).

Wetzel, David, *The Crimean War: A Diplomatic History* (Boulder, CO: East European Monographs, distributed by Columbia University Press, New York, 1985).

Whittam, John, 'War Aims and Strategy: The Italian Government and High Command 1914–1919', in Barry Hunt and Adrian Preston, eds, *War Aims and Strategic Policy in the Great War 1914–1918* (London: Croom Helm, 1977), pp. 85–104.

Williamson, S. R., 'Joffre Reshapes French Strategy, 1911–1913', in Paul M. Kennedy, ed., *The War Plans of the Great Powers, 1880–1914* (London: George Allen & Unwin, 1979), pp. 133–54.

Woodward, David R., *Trial by Friendship: Anglo-American Relations 1917–1918* (Lexington, KY: University Press of Kentucky, 1993).

Wright, Quincy, *A Study of War*, 2nd edn (Chicago, IL: University of Chicago Press, 1965).

Zeman, Z. A. B., 'The Balkans and the Coming of War', in R. J. W. Evans and Harmut Pogge von Strandmann, eds, *The Coming of the First World War* (Oxford: Clarendon Press, 1988), pp. 19–32.

Index